DATE DUE

DEMCO, INC. 38-2931

Praise for *My Friend the Fanatic*

My Friend the Fanatic reminds us of why we must look beyond the Middle East to appreciate whether Muslims can modernize—and how. Giving us a fresh take on one of the world's most pressing problems, Sadanand Dhume tells a profoundly human story replete with base instincts and high hopes.

—Irshad Manji, author of *The Trouble with Islam Today: A Muslim's Call for Reform of Her Faith*

Sadanand Dhume has gone beyond V. S. Naipaul to bring us a riveting portrait of Indonesia in flux. It is fluid, funny, and required reading for anyone interested in the future of Islam.

—Suketu Mehta, author of *Maximum City: Bombay Lost and Found*

Fascinating . . . A very fresh and quite urgent book on aspects of our great neighbour that we know absolutely nothing about.

—Phillip Adams, Late Night Live, ABC Radio National

Dhume plunged into the friendly squabble that is Indonesia. . . . He's a casually elegant writer with an eye for the big ideas and he's fascinated by the crunch between Islam and modernity.

—*Australian Literary Review*

Perfectly timed . . . elegantly written.

—*Australian Financial Review*

Takes on a big issue and delivers with flair.

—Vishakha Desai, President, Asia Society

A troubling series of events over the past few months is lending credence to Dhume's concerns . . . a marvelously fluid writer.

—*Asia Sentinel*

Highly well written and entertaining read . . . more than recommended.

—*Indonesia Matters*

A thoughtful, oftentimes quirky political travelogue . . . Dhume has a keen eye for detail, a wry sense of humour, and a rare humility. He paints for us a richly visual and varied landscape of the country while pulling together the disparate threads of Indonesia's political, religious and social history.

—*New Indian Express*

Shatters comforting certainties.

—Salil Tripathi, *Mint*

A fascinating intellectual journey through many layers of the country's rich cultural history . . . a deft exploration of how global currents of Arabized Islam are inexorably transforming Indonesia's easy-going syncretic Islamic culture. Dhume offers an engaging and deeply disturbing portrait of the world's largest Muslim country, a must read for every concerned world citizen.

—Nayan Chanda, author of *Bound Together: How Traders, Preachers, Adventurers and Warriors Shaped Globalization*

Sadanand Dhume has not only written a masterful travelogue, but has also turned the spotlight on a fundamentalist movement to which few outsiders have such meaningful access. *My Friend the Fanatic* should be required reading for anyone interested in the rise of radicalism in Indonesia, or in similar movements in other parts of the Muslim world.

—Jamie F. Metzl, Executive Vice President, Asia Society

My Friend the Fanatic describes a journey between Indonesia's extremes: the decadence of bohemian Jakarta, and the paranoia of the country's growing fundamentalist minority. In his encounters with exhibitionist sex writers, Javanese sorcerers, or repressive Osama-philes, Sadanand Dhume brings to bear a light, tolerant, and ironic eye. He has the wisdom to allow the people he meets to be themselves, not 'stand-ins for something larger.' He has the gift of making the most kitsch and sinister characters seem human, sad, and almost lovable.

—Richard Lloyd Parry, author of *In the Time of Madness: Indonesia on the Edge of Chaos*

MY FRIEND THE FANATIC

TRAVELS WITH A RADICAL ISLAMIST

Sadanand Dhume

SKYHORSE PUBLISHING

Skyhorse Publishing books may be purchased in bulk at special discounts for sales promotion, corporate gifts, fund-raising, or educational purposes. Special editions can also be created to specifications. For details, contact the Special Sales Department, Skyhorse Publishing, 555 Eighth Avenue, Suite 903, New York, NY 10018 or info@skyhorsepublishing.com.

www.skyhorsepublishing.com

10 9 8 7 6 5 4 3 2 1

Library of Congress Cataloging-in-Publication Data

Dhume, Sadanand.
My friend the fanatic : travels with a Radical Islamist / Sadanand Dhume.
p. cm.
ISBN 978-1-60239-643-2 (alk. paper)
1. Indonesia--Description and travel. 2. Islamic fundamentalism--Indonesia. 3. Dhume, Sadanand--Travel--Indonesia. I. Title.
DS620.2.D49 2009
959.804092--dc22
2009000234

Printed in the United States of America

For my parents

My grandfather inculcated in me Javanism and mysticism. From Father came Theosophy and Islam. From Mother, Hinduism and Buddhism.

Sukarno
SUKARNO: AN AUTOBIOGRAPHY

In Java, said one of my informants with the usual Javanese sense for cultural relativism, the spirits are unusually disturbing: 'I don't know how it is in America, but here they are always upsetting one.'

Clifford Geertz
THE RELIGION OF JAVA

Contents

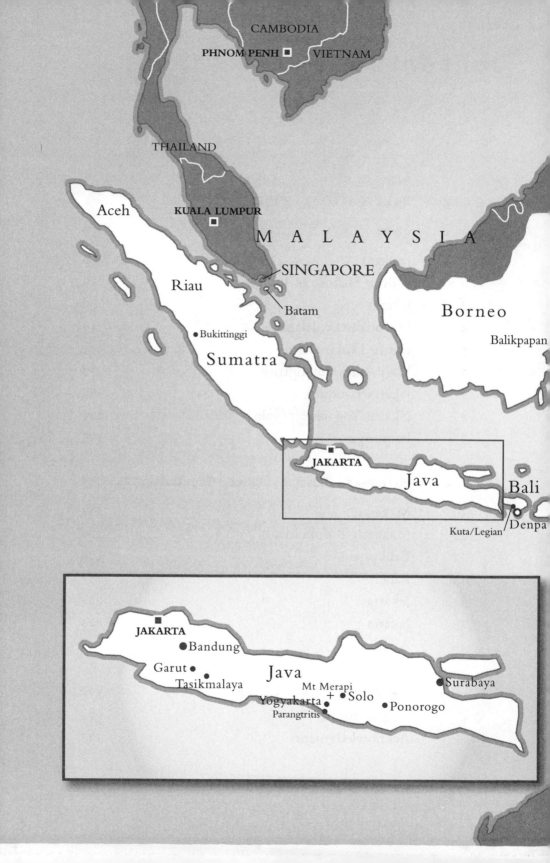

PHILIPPINES

Poso

Sulawesi

Maluku

akassar

Ambon

Bulukumba

I N D O N E S I A

Papua

Timor

250 Miles

0

0

500 Km

Darwin

A U S T R A L I A

Prologue

Bali
October 2002

By the time I arrived in Bali the exodus had already begun. Every flight out of Denpasar airport was packed and Qantas was said to have commissioned an extra aircraft specially for panicked Australians. In the last of the evening's light, in sarongs and printed shirts, thongs or sandals, here and there a surfboard tucked under an arm, they formed a ragged line outside the airport.

The sun had barely set when I reached Kuta, but it felt like the still before dawn. I walked past Bounty Bar, shaped like a pirate schooner and as deserted as a shipwreck. A bikini-clad mannequin stared out of a surfing-equipment store's darkened window. Ahead of me a small band of stay-behinds, their thongs and floral shirts at odds with their ashen faces, trudged towards a yellow-tape police barricade. I flashed my press card—I was here as a reporter for the *Far Eastern Economic Review* and the *Asian Wall Street Journal*—and ducked under the tape. Soldiers and policemen, machine guns slung from their shoulders, stood in a knot puffing on *kreteks*, clove cigarettes. Behind them stood a small Häagen-Dazs truck, its roof depressed as though it had been stepped on by a giant. The driver, I later learned, had been decapitated by the blast while he idled in traffic.

Ground zero smelled of gasoline and burnt wood. Uprooted tables, blackened beer bottles and mangled red plastic beer crates dotted the ashes of what had been the Sari Club the night before. Cars parked in front had been reduced to junkyard wrecks. The Balinese had already visited, leaving behind maroon, white and orange flowers in delicate banana-leaf baskets, their appeasement for the Gods.

For a while, searching for some trace of a human being, a shoe, a bracelet, a severed hand, I followed the spotlight of a video camera manned by another latecomer to the scene. But the site had already been cleaned up and all that remained was rubble. More than two hundred people died in the attacks: a smaller backpack bomb at Paddy's bar across the street had preceded the massive car bomb that did most of the damage. Three months later they would fill 140 bags with unidentified body parts for burial, but on that night it was as though the dead had been vapourised, leaving behind only ash and glass and plastic.

Less than a week earlier I had stood at the same spot, eager for the bustle of Kuta after four days in a sleepy east Balinese village. I had wolfed down a hamburger at the Hard Rock Café overlooking the beach then strolled to the Sari Club for a drink. It was empty except for a squad of bronzed and bare-chested Australians chugalug-ging Bintang beers under a large screen on which writhed Madonna dressed like a cowboy. The evening was still young; the sun's last salmon pink smeared the sky. Hours lay before the appearance of the first slender-hipped hookers. And it was not until close to midnight that the dance floor, packed and sweaty, would turn the club into a viable target.

I heard the crunch of the cameraman's receding footsteps. A few minutes later it was time for me to call it a night as well.

Until the Bali bombings every foreign journalist in the country could tell you two things: that Indonesia was the world's most populous Muslim country and that its Muslims were overwhelmingly moderate.

Islam was a relatively recent import to the archipelago. It washed up in the twelfth century, took root in the fifteenth and became dominant as late as the seventeenth. It arrived through trade rather than conquest, by Indian dhow rather than Arab charger. It was preceded by a millennium and a half of Hinduism and Buddhism, whose achievements included central Java's Borobudur, the world's largest Buddhist monument, and Majapahit, a Hindu–Buddhist empire whose influence stretched to present-day Cambodia. As the anthropologist Clifford Geertz wrote in comparing Indonesia to Morocco: 'In Indonesia, Islam did not construct a civilisation, it appropriated one.'

By the time the new faith took hold in the archipelago its influence in other parts of the world had already begun to wane. The high-water marks of Islamic civilisation—Abbasid Baghdad and Moorish Spain—had long receded and in 1492 Ferdinand and Isabella's armies completed the Reconquista by evicting the Moors from Granada. Portuguese gunships had already entered Southeast Asian waters when Majapahit sputtered its last in the early 1500s. Consequently, Islam was denied the long political supremacy it held in regions closer to the first flush of Arab power, and with it the chance to cement its hold on society. In 1619 the Dutch established their headquarters at Batavia, today's Jakarta. Except for a brief period of Japanese rule during World War Two, they stayed until 1949.

You still saw Dutch fingerprints here and there, in an odd word (*bioskop*—movie theatre, *rekening*—account), or in a sturdy old building, but it was the Hindu–Buddhist past that was felt most clearly. This was the only place in the world where you might call yourself Muslim yet name your children Vishnu and Sita, seek moral guidance in a wayang shadow puppet performance of the ancient Hindu epic the *Mahabharata*, and believe in Dewi Sri, the Goddess of the rice paddy, Ratu Kidul, Queen of the South Seas and Nini Tawek, angel of the Javanese kitchen. This comfort with the past, it seemed, fostered comfort with the present. The supermarkets stocked beer; Ramadan sales offered discounts on Capri pants. State-owned television housed a weekly show called 'Country Road', ninety minutes of Indonesians in denims and Stetsons line dancing, whirling imaginary lassos and crooning hits from deepest Texas and New Orleans.

At the same time, though, a deeper transformation of society was under way. Since the 1970s Indonesian Islam had begun to be stripped of its native foliage by a combination of rapid urbanisation, the implementation of uniform religious education by then president General Suharto's bitterly anti-communist regime and the efforts of homegrown and Middle Eastern purifiers of the faith. The old tolerance was giving way to an assertive new orthodoxy. You could see superficial signs every day—in the headscarves that dotted college campuses, in the shiny-domed mosques mushrooming in the countryside, in the prayer calluses on the foreheads of the devout. Demands for implementing the medieval Arab practices enshrined in sharia law, dismissed by the nation's founders more than fifty years earlier, had risen again. Church burnings, once unthinkable, barely raised eyebrows. Groups with names like Islamic Defenders Front and Laskar Jihad had taken to the streets, trashing bars and discotheques in Jakarta and battling Christians in a bloody civil war on the country's eastern fringe. Against this backdrop, the carnage in Bali was only the most visible expression of a much larger churning.

In the weeks after the bombings, Bali had the appearance of a familiar TV set peopled by an alien cast. Sunbathers gave way to police and soldiers, and to a contingent of set-jawed Australian investigators; reporters flooded the Hard Rock Hotel where officials tallied the body count at the daily press briefing. My time collapsed into a series of disjointed images: a Hindi film playing in the smoky waiting room at police headquarters, fresh plywood coffins stacked under the moonlight in a hospital courtyard, lunch alone on a sprawling white terrace by a deserted beach, a long row of red and white national flags at half-mast on bamboo poles, red silk umbrellas and the smell of incense at an interfaith prayer to keep the peace.

In Bali I felt the stirrings of a curiosity deeper than any I had ever felt before. Over the previous two years I had written about the growth of hardline Islam, but these articles, I now saw, barely hinted at the scale of the transformation under way. To understand where things were headed, what Indonesia would look like in ten years or twenty, I would have to pull together the disparate threads of a story that crisscrossed the archipelago.

Part One

Java

1

Jakarta

Hotel Borobudur, said to belong to Jakarta's most powerful army-backed mobster, sprawled across 23 landscaped acres in the heart of the city. In keeping with the national love affair with the acronym, the hotel disco was called MUSRO, short for Music Room. Five massive columns in the shape of rampant eagles, wings outstretched, curved around its entrance. Inside it was dim and smoky and my eyes took a few moments to adjust before I spotted the birthday girl. Her hair, usually straight, tonight cascaded to her shoulders in glossy black curls. Her leather skirt fell in jagged waves over spike-heeled boots. A crush of reporters wearing sweaters to ward off the aircon-ditioning surrounded her. Those in the first couple of rows thrust their battered tape-recorders under her nose; behind them jostled camera crews.

Djenar Maesa Ayu appeared unruffled, as though sheathed in an invisible bubble. The scrum parted for a moment to allow me to wish her happy birthday before closing back on itself, and as I made my way towards the salvers of peppered beef, barbecue chicken and fried rice lined up on a long table I heard a reporter shout out the one question they never tired of asking: 'Why do you always write about sex?'

Sometime swimwear model, daughter of an actress and a deceased film director, Djenar was the reigning wild child of Indonesian literature. She had recently threatened to strip before parliament to protest a proposed censorship bill. Her 31st birthday coincided with the launch of her second collection of short stories: *Jangan Main Main (Dengan Kelaminmu)* or *Don't Fool Around (With Your Genitals)*. The first story, *Suckled by Father*, was about a girl nursed not on her mother's breast but on her father's penis.

I owed my introduction to Djenar to the businessman and novelist Richard Oh. Richard was the Gertrude Stein of Jakarta, if you could picture Stein as a bald 44-year-old Chinese–Indonesian man with a smoking cigar between his fingers. His QB World bookstores, modelled on Barnes and Noble or Borders, dotted the city, and he owned a small publishing imprint called Metafor. He had established the Khatulistiwa Award, Indonesia's Booker Prize, and surrounded himself with a retinue of poets, writers and journalists. Unusually for the scion of a business family, Richard had studied creative writing in Wisconsin, where he developed a taste for literary fiction. I envied his easy familiarity with Proust and Kafka and Faulkner. Richard constantly urged me to catch up with authors I had barely heard of: 'Read W. G. Sebald. You have to read W. G. Sebald.'

By this time it was January, 2004, more than a year since the Bali bombings. In April 2003, six months after standing in the ruins of the Sari Club, I quit my job with the *Far Eastern Economic Review* and the *Asian Wall Street Journal* in a fit of bravado on being denied promised book leave. My years of writing about bank privatisation and debt restructuring and the fluctuating fortunes of noodle manufacturers and motorcycle importers were over. A new career as an author beckoned, beginning with the book about the changing face of Indonesia that had first come to me in Bali. Befitting my altered status—a step up or a step down depending on who was judging—I found myself struck off the American ambassador's guest list and welcomed to Richard Oh's entourage. But though my business card now said 'writer' the truth of that claim was tenuous. Once the first flush of purpose had passed, the reality of being unemployed without a bank balance to speak of sank in and my nerve faltered. I sought out a consulting assignment with the World Bank that took me to Aceh and padded my finances somewhat but left no time for other travel or serious writing. I accepted an invitation to the Australian National University's annual gathering of Indonesia experts in Canberra, and agreed to write a paper on ethnic politics and business, an exercise that somehow ended up taking months rather than the weeks I had intended.

The World Bank consultancy lapsed after six months. Shorn of excuses, I made a few desultory stabs at reviving things. I spent an afternoon with Ineke Koesherawati, the erstwhile star of such films as *Kenikmatan Tabu (Forbidden Bliss)* and *Gadis Metropolis II (Metropolitan Girl II)*, who had seamlessly transitioned from surf-soaked white shirts and flashes of dark lingerie to compering events for the headscarfed new middle class on how to achieve true Muslim womanhood. She seemed insulted when I compared her former screen persona to Jennifer Lopez. 'No, no, I was more like Pamela Anderson,' she insisted. I interviewed Puspo Wardoyo, a 47-year-old fried chicken restaurant magnate who had founded the nation's first polygamy award. His phone rang with the *azaan*, the Islamic call to prayer; his morose and childlike third wife had little Snoopies embroidered on her chaste white socks and nursed a barely disguised resentment towards wife number four. To balance the pious with the profane, I whiled away a long night with a transvestite dance troupe, the fabulously named Tata Dado and the Silver Boys. 'My body, better than Tyra Banks,' insisted Tata Dado, a rouged middle-aged man with the features of a butcher. But though each of these encounters captured something of the times, I had to admit that they didn't add up to much.

It was not as though I was entirely rudderless. If anything, the logic of the travels I had in mind dictated itself. I would begin in Java, home to half of Indonesia's population, the country's economic and political centre, and the heartland of the culture under siege. Then would come some of the so-called outer islands—Sulawesi, Borneo, Batam and, circumstances permitting, the Moluccas, also known as Maluku. In terms of themes, the broad changes in Indonesian society struck me as far more significant than the somewhat hyped threat from terrorism. Orthodox Islam was equally uncomfortable with the pop-culture present and the pagan past. To get a sense of these conflicts I would write about a massive Islamic reform movement called Muhammadiyah, the popular entertainer Inul Daratista, nominal Muslims who still worshipped the Queen of the South Seas, and the charismatic Bandung-based televangelist A. A. Gym. Only then would I address the question of terrorism. The odds of seeing the country's most famous terrorist suspect, Jemaah Islamiyah's Abu Bakar Bashir, appeared awfully slim, but I could visit the infamous school he founded, and also the prestigious Islamic school that helped shape Bashir's own world view.

Jemaah Islamiyah, though, was only the most prominent of a rash of organisations that shared the common goal of Islamists everywhere: the imposition of sharia law. What set Jemaah Islamiyah, an al Qaeda offshoot, apart was not its vision of an ideal society but its willingness to use violence to achieve its objectives. In parts of the country, such as south Sulawesi, the same goal was being pursued through administrative fiat. Other Islamists, such as the missionaries of the Borneo-based Hidayatullah network, preferred to dot the country with private enclaves run by strictly orthodox norms. Most ambitious of all was the Prosperous Justice

Party, or PKS. Modelled on Egypt's Muslim Brotherhood, and imbued with the same bedrock belief in the need to organise all aspects of society and the state according to Islamic precepts, it was widely seen as the party to watch in parliamentary and presidential elections scheduled for later that year.

Of course, my plans were just that, plans. In practice, an innate talent for procrastination reasserted itself. Some days I did nothing at all, on others nothing of consequence. There was always another book worth reading, another freelance magazine article, tempting as much for the familiarity as for the income, to dash off. Against this backdrop, Richard had taken on a certain outsized importance in my life. I had enjoyed his first two novels, which touched upon a subject many people found uncomfortable, the peculiar predicament of Indonesia's wealthy yet persecuted Chinese minority. Richard was at work on his third book. He had an agent in Spain and attended the Frankfurt book fair every year. He invariably made me feel poorly read, but I took a perverse pleasure in this, as though the repeated reminders of my unfamiliarity with the oeuvre of W. G. Sebald and A. L. Kennedy and Banana Yoshimoto, or more precisely that this mattered to me, hinted at an ambition less whimsical than it appeared. I began to think of Richard and Djenar—they were usually inseparable—as a bridge between the world of reporters and the world of writers. Their company strengthened the illusion that I had made the passage from one to the other, and I instinctively sensed that keeping that illusion alive was vital if I was not to simply give up. That both were larger than life figures in Jakarta helped. The glamour of their circle came as a welcome relief from the usual expats with their tired stories about scuba diving courses and bargain spas. This was the other Indonesia, the part whose aspirations belonged in *Vanity Fair* rather than in the Koran. What set Richard and Djenar apart from elites in other Muslim countries, with the possible exception of fiercely secular

Turkey and Tunisia, was not the fact of their existence—who hadn't heard of booze-fuelled parties in north Tehran or the libertinism of the posher parts of Karachi—but that there was nothing furtive about them. In Jakarta, as the camera crews swarming around Djenar underscored, a certain boldness still belonged in the public square.

Around me UB40's 'Red Red Wine' rose thickly above the clink of beer glasses. The gathering's sense of style showed on its feet: slim black stilettos, heavy buckled dress shoes, red canvas Adidas sneakers. I crossed a landing colonised by the star of the film *Ca-bau-kan* (in curly-toed cowboy boots) and his fans, and found Richard on a dim balcony in earnest conversation with a somewhat scruffy man he introduced as an up-and-coming writer. Richard held forth on his newest discovery, a Spanish existentialist of apparently vast profundity. Were we familiar with his work? We didn't know what we were missing.

The second floor of the disco formed a thick U-shape overlooking the dance floor. From where we stood we could see Djenar, on the opposite arm of the U, autographing books with a silver pen. She paused, broke the seal on a pack of Dunhill menthols, and lightly tossed the crumpled foil to one side. She lit her cigarette almost in slow motion before turning to accept a bouquet of marigolds and spiky green bulbs from three svelte women in black; each received a light peck on either cheek.

A makeshift stage on the dance floor below was decorated with naked white mannequins arranged like crash-test dummies, their arms and legs and necks at impossible angles. The cover of Djenar's book, a bright red background with PlayStation controls superimposed on a blurred pair of breasts, filled a large screen above them. After a few minutes the music died, the red on the screen faded, and an amateur video came on. It began with a man at a urinal, his pants down, his arse partially exposed; then it cut to a long-haired man in a denim jacket seated on a toilet.

'Who is that?' I asked Richard.

'Moammar Emka. He wrote *Jakarta Undercover*.' It was a bestselling exposé of sexual hijinks in the capital.

The rest of the brief film continued in a similar vein, a blur of urinals, toilet seats and frothing beer mugs punctuated by testimony from Djenar's friends and admirers. Then the birthday girl made her appearance onstage. The audience hushed and the sounds of clinking glasses faded. Djenar arranged herself artfully on a spotlit chair, one side of her leather skirt falling away to reveal a length of black-stockinged thigh, and began reading aloud about sucking thirstily on a penis.

By this time I had lived in Jakarta three years, but my relationship with the city went back further. Between 1980 and 1983 my father, a diplomat, was posted at the Indian embassy and I had spent a year here in 1981 when I was twelve. That Indonesia was better off than India was obvious even then. In Jakarta, Levi's jeans or Boney M cassettes didn't carry quite as much cachet as they did in New Delhi. The cars, mostly Toyotas and Hondas with the occasional Mitsubishi, showed up the backwardness of Delhi's ancient Fiats and Ambassadors. On the badminton court you saw Yonex in carbon graphite instead of Pioneer Sports in crude steel. Even the maids were better dressed, and for the most part better humoured as well.

I was homesick—evidence of Japanese industry didn't quite make up for friends left behind—and glad to return to India after a year. Over time Indonesia faded from my consciousness. As a student of journalism and international relations in America, and later as a foreign correspondent in India, I couldn't claim to have paid events in Indonesia particular attention. The country occupied only marginally more of my mindspace than, say, Malaysia or the Philippines. Nonetheless when the *Far Eastern Economic Review's* editors in Hong Kong broached the idea of moving me from India to Southeast Asia in 2000 I agreed almost without thinking. The prospect of living in Jakarta, not Manila or Singapore or Kuala Lumpur, was behind this alacrity. It wasn't merely misplaced nostalgia. With 220 million people Indonesia was the one country in the region that *mattered*. It was also at the cusp of two of the world's most important debates about Islam. Was the faith compatible with democracy? Was it compatible with economic development?

The city I returned to was barely recognisable. The Jakarta of my childhood had boasted no airport of glazed brick and plate glass, no straight and wide toll road to the city, no malls stocked with Australian wines and German toasters. The once-posh Hilton now looked drab beside the flash of the Grand Hyatt and the hushed opulence of the Dharmawangsa. I remembered the British Council library building, with its broken eggshell exterior, as imposingly modern; now it looked a runt dwarfed by giants.

By this time India's economy had been unshackled nearly a decade while Indonesia's was yet to recover from the 1997–98 Asian financial crisis. Yet the gulf between the countries I had sensed twenty years earlier had only widened. It was most conspicuous in those totemic symbols of the Suharto era—the skyscrapers on Jalan Sudirman. But I experienced it in smaller ways too: in the crisply airconditioned taxi that took me to work, in the efficiency behind the cash register at the department store, in the muted sophistication of Cinnabar where my colleagues in the foreign press corps gathered in the evening for a drink. Indonesia's rich were richer than India's; its poor, despite the setback, were less poor. Even the beggars, back since the crisis, were different from Indian beggars. Their limbs weren't mutilated. They wore thongs or scuffed sneakers; some carried guitars. They retained a few shreds of dignity.

This record of having done relatively well by its people was one of the things I admired most about Indonesia. Here was proof, if any were needed, of India's folly in extending the shelf life of

Nehruvian socialism through the 1970s and much of the 1980s, and of the wisdom of Indonesia's market-friendly policies and back-to-basics focus on literacy, health care and family planning. Not long after my arrival, a local activist in Pekanbaru in Sumatra took me to a village outside the city to show me poverty. He pointed at a one-room concrete shack with a tin roof. 'Look at how our people live!' he said. He was keen to make the case for greater autonomy from Jakarta, but I couldn't take my eyes off the row of small shoes lined up neatly outside the door. In poor Indian villages the children went barefoot, their bellies distended, their eyes dulled, their hair orange-brown billboards for malnutrition.

At Cinnabar the foreign correspondents and NGO expats complained about slumming it in Jakarta but, fresh from New Delhi, I could never empathise. Put simply, the city I had moved to was more civilised than the one I had left. The elevators in the foreign ministry did not stink of stale sweat; the taxi drivers weren't always out to cheat you; a foreign woman could walk the streets without the constant threat of being groped or accosted by a stranger saying, 'Hello madam, you want to fuck?'

Relative prosperity explained this only partly. I had spent three months in Kuala Lumpur, which was far wealthier than Jakarta yet at the same time somehow coarser, and had come to attribute this difference to culture. Below the emblems of Malay achievement— the Petronas Towers and the monorail—lay a terrible confusion. A Yemeni or a Pakistani might show up today and his children would be considered sons of the soil and given preferences in everything from college admissions to business contracts. The children of a Buddhist or Christian Chinese or of a Hindu Tamil who had lived there a hundred years remained foreign. The new Malaysian administrative capital, Putrajaya, was a Disneyesque conception of Araby, gaudy domes and soaring minarets and a copycat bridge from Isfahan in Iran.

This vulgarity was absent in Indonesia. With the exception of Islamists, the Javanese did not generally confuse being Muslim with being Arab. They had bent Islam to their culture rather than the other way round. In *Among the Believers*, V. S. Naipaul wrote: 'It was as if, at this far end of the world, the people of Java had taken what was most humane and liberating from the religions that had come their way, to make their own.' They had taken the best of Islam, its simple egalitarianism, its ability to infuse drab lives with dignity, without devaluing their earlier achievements. The Javanese retained their own history and architecture, their own names, their own dress and dance and music, their own rituals at birth and marriage and death, even their own conception of the afterlife. And it was these, expressed in a million subtle ways in gesture and carriage and voice, that gave their civilisation such a high gloss at what remained, after all, a very low level of income.

Three weeks after the book launch at the Borobudur, I joined Richard and Djenar's entourage at a south-Jakarta nightclub called Embassy. There were about ten of us: Djenar, her head on Richard's shoulder; Fira Basuki, a young novelist, glamorous in an early Bond film way with crooked teeth and ironed straight hair; a female copywriter with Ogilvy and Mather; Djenar's husband, who dabbled in real estate; and a couple of journalists. The club was closed to the public for the night. Cork-float candles in glasses sat on the small round tables that ringed the vacant dance floor. The handful near us that remained unoccupied had been claimed with small paper triangles lettered with the names of the fashionable— Roy, Dodo, Cici, Darwin.

A waitress in a quilted silver jacket brought over a bottle of Chivas and an ice bucket. Djenar passed around blue cans of soda that made the whisky taste strangely sweet. Shouting in my ear above the music, techno of some sort, Fira told me about her life.

Her father worked for an oil company and she had gone to university in Kansas. She had returned home a few years earlier and now, when she wasn't churning out chicklit, edited a glossy fashion magazine.

The music died and a woman's voice filled the room. 'Ladies and Gentlemen: Our star of the night.' The music picked up again, now dominated by a swiftly tattooed drumbeat. A spotlight fell on an elfin figure in the shadows. It was Moammar Emka, or so I guessed. He was dressed differently from the last time I had seen him, at Djenar's book launch. A massive gold headdress topped with long brown and white feathers perched precariously on his head. A gold lame cape trailed down his back. A gold bra, a gold girdle and a gold choker completed the outfit. His wispy beard was twisted into a spike. Emka tottered on heels to the middle of the dance floor escorted by a dozen shaking and shimmying belly dancers in sequins and glitter and a guard of bare-chested youths dressed as pharaoh's attendants. The drumbeat faded as he stopped and felt his falsies. '*Aduh*, they're slipping,' he squealed into a wireless mike.

Emka thanked the party's sponsors, which included an engine oil company ('Pennzoil, No. 1 Engine Oil in USA'), a hotel and a condom manufacturer. 'Hotel plus condom equals safe sex,' quipped Emka. Then, in an approximation of reciting an honour roll, he began to invite his closest friends to share the floor. A television hostess, first up, gave Emka's falsies a meaty squeeze. Then came an androgynous fashion designer, who ducked behind him and wrapped her head in the gold cape. Emka wagged a disapproving finger: 'Don't you dare wear a *jilbab*!' (The headscarf.) Laughter bounced off the walls. Then Emka called for Djenar.

'Djenar Maesa Ayu. Where's Djenar Maesa Ayu?'

She hung back a few moments, allowing a pocket of tension to build before joining the others under the spotlight. She bent and kissed Emka on both cheeks. The music picked up again and a video appeared on a screen with the clattering of typewriter keys and the words J-a-k-a-r-t-a U-n-d-e-r-c-o-v-e-r.

We were celebrating the release of *Jakarta Undercover 2: Carnival of the Night*, the sequel to *Jakarta Undercover: Sex'n the City*. I had recently acquired the comic version of *Sex'n the City*. In it an elfin man, his beard twisted in a spike, investigates the endless possibilities, for a price, of Jakarta's night-life. On every page he encounters leggy girls with names like Evi and Iva and Fia in unlikely places—a sushi bar, a hairdressing salon, inside a specially outfitted Mitsubishi Pajero. In real life the miracle of book royalties had transformed Emka from an impoverished east Javanese *pesantren* (Islamic boarding school) graduate to a minor celebrity who drove a BMW and hired nightclubs for his parties.

Once Emka and friends surrendered the dance floor it filled up and began to writhe and heave. The pharaoh's attendants patrolled its fringes with open bottles of Jack Daniels, pausing every few steps to pour the whisky straight into an eagerly upturned mouth. Everyone at our table declined, preferring to stick with the sweet Chivas. After a few minutes the belly dancers returned in new costumes. Spotlit on a counter across the floor from us, a slave girl in a bikini top made of coins and a diaphanous green skirt paired up with a pharaoh's attendant with kohl-rimmed eyes. She raised her ankle to his shoulder; he buried his face in her crotch. In the background, a schoolmarm's voice chanted, 'No sex before marriage. No sex before marriage. No sex before marriage.'

The earsplitting volume and the parade of dancers cramped conversation, but as the night wore on and the whisky kicked in Richard lit a cigar and became expansive. He told me to write and not worry about anything else—his publishing imprint, Metafor, would publish my book. Since my interest lay in non-fiction, he urged me to study Norman Mailer and Truman Capote. ('Capote invented the nonfiction novel.') At this I felt a jolt of accomplishment; for once, here were writers I knew though, of course, not nearly as well as Richard.

The next song that caught my ear consisted entirely of low moans. A dancer in a black bra, tiny black shorts and a gauzy black wrap climbed on the counter beside us and began to move in rhythm with the moans. Every now and then she whipped open the wrap to reveal an expanse of taut flesh. The moans picked up speed. The dancer ground her pelvis and writhed. A crowd of Roys, Darwins and Cicis formed around her. '*Buka! Buka! Buka!*' they chanted. (Open! Open! Open!) She let the wrap fall behind her on the counter. Someone put a camera phone to her rear and clicked. Djenar, who had been trying to make herself heard above the din, handed me her drink and approached the counter. She hoisted herself up with the help of the dancer in black. Then she placed one hand on the dancer's shoulder and leaned as far back as she could go. Thrusting her crotch out, Djenar slowly worked her way up the dancer's leg as though it were a pole in a strip club. The crowd went wild—cheering, clapping, whistling.

'Who says this country is fucked up?' shouted Richard.

2

A brief history of Indonesia

You could divide the history of independent Indonesia into three acts. The first (1945–65) was marked by upheaval and high drama and propelled by the charismatic Sukarno: Bearer of the Message of the People's Suffering, President for Life, or simply *Bung* (Brother) Karno. Sukarno had something of the strutting rooster about him. He carried a black and silver swagger stick tucked under an arm and showed a fondness for impeccably tailored uniforms. He devised his own ideology, Marhaenism, a brand of socialism centred on the small farmer and named for a struggling Sundanese peasant with a wife and four children and not much land. He was a world-class philanderer who, depending on who was counting, married between five and seven times and was said to have housed a nursery in the presidential palace for the access it provided to pretty young mothers. You couldn't imagine any of his contemporaries—India's Jawaharlal Nehru or the Egyptian Gamal Abdel Nasser—narrating an autobiography to an American journalist, Cindy Adams, who would go on to become a fabled New York gossip columnist.

The Sukarno era began on 17 August 1945, during the dying days of Japan's three-and-a-half-year occupation when, alongside his dour, bespectacled vice-president Mohammad Hatta, he co-signed Indonesia's proclamation of independence. Over the next twenty years the country lurched from one crisis to the next. Between 1945 and 1949 nationalist forces resisted Dutch attempts to reclaim their former colony. In 1948 they put down a communist rebellion in Madiun in east Java; between 1948 and 1965 they crushed an Islamic revolt in west Java, south Sulawesi and Aceh. Along the way (1958–61), they grappled with a CIA-sponsored rebellion centred in west Sumatra. Yet, even as he struggled to keep his country together, Sukarno devoted much of his energy and more of his rhetoric to confronting the West. He divided the world into New Emerging Forces (Nefos) and Old Established Forces (Oldefos) who were intent on pursuing neo-colonialism, colonialism and imperialism (Nekolim). Staking his claim to lead the former, he organised the 1955 Asia–Africa summit in Bandung, the precursor to the Non-Aligned Movement attended by, among others, Nehru, Nasser and Chinese premier Zhou Enlai. Three years later, irked by the Dutch refusal to hand over West New Guinea, Sukarno expelled 46,000 of their nationals and expropriated their businesses. (Eventually, under American pressure, the Dutch came around and in 1969 West New Guinea became the Indonesian province of west Irian, now called Papua.)

In his last years as president, Sukarno, who was never exactly the picture of stability, became increasingly erratic. In 1959, backed by the army, he ended the country's brief and chaotic experiment with parliamentary democracy—his term was 'chatterbox democracy'—and replaced it with a mild dictatorship he called 'guided democracy'. He drew closer to the Indonesian Communist Party (PKI), at the time the largest of its kind in the non-communist world. He began to propound his belief in Nasakom, a fuzzy blend of nationalism, religion and communism, though the largely pro-Western army and religious parties, both Muslim and Christian, ensured that the communists never wielded formal power. In 1963 Sukarno had himself named president for life. That year, outraged by British plans to amalgamate Sabah and Sarawak on Borneo into the new state of Malaysia—a dastardly case, he felt, of Oldefos indulging in Nekolim—Sukarno threatened to 'gobble Malaysia raw'. His supporters razed the British embassy in Jakarta. He launched a haphazard military campaign—with paratroopers and stray border incursions—while his army secretly cooperated with the British and Americans to ensure that it failed. The following year he told America to, 'Go to hell with your aid.' Then, in 1965, he withdrew Indonesia from the UN in a huff when it seated Malaysia (ungobbled) on the Security Council. He intended to replace the UN with a new international body: Conefo, or the Conference of New Emerging Forces. In the meantime he announced the creation of an anti-imperialist axis spanning Jakarta, Phnom Penh, Hanoi, Beijing and Pyongyang.

Sukarno gave his people pride and held them together by sheer force of personality, but stripped of this his record reveals soaring rhetoric and empty bellies. By the time he lost power Sukarno could claim one concrete achievement: the literacy rate, about 5 percent when the Dutch left, had risen to 40 percent. But set against that were stagnant rice yields, inflation at 500 percent, foreign investors in flight, seven years of falling per capita income and an official exchange rate that was a fiction compared to the fact of the black market.

Act Two (1965–98) saw solid achievement and fantastic greed bookmarked at either end by bloodshed. Its lead was a kind of anti-Sukarno, as much in persona as in policy. President Suharto spoke little and dressed soberly, most often in neatly pressed safari suits. He was a faithful husband and a doting father to his six children. To many he exemplified the archetypal Javanese values of internal calm and external composure. Insular to a fault, he made his first overseas trip at the age of forty and is not known to have broached the idea of an autobiography in English. Where Sukarno leaned towards permanent revolution, Suharto chose distant paternalism. He was *Bapak Pembangunan*, or 'Father of Development'; you wouldn't dream of calling him Bung. Where Sukarno quoted Rousseau and Voltaire, Garibaldi and Cavour, Jefferson and Lenin, and the Hindu reformer Vivekananda, Suharto's intellectual horizons didn't extend much beyond simple Javanese aphorisms: 'Virtue requires a firm mind' or 'Silence is an asset' or 'Wealth indicates one's ability to put worldly situations under one's control.'

Suharto ascended to power on a mountain of corpses. On 30 September, 1965 an abortive, allegedly communist-backed coup left six top generals dead. Over the next day, General Suharto, then commander of an elite combat unit, took control of the army and quashed the coup. He began the process of easing aside Sukarno that culminated with him seizing effective power five months later. By then he had presided over the annihilation of the PKI and the slaughter by death squads of an estimated half a million people, most of them in Java and Bali.

Suharto's New Order regime, as distinguished from Sukarno's Old Order, quickly severed ties with China, threw open the doors to fresh investment by the Oldefos and returned to the UN. As America's newest ally in Southeast Asia—the Vietnam war had deepened and the domino theory held sway in Washington—Suharto helped found the Association of Southeast Asian Nations as a bulwark against communism. At home he established a political vehicle called Golkar and a rubber-stamp parliament. The so-called Berkeley Mafia, a group of US-trained economists blessed by the World Bank and the International Monetary Fund, took the economy's reins. On their watch Suharto's countrymen would rapidly grow less poor while his family and friends grew obscenely rich.

Over the next three decades the economy expanded at an average of 6–7 percent annually. Foreign investment poured in, first a trickle and then a flood. In 1970, per capita income was $75; in 1996 it exceeded $1000 making Indonesia, already hailed as a miracle economy by the World Bank, officially a middle-income country. Manufactured exports exceeded those of raw materials; BMW dealerships had sprung up around the city; expatriate investment bankers clogged five-star hotel lobbies. In a city where a department store escalator had drawn gawkers a generation earlier, you could now dine in a revolving restaurant or play tennis on a rooftop court. Diplomats spoke of a permanent seat for Indonesia on the UN Security Council.

If Sukarno's weakness was women, Suharto's was wealth. His family, known as Cendana after the street that housed their compound in the tree-lined neighbourhood of Menteng, had the appetite of a pack of velociraptors. The Cendana family's reach extended into forestry and plantations, oil and gas and mining, telecoms and television, power and roads, real estate and hotels and food processing. Nothing was out of bounds—a monopoly on wheat imports, a cut from oil exports, an attempt to corner the clove market, a protected national car project.

Time reported that the family had homes in London (Hampstead, Hyde Park, Grosvenor Square), Los Angeles (Beverly Hills), Boston, Hawaii, Geneva and Singapore. It was said to own real estate in Indonesia the size of the Netherlands, a golf course in England and a secluded hunting retreat on a New Zealand glacier. It commanded private jets and yachts and fleets of Ferraris and Porsches and Rolls Royces. Two sons were regulars at the baccarat tables of London, Las Vegas and Atlantic City. Suharto had grown up impoverished in central Java in a small house with bamboo walls and a thatched palm roof and neither electricity nor running water. In 1997 *Fortune* magazine estimated his worth at $16 billion, which made him the world's sixth richest man at the time.

Yet, for all its baroqueness, you couldn't deny the New Order's achievements. Under Suharto's watch the literacy rate climbed from 40 percent in 1965 to 90 percent a quarter-century later. Life expectancy soared; birth rates and infant mortality plummeted. Before China's economic reforms began to pay off in the 1990s, Indonesia had rescued more people from poverty than any other nation: in 1970 about six out of ten Indonesians lived below the poverty line, by 1996 only one in ten. A once chronically under-nourished country was self-sufficient in food. It had substantially modernised its roads and ports and airports and power grid. A generation whose parents had not been to high school attended university; countless women had moved from the overcrowded rice paddy to the factory, or from the home to the office cubicle.

Act Three, or Reformasi, also began messily. In 1998 the Asian financial crisis collapsed the sole pillar of Suharto's legitimacy, the economy, and forced him to step down. Thailand, Korea and Malaysia also suffered, but a combination of binge borrowing abroad and weak institutions at home set Indonesia up for the steepest fall. The economy contracted 14 percent in 1998. At one point the rupiah lost nearly four-fifths of its value, plummeting from 2300 to 11,000 to the dollar. Inflation, in single digits for most of the New Order, hit 80 percent. Debt, much of it unpayable, ballooned to $140 billion. The poverty rate more than doubled to 27 percent—about 55 million people. Unemployment reached 20 million. The poorest yanked their children out of school; villages swelled with the newly unemployed; in the cities you heard stories of middle-class managers committing suicide. Jakarta became a capital sacked by its own people as mobs took to the street in a frenzy of rioting, rape and pillage, much of it aimed at the tiny but relatively wealthy ethnic Chinese minority.

After two presidents in 43 years, Indonesians saw a parade of three in the next five: Suharto's protégé, the hyperactive aircraft engineer B. J. Habibie, the wildly unpredictable blind Muslim liberal Abdurrahman Wahid and Sukarno's eldest daughter, the stodgy and matronly Megawati Sukarnoputri. In this time East Timor, annexed by Suharto in 1975, had voted to secede, and had been torched in retaliation by Jakarta-backed militias. In Borneo, Dayak tribes had revived an old headhunting tradition to rid their island of Madurese settlers. In east Java mobs periodically lynched those they suspected of being ninjas—allegedly black-clad black-magicians—and it was not uncommon to read of someone beaten to death for stealing a chicken or snatching a chain. Christians and Muslims had fallen upon each other in the Moluccas and in central Sulawesi. Muslim militias—Laskar Jihad, Laskar Jundullah, Laskar Mujahidin, Islamic Defenders Front—sprang up around the country, seemingly at will. Separatist movements simmered in the resource-rich provinces of Aceh in the west and Papua in the east. During Reformasi, bombs went off in shopping malls and churches. Here and there the police battled the army for control of smuggling rings and protection rackets, brothels and gambling dens.

The scale of national reinvention was staggering. Indonesia had morphed almost overnight—between 1999 and 2001—from one of the most centralised large countries in the world to one of the most decentralised. After elections in 1999, the first free vote in four decades, Suharto's rubber-stamp parliament had given way to one which bickered about everything from presidential power to personal perks. The army, unsure whether to reform or regroup, was in a sense at war with itself. The poodle press had developed a pitbull snarl. 'Mega's Mouth Smells like Diesel Fuel,' screamed a famous headline about the president in the popular newspaper *Rakyat Merdeka*.

The economy, meanwhile, remained adrift. Per capita income

hovered at pre-crisis levels. With both foreign and domestic invest-ment drying up, only consumption, much of it conspicuous, showed signs of life; Starbucks had opened shop in Jakarta, as had Ferrari. The anti-graft NGO Transparency International regularly ranked Indonesia as one of the most corrupt places on earth, though without Suharto graft too had become more democratic: local governments invented new taxes; publishers swayed school syllabi; policemen and soldiers moonlighted as guards and, for the right price, as assassins. To the outside world the former miracle economy, once compared with Korea and Taiwan, now belonged in the same breath as Nigeria and Bangladesh.

3

Jakarta

In Jakarta I lived in an apartment complex called Puri Casablanca, four tall pink towers on the edge of the central business district or, as the website boasted, 'strategically located in golden triangle.' Each tower was named for a flower: Allamanda, Bougainvillea, Cattleya and Dahlia. This wasn't the top end of the market—the Four Seasons or the Dharmawangsa with their BMW and Jaguar lined underground parking—but it wasn't quite the bottom either. A profusion of fresh flowers greeted you in the lobby; the marble floors gleamed with polish; the water in the kidney-shaped swimming pool stayed a clear pale blue all year round. The New York Deli next to it, where the servers were Deep Purple fans, dished up Rubens and Rachels and Turkey Clubs with American meats and Australian cheeses and Kettle Chips in four flavours.

Propped against the living room wall of my apartment, on the eighth floor of Allamanda, was a black and white cartoon by an artist from Yogyakarta. It showed the *dangdut* performer Inul Daratista onstage, her famous backside encased in tight striped pants.

Across from her, on another stage, stood her nemesis, Rhoma Irama, an older dangdut star. Rhoma had once borrowed his look from Elvis Presley and his sound partly from Deep Purple, but he had since found God and placed his voice in the service of the faith. My cartoon showed him belting out *nasyid*, devotional Islamic music.

Dangdut, onomatopoeically named for the Indian drumbeat that ran through most songs, was popular music, the music of the street. Inul Daratista ('The Girl with the Breasts') was the stage name of Ainul Rokhimah, a 25-year-old peasant girl from the *abangan*, or nominal Muslim, heartland of east Java. Inul was something of a hero to me. She had started out performing at village weddings and circumcision ceremonies for 10,000 rupiah (about a dollar) a song and now charged, as the papers breathlessly reported, 70 million rupiah for a forty-minute appearance. This metamorphosis from impoverished yokel to superstar, as the papers peevishly reported, owed less to Inul's voice than to her backside. She had invented a dance move called drilling that had quickly become all the rage. It involved, to put it simply, rotating her behind faster and faster in a blur of tightening circles.

The previous year drilling had drawn the wrath of the Council of Indonesian Ulama, a powerful quasi-official group of mullahs. They called Inul 'devilish' and 'lustful' and as proof of her malign influence brought up a man who claimed that a pirated VCD of her act had led him to rape a child. Rhoma Irama, ageing and ill-tempered, joined the chorus of outrage. Concerned about her future in the industry a cowed Inul approached Rhoma for his blessings, but this only brought on public humiliation. 'She performs trash,' announced Rhoma at a press conference. (This from a man with a fondness for white leather bodysuits.) Rhoma proceeded to ban Inul from performing any of his songs.

In the end, however, Inul appeared to have the last laugh. The former president Abdurrahman Wahid and a clutch of women's groups rallied behind her. Though his eyesight prevented him from appreciating the finer points of drilling, Wahid declared that it ought to be protected as an art form. Hundreds of noisy feminists drilled in solidarity at the Hotel Indonesia circle. The pious Rhoma's reputation received a jolt when a tabloid journalist reported him exiting a starlet's bungalow at dawn. Since then Inul's popularity had acquired new proportions. She had become the best-paid entertainer in the country. She was on television advertising everything from motorcycles to mosquito coils and playing herself in a miniseries based on her life story. On the streets they sold Inul pencils—made of rubber, supple and flexible.

Crown Entertainment Center belonged in a Moammar Emka book. On the street outside toothless vendors peddled pirated porn DVDs with loud cries of, 'hello mister chicky-chicky.' Though rooted in the small business hustle and open sewers of the Chinese neighbourhood Glodok, the centre itself was rather more upscale than its surroundings and included a spa, a disco, a massage parlour and private karaoke rooms.

About two months after the *Jakarta Undercover* party I shook off my lethargy one evening to visit Crown. I took the elevator to the seventh floor, passed through a metal detector and then up a sweeping stairway that terminated at a sign that said 'VVIP Ladies'. Most of the staff milling about were girls in snug navy blue dresses with flawless skin and shampoo commercial hair. A covey of them clustered by a flickering computer screen in a low, open booth shaped like a horseshoe.

The show wasn't due to begin for another half hour and the disco's doors were still shut. I waited on the lip of a wall-high waterfall facing the booth. Security was tight on account of the night's special guest; men in safari suits with cropped skulls and beefy forearms barked instructions into their walkie-talkies. A couple of them looked pointedly at my beard and my black messenger bag, but nobody said anything. To my right, one-third of a long banner touted a new brand of mild kretek; the other two-thirds was given to a picture of Inul sheathed in black leather, silver chains on her hips, her hair piled high in caramel-coloured curls. An older woman, a *mamasan*—chunky legs, painted red lips, pencil eyebrows—lowered her bulk beside me and placed a sleek new Sony digital camera in my hands. Would I explain how to use it? I turned it on and showed her which button to click. When I aimed the camera at her she exclaimed in horror, 'No, no,' and pointed at one of her girls, young and chubby in a tight black skirt and a T-shirt with a sepia-tinted picture of Britney Spears. 'I'm ugly. Take her picture instead.'

At length the doors swung open on a dark and cavernous room with dozens of round black tables on three sides of a dance floor. A stage under a canopy shaped like a large crown, of the kind I associated with either Henry VIII or the King of Hearts, abutted the fourth. Blue light bounced off two drum sets and a synthesiser. On a screen above them a dandelion exploded in a million pieces. The room quickly began to fill, for the most part with middle-class twenty-somethings, not the sort you would usually find at a dangdut concert. Waiters in canary yellow Formula One pit stop crew uniforms threaded their way between tables with tall bottles of Beer Bintang. A sign came on screen, a red circle with the words 'Ngebor is not a Crime.' *Ngebor* was Indonesian for 'drilling'.

As befit her status, Inul was late. While we waited, a boyish and somewhat nervous host did his best to amuse the swelling crowd. He boasted about the building's amenities: bar, spa, disco, cigar cellar. He talked up a 70 percent discount on the karaoke rooms that night and a 50 percent discount on 'beverages'. The American word in a sentence of Indonesian sounded odd to my ears. He offered a prize for anyone wearing glasses with spots on them, for anyone in batik underwear. Nobody came forward. He asked us to guess Inul's shoe size. (Thirty-nine, it turned out.) As the audience's impatience grew palpable, he persuaded three college girls to drill. They came onstage giggling and did their imitation, shyly and slowly. At last the host darted into the wings and a thrill of anticipation ran through the room. The drummers took their places, then two long-haired men on electric guitars and a short-haired man on the synthesiser. Perhaps to make up for the delay, they skipped a warm-up and immediately fell upon their instruments with a vigour that suggested a secret contest to see who could burst your eardrums first. A few moment later Inul glided onstage in a silver latex bodysuit, silver chains around her neck and dangling from her hips. The music died while she struck a brief pose under a spotlight, middle finger and thumb together like an Indian dancer. Then it resumed, faster and, if this was possible, louder. Inul shook her big curly mane over her face like a heavy metal rocker. 'Hho! Hho!' she barked. A crush of fans, camera phones aloft, surged to the edge of the stage. 'Hho! Hho! Hho!' screeched Inul, her hair a blur.

I had been looking forward to a performance both devilish and lustful, but the person onstage resembled an over-caffeinated gym instructress more than an erotic temptress. She dropped her hair over her face again and pulled it back with a sharp jerk. Flailing her arms violently, she played air guitar. The papers, you had to admit, were right about her vocal limitations; I cringed each time her voice reached for a high note, like a piece of chalk on an unfortunate blackboard. After about half a dozen songs, including a popular one about herself, Inul sauntered to the edge of the stage. 'If I sing a song by *Pak* Rhoma he'll call the police,' she said mimicking a phone with thumb and little finger. The room filled with hisses and boos. Inul nodded at the band to resume its assault, took three strides towards the centre of the stage, and halted. Swivelling on one heel, she pumped the other leg like a piston—knee bent, knee straight, knee bent. As she gathered momentum her ample latex-clad behind bore down in circles, lower and lower, faster and faster, lower, faster, faster, lower. The effect eluded words. It was mesmerising as only a silver bottom rotating at high speed could be.

Barely 45 minutes after she stepped onstage Inul was gone. In the elevator on the way down her fans whispered about the millions this appearance had commanded.

I first heard about Herry from Santi Soekanto, a journalist who spoke impeccable English with a faintly English accent, cloaked herself head to toe in a black abaya and occasionally wrote about Islam in the *Jakarta Post*. Around the time of the Inul concert my Chinese–Indonesian assistant, a 22 year old just out of college named Maretha, had left me for a better paying job in public relations. This came as a bit of a relief, for though Maretha was neat and tidy, conscientious about clipping and filing stories about politicians and preachers, and persistent in setting up interviews with the likes of the reformed metropolitan girl and the polygamous fried chicken magnate, I had come to what ought to have been a mind-numbingly obvious realisation: that a Chinese girl with a well-thumbed Bible in her handbag wasn't about to open any of the doors I most needed opened. I had hoped to work with Santi, but when she declined I asked her to suggest someone else, someone more intimate than me with the landscape of Islam. She emailed me three résumés, one of which belonged to a Herry Nurdi, the managing editor of the fundamentalist mouthpiece *Sabili*.

Like so much else, *Sabili* was a creature of Reformasi. The New Order had shuttered an earlier incarnation, launched in 1989 by activists using false names and, it was generally believed, Saudi funds. Its views were deemed too strident even at a time when President Suharto had begun to shed his former aversion to mixing Islam and politics. In 1998, in the first flush of democracy, *Sabili* had sprung up again and now, just six years later, rivalled mainstream publications in its clout. I had seen it sold outside mosques and recalled seeing Osama bin Laden on its cover. A few months after the Bali bombings *Sabili* had named Abu Bakar Bashir, the elderly Yemeni-Indonesian who allegedly headed Jemaah Islamiyah—the terrorist group believed responsible—its man of the year. 'If Bashir, most of whose life has been devoted to upholding Islamic sharia law, should be called a terrorist, being terrorists might as well be our goal,' said the article.

One morning, about a week after the Inul concert, Herry and I met at Puri Casablanca, in the lobby of Allamanda. My first impression was positive: he wore a neatly pressed full-sleeved batik shirt, which either meant that this meeting mattered to him or that he had somewhere important to go afterwards. He was half a head shorter than me with deep brown skin, a beard thicker on the neck than on the face, and a shaved upper lip. His haircut evoked a world of terse barbering. He had a callus like a thick hyphen on his forehead, proof of hours spent prostrated in prayer. His jaw was slightly askew giving him a crab-like look; his walk, an almost sideways shuffle accentuated this impression.

In a café near the swimming pool I explained my situation and the kind of book I hoped to write. Herry's eyes brightened with understanding and I found myself taking an immediate liking to him. I outlined my rudimentary thesis: that Indonesia was being shaped by two essentially opposed forces, Islamisation and globalisation, and that of the two Islam was the more important. When I had finished Herry asked me a question.

'What do you think of Naipaul?'

I measured my response.

'His work about India is far superior to anything he ever wrote about Indonesia. You can't spend three months in a country and expect to write about it with nuance.'

Naipaul had, of course, mocked Islam in the non-Arab world, its mimicry and its acute discomfort with a pre-Islamic past. You couldn't expect the managing editor of *Sabili* to be a fan. So my response, though not strictly untrue, was tailored for his benefit. Herry nodded his agreement and then told me about a *Washington Post* reporter who had written a negative piece about *Sabili* after it named Bashir man of the year. I wasn't the one being interviewed, but I felt as though I had passed a test.

I asked Herry to tell me a little more about himself. He was from Surabaya in east Java. He was married and had a three-year-old daughter; a second child was on its way. I said he looked a little young for a managing editor. He was 27 years old, he said. He had never been to college, but had worked his way up at *Sabili* and now ran a team of reporters. His pride in the magazine was evident. It sold eighty thousand copies a week, he said, more than any other news weekly in the country, though few people knew that.

'Do you have any more questions for me?' I asked.

'I hope you'll be fair when you write about Islam.'

'I'll do my best.'

We agreed to travel together to the places that required his mediation; others, such as the fleshpots of Batam, I would see alone. I would pay him for his time, but as we shook hands before Herry shuffled off for his next appointment I got the feeling that he had agreed to do it more for the adventure than for the cash.

I felt confident of keeping my promise of fairness. Writers on Islam tended to fall somewhere between two poles. At one end were those who liked to quote chapter and verse from the Koran and episodes from the life of the Prophet to prove that the faith was inherently violent. Did not the Koran command Muslims to 'slay the idolators wherever you find them,' and hadn't Mohammed himself ordered the beheading of seven hundred prisoners from the Jewish tribe

Banu Qurayza in Medina? At the other end were those who insisted that Islam was a 'religion of peace', and who liked to suggest that jihad really only meant striving for self-improvement, never mind all the suicide bombers and militia members who begged to differ.

I placed myself in the middle. As a lifelong atheist I had little sympathy for organised religion; Islamic orthodoxy's stark division of humanity between believers and unbelievers, and its treatment of non-Muslims and women struck me as especially distasteful. All non-Muslim worship was banned in Saudi Arabia and a certain barbarism touched the Islamic approach to divorce. I also accepted that the Prophet's life, shot through with war and conquest, allowed violent Muslims to sanctify their behaviour in religious terms unavailable to, say, Buddhists or Quakers. That Mohammed was as much a political leader as a spiritual one made it harder for Muslim societies to accept the separation of mosque and state. That the Koran was seen as the literal word of God, unchanging and unchangeable, made coming to terms with modernity harder for orthodox Sunni Muslim societies than for most others.

At the same time, though, Muslims hardly had a monopoly on religious intolerance and it didn't take a genius to mine examples of the absurd and the cruel from the holy texts of most any faith. I had encountered my share of Hindu and Christian bigots and most Muslims of my acquaintance—Indians, Pakistanis, Indonesians—were as open-minded and as averse to violence as anyone else. For the most part I felt, with the light condescension of the atheist, that practising Muslims, like people of any religion, turned to faith for what solace it offered in an imperfect world. While I couldn't share their enthusiasm, neither would I begrudge it.

As for Islamism, it was hard to think of many things more daft or dangerous than the utopian idea of running a modern society by the medieval norms enshrined in the sharia. The experiment had failed in every country that tried it—Saudi Arabia, Iran, Sudan, Taliban-era

Afghanistan. But here too my curiosity dwarfed whatever distaste the sharia-minded inspired. I might never grow to admire Islamism, but I'd do my best to understand its followers.

I didn't hear from Herry for a week and then he called one afternoon to say he would come over. As usual, my apartment was a wreck with books and papers piled high on the dining table and a stack of short stories printed from the *New Yorker*, *Ploughshares* and half a dozen obscure journals taking up half the living room couch. As I began tidying up I came upon a transparent plastic pouch filled with garlands made from gnarled brown rudraksha beads. The beads were considered holy by Hindus and I had bought them as presents for my father and an uncle before a reporting trip to India that fell through at the last minute. They were the seed of a plant that grew only in Nepal and Indonesia, and the Indonesian variety was said to be the superior. My first instinct was to hide the garlands. A part of me needed my new Islamist employee's approval; I didn't want him to think me superstitious. Another part of me revolted against this instinct to pander to Herry by effacing myself. In the end I resisted the urge to squirrel the rudrakshas away in the bedroom and let them remain on the dining table. They were hardly that visible anyway amid all the clutter, I reasoned.

Herry had a bright orange plastic tag with the word 'guest' clipped to his blue quilted jacket. The concierge had made him wear it. They never handed my American or English friends a tag, but the rules were apparently different for obviously Muslim-looking men. This was a true mark of Third Worldness, shared equally by Indonesia and India. Locals treated foreigners (not counting Africans) better than they did each other.

Herry apologised for not having found the time to see me sooner. *Sabili* was in a spot of trouble for attacking Susilo Bambang Yudhoyono, or SBY as he was popularly called, the former general who had emerged as Megawati's leading challenger in the forthcoming presidential election—the first round of voting was barely two months away. *Sabili* had accused SBY of not being a real Muslim, but a 'mystic'. By this they meant the Islam he followed still incorporated pre-Islamic beliefs; he was not fully Arabised. According to the classic typology made famous by Clifford Geertz, Javanese Muslims could be divided into three categories. The devout—those who took seriously the obligation to pray five times a day, fast during the month of Ramadan, make the hajj pilgrimage to Mecca and so on—were called *santris*. Nominal Muslims of the lower classes were called abangan, which means 'red' in Javanese. They were mostly peasants and practised an easygoing folk Islam shot through with pre-Islamic beliefs and practices. The third category consisted of the aristocratic nominal Muslims known as *priyayi*, or to borrow Geertz's evocative description, 'white collar nobles'. These were Java's gentry, known for their refined etiquette, their love of the arts and their penchant for mystical meditation. For the most part, they differed from the abangan more in class than in outlook, a Javanese version of the divide between high church and low. Like the abangan, the priyayi were concentrated in east and central Java.

I found the attack on SBY ironic. Not long ago priyayi ruling elites who were descended, as legend had it, from Kshatriyas, the warrior caste of the old Hindu kingdoms, would have worn the accusation of being a mystic with honour. I thought of *Bumi Manusia* (*This Earth of Mankind*) the first book of Pramoedya Ananta Toer's *Buru Quartet*, in which the protagonist's mother reminds him of his lineage on his wedding night: 'You are a descendant of the knights of Java...' But now, in this democratic age, any hint of the past had evidently become something to hide.

Herry chuckled. 'They sue *Sabili*.'

I asked him which presidential candidates had the soundest religious credentials. He told me how General Wiranto, an Islamist favourite, prayed five times a day now but was known to have been less devout earlier in his career when the army was synonymous with an aversion to orthodox Islam. Herry thought it ironic that Wiranto's wife was tented head to toe whereas the wife of Amien Rais, a candidate more formally rooted in Islam, chose only the jilbab, that too in bright colours. While he was speaking, something in my balcony appeared to catch Herry's eye. He stood up abruptly and peered outside. 'It's time for me to pray,' he said. 'Where can I wash?'

A few minutes later Herry emerged from the bathroom wearing a white skullcap that seemed to add ten years to his demeanour. Stepping out on the balcony, he craned his neck to establish which way was west. He came back inside and dropped his quilted jacket on the living room floor. I was overcome by awkwardness. What was I supposed to do with myself while he prayed? Would it be disrespectful to check email? Did he need privacy? In the end I tiptoed into another room. There I read an essay by Jamaica Kincaid while Herry prostrated himself in prayer, his head bowed towards my front door and the Koreans across the hall, whose apartment, I now knew, faced Mecca.

'It isn't good,' said Herry. 'The jury trying to be like Simon Cowell. Sometimes so sarcastic to contestant.' We were in a Silver Bird, a black limousine taxi, a few days after his visit to my apartment discussing 'Indonesian Idol', only just into its first season. 'Mohammed the Prophet once said that a sign of approaching doomsday is many people trying to be singer. I see that now. In America, in Europe.'

'In Indonesia too,' I added helpfully.

'In Indonesia too. He said there are fifteen signs. I can't remember them all. One was an invasion near the river Euphrates. Maybe that is Iraq.'

'What will happen on doomsday?'

'I don't think there will be life if there's doomsday. Maybe it's better if it's after I'm dead.'

A few minutes later we arrived at a women's hospital, one of the many good works of the vast Muhammadiyah movement dedicated to the purification of Islam. We were to see Din Syamsuddin, a senior man in the organisation, the following week and I wanted to visit one of its schools or hospitals before that. Herry had figured that it was better to simply show up rather than make an appointment in advance, but now we found that nobody would see us. The doctors were all busy; the nurses weren't willing to talk. We waited in a walled courtyard, side-by-side on hard plastic chairs, our backs to a wall with 'Allah' written above us in Arabic. I tried not to breathe the antiseptic hospital smell too deeply.

Women at Muhammadiyah meetings covered their heads and the hospital was no different. The female staff—nurses, receptionists, phone operators—all wore the jilbab but, to my mild surprise, many of the patients didn't. I commented on this to Herry, on how Indonesia was tolerant in the sense that jilbabs didn't appear to bother the un-jilbabed majority and bare heads were acceptable even in a place like this. He agreed. But it wasn't like this everywhere, he added. He recalled visiting Aceh a few years earlier when they had first begun implementing a watered-down form of sharia. 'I saw two uncovered women dragged off the street opposite the Masjid Raya to have their heads shaved as punishment,' he said. His voice expressed neither approval nor revulsion. I couldn't make out whether this was because he was a journalist or an Islamist.

As if on cue, a woman in a tight white dress crossed the courtyard on her way out. Her shiny black hair fell to her waist. She carried a large handbag shaped like a sheep with a zipper down its back; the bag swayed with the roll of her hips.

'How do you feel when you see someone like that?' I asked.

'I don't like it, but there's nothing I can do. I'm not angry, but I feel pity for them. First, I feel that they are not free. They can be called sexy because of their clothes. There's a stigma. To be sexy you have to wear a short skirt or tight clothes.'

He hadn't yet learned how to be angry at the sight of a woman's bare head, I thought. That level of intolerance was hard to manage in Indonesia, especially if you lived in Jakarta. There were simply too many bare heads in the shopping malls and shampoo commercials on television. It would have meant being permanently enraged.

We made another round of the doctors without luck and then returned to our perch and talked about books for a while before Herry shuffled off to refill his phone card. When he came back he wanted to tell me about his family. His wife was expecting their second child, due any day now.

'I want to get married again,' he said.

'I bet your wife would have something to say about that.'

'I said to my wife, "How about if I marry again?" She said, "That's fine, but I won't go to your wedding party. You do it yourself."' He laughed. 'If I marry again, it's not an Indonesian, but I want one from Jordan.'

'Why Jordan?'

'Because I want to enter Palestine.'

'You'll find it hard to find a Jordanian bride.'

'Yes, it's difficult. But if we go to Mecca and Medina maybe we can find.'

I remembered a conversation with a Saudi tourist at a Jakarta pizza parlour who had claimed that his countrymen liked German women best. It had something to do with bloodlines.

'Why not marry some other foreigner, a European or an Australian, and convert her?'

'It's difficult enough with a Muslim. I see women in Jordan. They go out without the jilbab. The lifestyle is very glamorous. The shoes are Gucci, the watch is Alexander Christi, the bag is—'

'What is Alexander Christi?'

'It's a brand.'

He continued. 'But what's really interesting is that I went to Mecca and Medina and there are no women with any part of their body showing. Everything is closed very tightly.' He brought his fingers to his eyes to make slits. 'But if you go to Jeddah, only two hours away, maybe you can find women with—' He put his hand on his belly to indicate a bare midriff. 'Maybe you will see them in the supermarket.'

A nurse came by and said that there was still nobody available to talk to us.

In the evening we set off in search of a television serial being shot in a Jakarta suburb that called itself 'City of a Million Charms'. We only needed to find one person in the city of a million charms. And though we had no address we knew it would be easy. As our Silver Bird nosed into the city, I rolled down the window. 'Where's Inul?' I asked a pair of schoolgirls still in their uniforms. They pointed down a street and reeled off directions. They knew. Everyone knew. 'I read that she paid 8 billion rupiah for her house in Pondok Indah,' said the Silver Bird driver.

This was our first full day together, but Herry and I had already established an easy familiarity. As journalists we possessed the plasticity of character that comes from ingratiating yourself with the unlikeliest people. Even so, the ease of our banter surprised me. When we spoke in English, about half the time so far, Herry's words could suggest crudeness. In fact his English, though self-taught, matched my Indonesian, and I had had the benefit of lessons and of three years of practise, four if you counted pre-teen efforts. In Herry's mind I detected a restless, burrowing quality. His interests spanned books and politics and current affairs. His sense of humour leaned towards the impolitic; he said he often wondered whether the large number of Indians who seemed to die all the time in accidents was a form of population control. Of course my rush of goodwill towards him, the almost giddy optimism I felt on reviving my project, sweetened my judgement. After the failed hospital expedition we had lunched at one of the polygamous chicken magnate's restaurants before returning to Puri Casablanca to go over our itinerary in detail. Herry had thrown in a couple of good suggestions. His self-confidence verged on cockiness. Access would be no problem at all.

The driver located the house without any trouble and soon Herry and I found ourselves in a well-lit living room. Fat black cables trailed the floor. Bright lights burned on tall aluminium stands. Stuffed toys—four koala bears, three teddy bears, a sheep, a moose, a kangaroo—gave the shelves and sofas a nursery quality. They were in the middle of a shot. A TV monitor showed a mousy-looking woman in knee-length lycra pants and a frilly brown blouse doing dishes. That's a maid, I thought and continued to scour the room for Inul. A few minutes later the evening call to prayer settled like a blanket over the city of a million charms. 'Cut,' shouted the director. I still hadn't spotted Inul. The maid in the frilly blouse walked up to the monitor and everyone's eyes followed her.

'What will you eat *Mbak* Inul?' someone asked.

'Vegetables and liver.'

I looked at her again, carefully. Minus the latex bodysuit, the silver chains on her hips, and the elaborate coiffure Inul appeared diminished, shrunk two sizes, like a Lhasa apso after a bath. She looked like I imagined she might have not so long ago when she was whirling amid the freshly circumcised in east Java. Before we had a chance to accost her, Inul sauntered into another room while a minion scurried off to fetch her dinner. By now it had started to pour. The rain drummed hard on the roof and the scent of wet earth rushed in through an open door. The director announced that they would break until the shower subsided. Sensing our opportunity, Herry and I approached a secretary, who said we could interview Inul while they waited. After a few minutes she emerged from a bedroom, slipped off a pair of black thongs bedecked with pink plastic orchids, and arranged herself cross-legged on a sofa, a pillow on her lap. She looked at us without interest and scratched distractedly between her breasts.

I proffered a somewhat halting preamble about writing a book and apologised for my Indonesian. Inul smiled sympathetically, revealing braces on her lower teeth. Light bounced off a stone set in one of her incisors. She saw it catch my eye. It was a diamond, a blue diamond, she said. For some mysterious reason the diamond restored her star power, as though someone had pulled a secret lever; for a few moments I was bedazzled, at a loss for words. I had interviewed a president and two foreign ministers and too many ambassadors and members of parliament and CEOs to count, but this was of a different order. They didn't carry the weight of a year's worth of clippings; they didn't have diamonds in their teeth. Inul rested her hand on my arm and told me to relax. Stepping in deftly, Herry revealed that he too was from east Java, from Surabaya. They lapsed into a few words of Javanese. He switched back to Indonesian and told her he was with *Sabili*. She nodded and said of course she knew *Sabili*.

My composure recovered, I began by asking Inul about her run-in with the Council of Indonesian Ulama. I had already rehearsed the interview in my head. I knew what she would say. She would attack the mullahs. She would say something spirited about freedom of expression or a woman's right to rotate her behind any which way she liked. My imagination had assigned her a role; she would fulfill it.

'Right now it's the era of Inul Daratista's drilling,' she said. 'It has caused a commotion. People are copying it. I don't like it. I don't forbid it, but I don't like it.'

'Why not?'

'I am trying to change from the Inul Daratista they used to call very pornographic. This is to become better. They ought to take as an example how I have learned to be better, not how I was bad before. Yes, of course, drilling is still drilling, but there are definite boundaries. There are so many dances now. They're dancing in all kinds of ways.'

Though I had asked the question she looked at Herry while she answered. He leaned forward, his eyes brimming with empathy.

'And they all blame Inul?' he asked.

'Yes. In the end they all blame me.'

She shifted to face Herry better.

'What worries you the most?' he asked.

'I don't feel worried about my career. The world is like a rotating wheel. Sometimes I'm up and sometimes I'm down. My only concern is that I'm able to perform my prayers to God. That's all. And how I can be devoted to my husband.'

'This is interesting,' said Herry gently. 'The Council of Ulama attacked you, but you have religious motivation that, according to me, has been underscored by your words.'

'To tell you the truth, people don't know what our family is like. Everyone in my family is a fanatic. We are all fanatics about our faith.'

Herry brightened visibly. 'How are you fanatics?'

'Ehm, my father, if I returned home from a show after midnight he would not let me in the house. And if we ever forgot to pray father would always undo—'

'His belt?' I thought I detected a note of eagerness in his voice.

'His belt so that he could hit us children.'

By now Inul was fully warmed up.

'Look at those other girls. Look at those girls in Bali how they dance. The dancers there are more pornographic. They're like this—' She rubbed her palms together, slowly and suggestively.

Herry nodded. She had evidently touched a chord in him.

After the interview we posed for pictures, me with my arm around Inul's shoulder, then Herry sitting stiffly beside her, a lopsided grin on his face, but careful not to touch her. The rain had stopped and we watched a few more minutes of the dishwashing scene before deciding that it was time to return to Jakarta. Back in the Silver Bird Herry was pensive. He said he felt bad. He had had no idea of Inul's piety, or of her family's. He had allowed his reporters to savage her and now he felt contrite. I had had no idea either. I wasn't quite sure what to make of it, except that it put drilling in a whole new light.

4

Nationalists v. Islamists

The basic split in Indonesian politics was between nationalists, who thought of religion as a largely personal matter and Islamists, the sharia-minded, who believed that Islam ought to regulate society and the state. This split could be traced to contending views of history.

For the most part nationalists saw Indonesia as a successor to the great Hindu–Buddhist Majapahit Empire (1293–circa 1500), the political and cultural acme of Javanese civilisation. The nationalist past embraced Gajah Mada, a fourteenth-century prime minister famous for vowing to eat only unspiced food until he had united the archipelago; and Joyoboyo, a twelfth-century east Javanese ruler who personified the ideal of Ratu Adil, the just king, and authored a book that reputedly foretold colonisation by the Dutch, their displacement by the Japanese, and eventual independence. This conception of pre-colonial unity fuelled the independence struggle, strengthened subsequent claims to Dutch West New Guinea and Portuguese-ruled East Timor, and gave a natural place in the country to Hindu Bali and the Christian parts of eastern Indonesia.

Islamists tended to take a narrower view. All that mattered, they believed, came with the advent of their faith. The vast Buddhist complex of Borobudur and the finely carved Hindu temples of Prambanan were dismissed as relics of polytheistic barbarism. Christian majority regions symbolised missionary encroachments to be erased with the passage of time. If Islamists looked to a glorious past, it was to Baghdad and Moorish Spain. If they needed heroes, they could find them in the faith's early years in the Arabian peninsula or, at a stretch if archipelagic roots were required, in the first sultanates in Sumatra and Java.

The story of Islamism's ascent and nationalism's eclipse breaks naturally into four acts rather than three: Old Order, New Order One, New Order Two and Reformasi. In Sukarno's Indonesia (1945–65) Islam as a faith was largely heterodox; as an ideology it was bested by both nationalism and communism. During the first 25-odd years of Suharto's rule (1965–90) orthodox piety soared, but Islamism remained out in the political cold. Suharto's later years (1990–98) and Reformasi (1998 onwards) saw both orthodox practice and Islamist politics metastasise as never before.

The contest began at independence in 1945 with the defeat of an early attempt by Islamists to force Muslims to follow sharia. Worried that the fragile new nation would fracture, Sukarno helped scuttle the so-called Jakarta Charter, a constitutional amendment which would have based the state on, 'belief in God with the obligation of adherents of Islam to carry out Islamic law.' Instead he backed Pancasila, the national ideology, which guarantees equality for the followers of all five of Indonesia's recognised religions: Buddhism, Christianity (Protestant and Catholic), Hinduism and Islam. Pancasila consists of five somewhat fuzzy principles: belief in one God, just and civilised humanitarianism, national unity, democracy through consultation and social justice.

Sukarno himself was perhaps the best reflection of his times. Sukarno's father was a priyayi Theosophist, his mother a Balinese Hindu. The first president was named after Karna in the *Mahabharata*, offspring of Surya, the Sun, and Kunti, the mother of the Pandava brothers. Like most Javanese of his time and class, Sukarno displayed an eclectic, inclusive approach to faith, one rooted in the essential Javanese belief that many are the paths to God. He built the massive Istiqlal mosque in Jakarta and went on the hajj; but he was also known to consult *dukuns*—Javanist seers—and to revere an ancient kris, the spiritually potent dagger traditionally handed down from father to son. He studied the Koran while imprisoned by the Dutch and claimed, in his autobiography, to bow to Mecca five times a day. He also read the Bible with a Dutch pastor, could quote verbatim from the Sermon on the Mount, and boasted of holding three of the Vatican's highest orders while the president of Ireland claimed only one.

The new nation's symbols reflected an intense awareness of history. The national coat of arms depicted the semi-divine eagle Garuda from the Hindu epic *Ramayana*, with the words in old Javanese of a fourteenth-century Majapahit poet, *Bhinneka Tunggal Ika* ('Unity in Diversity'), penned originally to unite quarrelling Buddhists and Shaivites, devotees of the Hindu God Shiva. Garuda also loaned his name to the national airline. An elite liberal arts university in Yogyakarta was named for Gajah Mada. Ganesha, scribe of the *Mahabharata* and God of wisdom, graced the shield of its technical peer and Sukarno's alma mater, the Institute of Technology in Bandung. The army housed divisional commands named after Brawijaya, the last Hindu king of Majapahit, who was said to have embraced Islam, and after Diponegoro, a mystical Muslim Javanese prince who led a nineteenth-century revolt against the Dutch. But it also commemorated the pre-Islamic west Javanese kingdom of Siliwangi, the Sumatra-based Buddhist trading empire of Sriwijaya, and Tanjungpura, a shadowy Majapahit-era kingdom in Borneo.

Though Islamism found no friend in Sukarno, during his rule it was communism rather than nationalism that was aimed like a proverbial dagger at its heart. In the elections of 1955, just seven years after being put down by the army in Madiun, the Indonesian Communist Party (PKI) bounced back unexpectedly, winning more than 6 million votes, about 16 percent of the total, which placed it fourth after Sukarno's nationalists and two large Muslim parties. For a country officially 90 percent Muslim, Islam's political appeal was underwhelming. Masyumi, the more strictly scriptural of the Muslim parties, drew 21 percent, about half of it outside Java. Nahdlatul Ulama (The Awakening of the Ulama), the political vehicle of Javanese mullahs, pulled in 18 percent, almost all in Java. The PKI drew its support from the same island: Javanese made up 85 percent of its voters; in the densely populated abangan strongholds of east and central Java one in two voters supported the party.

Despite the strong showing, the communists were locked out of formal power. The pro-Western army leadership, with its memory of the PKI rebellion in Madiun, made no effort to hide its hostility; nor did the Muslim and Christian parties that excluded the PKI from the series of short-lived governments that riddled the 1950s. But the party, confident of both history's and Sukarno's favour, took these setbacks in its stride. It was easily the best organised political force in the country. New recruits continued to flock to PKI organisations for peasants, women and youth. It controlled an influential artists and writers collective and the largest trade union. It frequently flexed its street muscle, rallying the placarded poor to press its demands and, increasingly, to back Sukarno's pronouncements against the Oldefos and Nekolim.

In 1960 Sukarno tightened his tango with the communists; chatterbox democracy had been replaced by the guided sort the previous year. He began championing the blend of nationalism, religion and communism he called Nasakom. He banned the puritanical Masyumi (along with the small but influential socialist party) for backing the west Sumatra-based, CIA-sponsored rebellion, and subsequently imprisoned many of its leaders, including a former prime minister, Mohammad Natsir. By now the PKI had emerged as the president's most vocal ally. In 1962 Sukarno invited Chairman D. N. Aidit and his number two, Nyoto, into his cabinet as ministers without portfolio. A year later the party began a sporadic campaign to seize land for the landless. By 1965 the PKI was the largest communist party outside China and the Soviet Union. It claimed 3 million members, thirty thousand of them trained cadres, and between 15 and 20 million supporters.

Act Two (1965–90) begins in Jakarta on the night of 30 September 1965 with an abortive coup led by left-wing elements of Sukarno's presidential guard. At first events appeared to unfold according to a carefully laid plan. Rebel troops killed three conservative generals in their homes and took three others, along with a lieutenant unlucky to be in the wrong place, to Lobang Buaya, the 'Crocodile Hole', an abandoned rubber plantation abutting an air force base used as rebel headquarters. There the four prisoners were executed and all seven bodies thrown into a deep well. The next morning the rebels identified themselves on the radio as the 30 September Movement. They promised to eradicate corruption and to bolster President Sukarno. They said their movement was an internal army affair, and that they had acted to preempt a CIA-backed coup against Sukarno by a council of generals.

In hindsight things might have turned out differently for the 30 September Movement if not for a series of elementary blunders. The army chief, General Nasution, escaped his would-be assassins by clambering over a wall into his neighbour's garden. More decisively, Suharto, then a major general and commander of the elite Army Strategic Reserve Command was—suspiciously, accidentally or providentially depending on your point of view—never targeted. Early on the morning of 1 October he drove himself to his headquarters in the heart of the city. Over the course of the day he took command of the army and bluffed, cajoled and threatened the poorly organised rebels into submission, a task simplified by their failure to supply troops outside the presidential palace with sufficient food and water. A few hours after nightfall Suharto controlled Jakarta and the coup was effectively over.

The extent of PKI involvement in the 30 September Movement remains a matter of scholarly squabble. On the one hand, the murdered generals were staunchly anti-communist. In the fog of the coup's unfolding, Aidit along with Sukarno and the pro-communist air force chief, Omar Dhani, had visited the rebel-held air force base, as had members of a communist youth group and Gerwani, the women's wing of the party. Yet the communists neither publicly backed the coup nor called on their supporters to rise in its support. Aidit was the only senior party leader in Jakarta at the time. Moreover, with both momentum and the president on its side the party had the least to gain from a crude power grab. The Indonesianist Benedict Anderson has argued convincingly that the coup was really an internal army matter propelled by young officers appalled by the lavish lifestyles of their superiors. Regardless of which version you believe, the consequences of that night at the Crocodile Hole would, as they say, change the course of history.

Indonesian communism had cleaved to local circumstances. For the most part the peasants and urban poor who flocked to the party had little interest in the finer points of dialectical materialism, much less in formal atheism. Nonetheless being poor and a PKI supporter were strongly correlated, as were being poor and abangan. The army egged on the reprisals, which began within days of the coup's failure. It broadcast concocted stories in which PKI cadres had gouged the murdered generals' eyes, castrated them in front of Gerwani members, and afterwards, lust following bloodlust, collapsed in nightlong orgies. Army officers, at times with covert American assistance, supplied the civilian death squads that did most of the dirty work with trucks, weapons and lists of communist sympathisers. The land-holding mullahs of Nahdlatul Ulama, santris who had felt the hot breath of the abangan challenge to their wealth and status, were among the most diligent killers. Often the murdered were singled out as much for their impiety as for their politics. (In Bali, high caste Hindu landlords played a similar role; elsewhere devout Catholics did their part.) As the madness spread, heads were hung in doorways, penises nailed to telephone poles. Irrigation canals and rivers filled with headless torsos and arms and legs. In an extra twist of cruelty aimed at victims' families, bodies were left to rot without burial so that their spirits would never rest.

Sukarno, compromised by his links to the PKI and his visit to the air force base, called for calm but was ignored. (He died five years later under house arrest in Jakarta.) A former bodyguard betrayed Aidit, stranded in central Java without transport to take him to Jakarta; the army shot him near Solo, threw his body down a well and quickly planted a grove of banana trees over it. Nyoto, stopped on his way out of the presidential palace after a cabinet meeting, met a similar end. It took six months for the worst of the violence to wear itself out. Apart from the half million killed, six hundred thousand to seven hundred and fifty thousand people were imprisoned, including the writer Pramoedya Ananta Toer. *Time*, with typical Cold War certainty, called the elimination of the PKI, 'The West's best news for years in Asia.'

At first it appeared to be even better news for Islamist politicians, who, with some justification, expected rewards for services rendered. But though the bloody beginnings of the New Order seeded the coming bloom of orthodoxy, it would be about twenty years before the first significant harvest, another five before Suharto himself began to reach out to the Muslim supremacists, if not quite full-blown Islamists, his policies had inadvertently bolstered. Until then Islamists of all shades would measure his rule in disappointments.

If anything General Suharto was even more Javanese than the worldly Sukarno. He had grown up near Yogyakarta in central Java, the fulcrum, with nearby Solo, of the island's Indic culture. He prided himself on his knowledge of Javanism, the indigenous faith of the Javanese—an Animist–Hindu–Buddhist core lightly varnished with Islam—and was known to retreat to remote holy caves to meditate and gather spiritual strength. He spoke Javanese better than he did Indonesian. He regularly consulted dukuns and his closest aides included army officers known for having mastered Javanism's most complex spiritual and philosophical conundrums. The general's wife, Ibu Tien, claimed descent from the medieval kings of Solo and adopted their stately high culture as a model. Over the centuries the Hindu–Buddhist ideal of Ratu Adil had retained a grip on the Javanese imagination, and from the outset Suharto—distant, restrained, master of his emotions—made the just king's personality traits his own. He subscribed to the Javanese idea of power as concentration and weakness as diffusion. He was refined in the Javanese sense, oblique in speech and careful to never show exertion. Until the final months of his 32-year reign nobody saw him lose his temper.

The New Order cloaked itself in Javanese symbolism. The presidential order of 1966 that effectively handed Suharto power was called Supersemar. While ostensibly this stood for the date of its issue—*Sebelas Maret*, or 11 March—Semar was also the guardian God of Java and for the general to begin his reign with such a proclamation signalled its divine acceptance. A few years later Suharto lectured students angered by early signs of corruption in his government about the Javanese manner of protest: dressing in white and sitting patiently from dawn to dusk for an audience with the king. He made the military adopt one of his favourite aphorisms: 'Lead from the front. Motivate from the middle. Animate from the rear.' As a symbol for his political vehicle, Golkar, he chose the sacred banyan tree. He named the communications satellite that marked the symbolic unification of the archipelago in 1976 'Palapa', after Gajah Mada's fourteenth-century vow to do the same.

The army, led disproportionately by priyayi and Christians and manned mostly by abangan, saw itself as the guardian of Pancasila, which made it almost as mistrustful of Islamism as it had been of communism. Shortly after taking power Suharto released Masyumi leaders jailed by Sukarno and allowed the partial rehabilitation of the party, but under a new name and defanged by the exclusion of its top leadership including Natsir. A few years later the general merged four Muslim parties into one and gave it a decidedly un-Islamic name: United Development Party. He went on to ban religious symbols from the sham elections held every five years to legitimise his rule and to bar the jilbab from classrooms. He picked a devout Javanese Catholic, Leonardus Benjamin 'Benny' Moerdani, to head the army. In the most prominent example of the government's non-sectarian resolve, in 1984 troops ended a spree of looting and church burning, ginned up by a rabidly anti-Chinese preacher near Jakarta's Tanjung Priok port, by shooting dozens of rioters. Pancasila reached its zenith the following year when Suharto had parliament decree that all mass organisations, including Islamic ones, had to adopt it as their 'sole basis'. But by then the doctrine's social underpinnings were already beginning to feel the weight of change, for the partisans of Pancasila had unwittingly created the conditions for their own demise.

For the last fifty-odd years of their rule, the Dutch, on the advice of the unforgettably named orientalist C. Snouck Hurgronje, followed a two-pronged strategy towards Islam: encouraging it as a faith while suppressing it as an ideology. From the first the New Order, paranoid about a PKI comeback, mirrored this approach. It encouraged public displays of piety and enforced religious education in schools just as enrolment soared. It embarked upon an ambitious mosque-building program that reached deep inside villages. As the number of students graduating high school rose, it expanded a network of state-funded Islamic universities to accommodate the religious-minded among them along with a swelling number of graduates of pesantren, or traditional Islamic boarding schools.

The government erected these props for piety against the backdrop of a quickening economy. The policies that brought tarred roads and power pylons, town hospitals and village clinics, motorcycle factories and Japanese businessmen also spawned migration and urbanisation, karaoke bars and massage parlours, drug addicts and petty criminals on street corners. Amid this upheaval, the first generation formally schooled in the faith turned to the mosque for answers.

Events in the Middle East gave orthodox Islam new impetus. After the OPEC crisis of 1973, Arabs flush with petrodollars added heft to longstanding local efforts to purify the faith, bankrolling mosques, underwriting scholarships and paying for translations of Islamist ideologues such as the Egyptians Sayyid Qutb and Hassan al-Banna and the Pakistani Abul Ala Maududi. The fall of the Shah of Iran in 1979 sent frissons down the spines of a generation of student Islamists and accelerated the Islamisation of neighbouring Malaysia. Then, in the 1980s, the Americans and Saudis responded to the Soviet invasion of Afghanistan by arming, training and indoctrinating violent Islamists from around the world, and by resurrecting the long-dormant idea of a global jihad against unbelievers.

In Indonesia, it took until the mid-1980s for the first social changes to become visible, for Friday worshippers to spill onto sidewalks, for Arab names to begin edging out Sanskrit ones in kindergartens, for offices to sound with the throaty *assalam aleikum* as much as with the bland *selamat pagi* (good morning), for the jilbab, the Ramadan fast and the hajj pilgrimage to become status symbols, for the Koranic study group to replace the common room at the heart of student life on campus. In response, from the late 1980s onwards the New Order softened its opposition to Islam's encroachment on the secular sphere. It relaxed the ban on the jilbab in government schools and expanded the authority of Islamic courts. Arabic lessons made their debut on television.

Suharto's transformation from Pancasila's Javanese strongman to the chief patron of Muslim supremacists defines Act Three (1990–98). His reasons remain a matter of conjecture. Perhaps the ageing general came to acknowledge the changes taking place around him. Perhaps he looked to balance the power of an army whose support he could no longer take for granted; his old comrade in arms, the Catholic general Benny Moerdani, is said to have been the only man brave enough to caution him about his children's spiralling greed. At any rate, in 1990 Suharto ignored murmurs of concern from the army and backed the well-publicised creation of the Indonesian Muslim Intellectuals Association, known as ICMI (pronounced itch-me), and headed by his protégé, B. J. Habibie. An Islamic newspaper, *Republika*, and the Center for Information and Development Studies, an Islamic think tank, followed in its slipstream.

ICMI's birth marked a watershed. For decades New Order dogma had warned against SARA (*Suku, Agama, Ras, Antargolongan*)— divisions based on ethnicity, religion, race and so-called inter-group relations. Now it publicly supported the notion that there was a difference between an Indonesian intellectual and a Muslim Indonesian intellectual, an Indonesian journalist and a Muslim journalist, an Indonesian economist, civil servant or army officer and his Muslim colleagues. Each of these new self-consciously Muslim bodies had an alleged Christian counterpart. But whereas

Christians, many of them Chinese Catholics, ran or owned the country's premier think tank, the Center for Strategic and International Studies, and its leading newspaper, *Kompas*, neither could be accused of an even remotely sectarian outlook. If they showed a lack of sympathy for Islamism it was rooted in an almost slavish fealty to Pancasila.

A flurry of symbolic events—each in itself a mere ripple, but together adding up to a wave—followed the birth of ICMI. For the first time, Suharto donned the simple white robes of the hajj pilgrim and flew to Mecca, television crews in tow. The first Islamic bank, Bank Muamalat Indonesia, swung its doors open for business. The Saudi-funded proselytisation group Dewan Dakwah Islamiyah Indonesia, founded by the former Masyumi leader Natsir, was allowed to propagate in villages that had converted to Christianity, Hinduism or Buddhism in the wake of the pogroms of the 1960s. Prosecutors jailed the eccentric Catholic editor of the tabloid *Monitor* for blasphemy after he published a readers' poll of most admired figures in which the Prophet placed a lowly eleventh. (One place below the editor, ten below Suharto.)

ICMI's enduring contribution to intellectual discourse was the idea of *proporsionalisme*: that as 90 percent of the population, Muslims deserved similar representation in government, business and the military. In 1993 Suharto duly halved the number of Christians in his cabinet and eased Benny Moerdani into retirement. More overtures to Islam, both real and symbolic, followed. The national lottery was scrapped. The president's new devout supporters public-ly gathered funds to build a grand mosque in his name—in Sarajevo. The arrest of an elderly and aristocratic Javanist for calling the Prophet a dictator—though he said he meant it as a compliment—jolted the old priyayi elite. Public life remained tightly curtailed, but large demonstrations for Bosnia and Palestine routinely found sanction. Meanwhile piety continued to skyrocket. In 1983 the hajj drew about fifty thousand Indonesians, fifteen years later four times as many.

It's impossible to gauge the depth of Suharto's conversion. Starting in the 1980s he had hired a mullah to help him read the Koran and after the hajj he adopted the first name Mohammed and the prefix hajji. Yet evidence lingered that the general's spiritual and cultural compass remained pointed towards central Java. In 1997, a few months before the first wave of the Asian financial crisis broke in Thailand, a dukun is said to have warned that the nail of Java, planted by the Gods to keep it stable, had come loose. A worried Suharto ordered an elaborate 'cleansing of the world' ceremony near Borobudur to set it right. On stepping down the following year, he said it was to become a *pendeta*, a priest, a nod to the old Hindu tradition of the aged king retiring to the forest for the life of the ascetic.

In the final years of Suharto's rule the pace of riots and church burnings, aimed mostly at the Chinese, accelerated; but it wasn't until the anything-goes fourth act, Reformasi, that the last restraints vanished. Anti-Christian violence told part of the story: mobs attacked only two churches in 21 years of Sukarno's rule. In 32 years of Suharto that figure rose to 455, the majority after 1996. With the economy in freefall, 76 attacks in just thirteen months took place under his successor, Habibie. Militants who had fled the country during the heyday of Pancasila, including Abu Bakar Bashir, felt safe enough to return. The militias that sprang up almost overnight recruited and trained in public before honing their skills on bars in Jakarta and Christian villages in central Sulawesi and the Moluccas. Christmas Eve in 2000 was commemorated across the archipelago by a series of co-ordinated bombings of churches and priests.

Meanwhile Pancasila continued its slow fade. Some Muslim organisations that had swallowed it under duress in the mid-eighties spat it out undigested; Islamic universities quietly dropped it from curricula. Pilloried in the press for corruption and high-handedness, Pancasila's old guarantor, the still largely non-sectarian army, retreated from a formal role in politics. Decentralisation brought compulsory jilbabs for female civil servants in some parts of the country, talk of amputations and public flogging in others. The Justice Party, modelled on Egypt's Muslim Brotherhood, made its electoral debut. For the first time in decades you heard calls for the revival of the Jakarta Charter on the street and in parliament. On television there was the ubiquitous A. A. Gym. In the papers there were advertisements for Muslim-only housing estates and once-mainstream bands that now only played for the pious. Unshackled from government oversight, mullahs railed against condom adver-tisements and dancing that was too salacious for their tastes.

And yet the survival of the old truism about moderation wasn't entirely unjustified. Islamists and their orthodox allies were still a minority, albeit a much larger one than was generally assumed and one with momentum on its side. A woman, Megawati Sukarnoputri, occupied the presidential palace; nominally non-sectarian parties still dominated parliament. The national coat of arms and the words 'Bhinneka Tunggal Ika' remained unchanged and even the enfeebled Pancasila had not been officially jettisoned. There was still beer in the supermarkets, miniskirts in the malls, Garuda stewardesses in tight sarongs. There were condom advertisements and salacious dances for the mullahs to attack. Sukarno, in his grave 34 years, would have had no trouble recognising most of his countrymen. They remained laid back and culturally promiscuous, eager to embrace everything from the Taiwanese boy band F4 to the English Premier League. (Manchester United T-shirts were everywhere.) Where else in the Muslim world could Djenar Maesa Ayu elucidate on unusual parental bonding and Moammar Emka throw a bookless book launch? But the question remained: For how long?

5

Garut/Tasikmalaya

Herry's older daughter was named Irhamni Jekar Andjani. Irhamni
was Arabic for love. *Jekar* meant 'flower' in Javanese. Andjani, the
mother of the monkey king Hanuman in the *Ramayana*, came from
wayang puppetry. For his second daughter he had chosen Rahma
Jekar Drupadi. Rahma Jekar, again Arabic and Javanese, mirrored
Irhamni Jekar in meaning. Drupadi too belonged to the wayang; in
the *Mahabharata* she married the Pandava brothers. Islamists didn't
usually bother with Javanese culture except, of course, to condemn
its countless deviations from the true faith. In most matters Herry
had broken firmly with his past. He prayed differently from his
abangan parents; his manner of kneeling and prostration would raise
no snickers in Cairo or Baghdad. His mother, he said, remained
stubbornly bareheaded; his wife wore the jilbab. He had found Arab
first names for his daughters. (His own, echoing a 1970s pop star's,
showed shallower roots.) Yet Herry had not rejected Java entirely.
He held on to a sliver of its beauty in his daughters' names.

Three days after our encounter with Inul, Herry suggested

breakfast at Hoka Hoka Bento, a Japanese fast food joint, while we waited at Gambir station for the train to Bandung. He ordered rice, vegetable rolls and chicken teriyaki, I the beef teriyaki. When the food came he eyed my plate and said with a laugh, 'For an Indonesian it's not a meal without rice.' We found a table under a speaker blaring the opening bars from 'Indonesian Idol', grafted like bone marrow from 'American Idol'.

I asked Herry about his baby daughter, born just the previous day. Rahma, he said, weighed only 2.9 kilograms. She was a small baby. He placed his hands on either end of his brown plastic tray to illustrate.

'How many children do you want?' I asked.

'With one wife?'

I nodded. He held up four fingers.

'And with the second?'

He raised four fingers again.

'No discrimination,' I said.

'When I go to Mecca, I pray at the Kaaba to make my family a Muslim family and to make every member of this family either the pen or the sword of Islam.'

'You're the pen, I guess.'

'Yes, that's why I said pen first.' He laughed. Then he became serious. 'But every Muslim must know how to fight. For example, in a war or conflict a Muslim must know how to fight. I was in Ambon. They cut down electricity poles there to make bombs.' He meant the civil war (1999–2002) between Muslims and Christians in the Moluccas in eastern Indonesia.

'How?'

'Because it's hollow. They use it like a bazooka. In a war, every Muslim must fight.'

'How close were you to the fighting?'

'In front of my face. Mainly Molotov cocktails, bomb *lontar* from electricity poles, and automatic and semi-automatic weapons.' He worked the top row of his teeth with a toothpick.

'Weren't you scared?'

'What are you talking about? I was so scared that when I went home I couldn't eat for three weeks without vomiting.' He continued. 'The first conflict I saw was Sampit.' (In Borneo, where in 2001 indigenous Dayak tribals went on a rampage against settlers from Madura, an island off the northeastern coast of Java.) 'We were in a van and the Dayaks stopped us. They were sniffing hands. They sniffed one person's hand and said, "Java." They sniffed another and said, "Java." And then they sniffed one and said, "Madura." They took him away and chopped off his head.'

'Was he really from Madura?'

'I don't know. I was too scared to ask questions.'

The executive-class train offered both airconditioning and entertainment. On a screen at one end of our carriage pranced the boy band Westlife. Indonesians had a thing for Westlife; you were never too far from one of their songs. When we had settled in Herry reached into a fawn knapsack and handed me a book, a bootleg photocopy but well-bound, with a sturdy cardboard cover. I looked at the title: *Ex-Libris, Confessions of a Common Reader* by Anne Fadiman.

'My favourite book,' said Herry. 'I copy from British Council.'

'Where's she from? English or American?'

'English.'

After a few minutes, once the train had started, Herry slouched in his seat and dozed off. As the unbroken green of rice paddies flashed by outside, I turned to the book. It soon became obvious that Anne Fadiman was an American writing about her unmistakably American, albeit unusually eggheadish, life. For a moment I wondered if Herry had really read his favourite book. Maybe with his limited English he had digested it the way I did the Indonesian newspapers, with a few gulps of guesswork. And yet the error seemed too basic for that. At the Muhammadiyah hospital Herry had confided his love of Gogol and Solzhenitsyn, but now this struck a false note. It wouldn't have taken much to figure out that such things easily impressed me. I swatted aside my suspicions. It was remarkable that Herry read any English at all. It was remarkable for a boy from Surabaya without a college education to have *heard* of Gogol and Solzhenitsyn. This was a country where, Richard Oh's best efforts notwithstanding, Agatha Christie passed for literature.

From Bandung we took a rickety two-hour taxi ride to the town of Garut, where the streets were potholed, the streetlights too widely spaced, as though to provide reassurance more than illumination. Though it was barely seven, the sparseness of traffic made it feel like midnight in Jakarta. Herry had arranged for us to see Din Syamsuddin, secretary general of the Council of Indonesian Ulama, vice-president of Muhammadiyah and frontrunner to lead it and, needless to say, no fan of Inul. He was in west Java campaigning for Amien Rais, a fellow Muhammadiyah man, the presidential candidate whose wife wore colourful jilbabs.

Outside the hall where Din was to speak skullcapped men peddled small bottles of honey and nostrums for aches and pains. We fingered the display for a few minutes—the honey, oddly enough, was from Bali—before filtering inside with the rest of the audience and settling in the back row. The program began with a skinny boy intoning a prayer, nasal and sweet. By now I had heard it many times in many places and though it remained foreign to my ear I could see how it might sound beautiful to the habituated. I had profiled Din in the *Far Eastern Economic Review*, and had travelled with him before. These gatherings held a dreary sameness—fake flowers on the table, men in rimless black velvet *pecis* on one side of the room, jilbabed women on the other, endless speeches by faded local notables before the main act, endless questions dwelling on do's and don'ts after it. Here you could see the lack of imagination in the green doors, the green window sills, the shiny turquoise-green curtains. The banner above the stage misspelled Din's name.

Chubby and clean-shaven, with greying temples and a handshake like butter gone bad, Din couldn't have been further from the popular caricature of the America-bashing mullah. But his state-owned bank manager's mien shed its diffidence the moment you placed him behind a podium. His stump speech hadn't changed that much since the last time I had heard it. He railed against *pornografi* and *pornoaksi*. He expounded upon the nation's 'multi-dimensional multi-crisis'. He cautioned against moral permissiveness. He showed off a little. ('The US ambassador wanted to call on me, but I refused to see him three times.') He drew disparaging laughter with a dig at a television channel called TPI. The P stood for *pendidikan*, the Indonesian word for 'education', but Din called it 'Televisi Pornografi Indonesia.'

'How is TPI pornographic?' I whispered.

'Mystic,' said Herry.

The channel, its eye firmly on the lower end of the market, churned out an endless variety of shows about ghosts and spirits. You couldn't really blame Din for his ire; his organisation had spent nearly a century trying to wipe out such beliefs.

Muhammadiyah was founded in Yogyakarta in 1912 by a batik trader named Ahmad Dahlan. As a young man Dahlan had studied for many years in Mecca, where he came across the writings of the Egyptian thinker Muhammad Abduh (1849–1905). In order to overcome Egypt's, and Islam's, subjugation by the West, Abduh came up with a two-pronged solution—the purification of the faith, or returning it to its pristine form as practised during the time of the Prophet, and the development of a modern system of Islamic education emphasising both religion and science. Half the strategy called for a return to the past, the other half for an embrace of the present. There was a famous story about how early in his career as a reformer Dahlan discovered a mosque in Yogyakarta improperly aligned with Mecca. Ignoring howls of protest, he insisted that the worshippers face the holy city in prayer even though this meant misalignment within their own mosque. It was a metaphor of sorts for the organisation he founded.

Dahlan started with twelve followers in 1912. His movement now claimed 30 million. It stood for education, social work and the modesty of women; it built prayer rooms and mosques, clinics and hospitals, poor houses and orphanages, and, especially, schools and universities. But the bedrock of Muhammadiyah's belief, shared by Abduh's followers everywhere, was the primacy of the Koran and the Sunnah, the words and deeds of the Prophet. Abduh's ideas about science were medieval: he believed the key to progress lay in acquiring a fixed body of knowledge rather than in mastering a new way of thinking. Nonetheless in Egypt you could view him as someone who cracked open the door to modernity. In Indonesia, however, Abduh's teachings amounted to a declaration of war against Javanese culture. Muhammadiyah opposed the *slametan*, the communal feast at the heart of Javanese tradition. It opposed the wayang. It opposed seers and spiritualists of every hue.

Its national spread and largely urban membership made Muhammadiyah arguably the most influential Muslim organisation in the country, though the other major grassroots santri group, Nahdlatul Ulama, allegedly 40 million strong, claimed more adherents. Intense loyalty to mullahs and their descendants, rather than solely to texts, marked Nahdlatul Ulama. (Academics called Nahdlatul Ulama's approach to Islam traditionalist; Muhammadiyah's took the label modernist.) Nahdlatul Ulama's mainly rural Javanese followers visited the graves of Muslim saints and recited magical

(Muslim) spells before prayers, practices looked down on as backward by Muhammadiyah. Nahdlatul Ulama santris in turn looked down on the abangan.

Nahdlatul Ulama's leader through most of the 1980s and 1990s, the enlightened polymath and former president Abdurrahman Wahid, had given it a more liberal slant than Muhammadiyah. Wahid was a remarkable figure, the one person in Indonesia's pantheon of moderate Muslim leaders who was moderate by any yardstick and not merely by the special one generally used for Islam. He had opposed the creation of ICMI and had stood up for Arswendo Atmowiloto, the editor jailed for publishing a poll featuring the Prophet. He was among Inul's most ardent supporters. Of course, the pluralism preached by the former president's coterie of Jakarta-based intellectuals didn't always match the actions of the heavy-handed mullahs who ruled the boondocks; in 1996 Nahdlatul Ulama members were at the forefront of a spate of church burnings in east Java. Nonetheless Wahid, a firm opponent of sharia, embodied the fact that though the pious were generally the people most receptive to Islamism's appeal, piety alone did not make one an Islamist.

As I had expected, the evening droned on endlessly. More than one person in the audience wanted to know why they couldn't simply issue a fatwa to vote for Amien. There were the usual discursions about Christian duplicity that ended with exclamation points rather than question marks. While this was going on Herry stepped outside to take a phone call. When he came back he looked shaken. 'I'm sorry, but I have to return to Jakarta tomorrow morning,' he said. Susilo Bambang Yudhoyono supporters had summoned him for a meeting to clear up the magazine's accusation that SBY was a mystic. I could see that Herry wasn't looking forward to it. Though personally devout, SBY leaned politically towards nationalism. Herry nursed a special loathing for him. He blamed the former general, who had been Megawati's chief security minister before resigning to run for office, for rounding up militants in the wake of the Bali bombings. Predictably, *Sabili's* research had thrown up other suspects: Mossad and the CIA. It also claimed that the larger of the two explosions wasn't caused by a car bomb but by either a 'micro-nuclear device' or a rocket launched from a foreign ship. SBY had failed to pursue these promising lines of inquiry.

In many ways Din's career reflected the changes of the past two decades. In 1986, during the heyday of Pancasila, he won a Fulbright to study in America; the embassy had been reaching out to young Islamic scholars and the army-dominated establishment felt that a Western education would produce outward-looking mullahs inoculated against extremism. Freshly armed with a doctorate in Islamic studies from UCLA, Din returned home in 1990 to an atmosphere of ferment—orthodox Islam stronger than ever before, its political twin newly unshackled. He joined ICMI and Golkar and almost immediately earned a reputation as an attack dog for the new New Order. He helped scrap the popular government-run lottery on religious grounds. He led the charge against Arswendo Atmowiloto, and demanded prison for the elderly Javanese aristocrat who made the mistake of calling the Prophet a dictator.

The passage of time had done little to mellow Din. When I first arrived in Jakarta he was busy drumming up support for the militia Laskar Jihad in the Moluccas. He routinely cast aspersions on the international investigation into the Bali bombings and spoke approvingly of the World Trade Center attacks. As he liked to point out, tweaking and enlisting a factoid served up in an American public diplomacy campaign, the attacks, 'caused forty-five thousand Americans to enter Islam.' For all this Din had always struck me as more the shrewd politician than the religious zealot, as someone who mirrored public opinion at least as much as he shaped it.

When we went up to him as the hall was emptying he greeted me warmly. 'Why didn't you tell me my good friend was coming?' he chided Herry. 'Funny combination, *Far Eastern Economic Review* and *Sabili*.'

The next morning Herry returned to Jakarta and I continued with Din and company to a wedding in Tasikmalaya, another west Java town. Din's entourage included three somewhat confused-looking middle-class girls (jilbabs, lipstick, tight sweaters) and four or five young men who strutted as though they felt special in blazers. A certain earnestness and energy animated them all. After Din's speech one of them, a large girl with goldfish lips, had asked about how best to guard against secularism.

In Tasikmalaya the bride was beautiful, her head wreathed in long strands of jasmine, a flower-shaped crystal brooch at her neck, her silver stilettos crossed over slender ankles. The groom was handsome. He wore a kris in his waistband, flat silver slippers on his feet and a matching crystal flower in his black and white turban. Din blessed the newlyweds and told the guests that marriage had three functions in Islam: reproduction, education and the widening of the Muslim family, the *ummah*. 'Gays and lesbians go against the laws of mankind,' he added.

Afterwards I shared Din's minivan as our convoy sped towards a nearby mosque where he was to preach. If you set aside his politics for a moment he was awfully easy to like. Born in Sumbawa, a tiny island east of Bali, he had never fully shed the eager-to-please manner of a small town boy. Once he had told me how Muhammadiyah disapproved of Suharto's penchant for meditation; but in the next breath he shared an anecdote about visiting the ex-president in Cendana and being rewarded with a nod of recognition. There remained a touch of awe in the way he mentioned presidential candidates and five-star hotels, as though he couldn't quite believe how far he had come. Din had called Inul immoral, but now he brushed this aside as trivial. I didn't press the matter. Instead we discussed the elections; he told me of having been scouted as a potential vice-presidential candidate, and about an interfaith dialogue he had organised at the Intercontinental.

Garut and Tasikmalaya were in the heart of west Java's Islamic belt, the site of the Darul Islam (Abode of Islam) revolt against the government in the late 1940s and 1950s led by a charismatic medical student turned preacher named Sekarmadji Kartosuwirjo. Towards the end of their occupation Kartosuwirjo involved himself in the Japanese organisation of the anti-European Muslim militia Hizbullah, the armed wing of Masyumi. In the upheaval that followed Sukarno's declaration of independence in 1945 and the subsequent Dutch attempt to retake the archipelago, Kartosuwirjo's supporters consolidated an area of influence around Garut. In 1949 the Dutch—in command of most major cities but unable to wipe out guerilla resistance and increasingly under American pressure to give up—granted Indonesia formal independence. By then Kartosuwirjo had declared himself the imam of the Indonesian Islamic State. As the Prophet had with the Arabian town of Yathrib, he changed the name of the village where he made the declaration to Medina. And with the Dutch out of the way he turned to fighting the Sukarno government and the nationalist troops of the army. By 1953 the rebellion had spread to devout Aceh and south Sulawesi. Kartosuwirjo's followers battled the government for twelve years before soldiers captured him in 1962 and placed him before a firing squad. The rebellion sputtered on for another three years in south Sulawesi. In all it claimed forty thousand lives. Its principal legacy was the shadow of mistrust that still lingered between many santris and the army.

Kartosuwirjo's enthusiasm for sharia, coupled with a certain brutality towards unbelievers, had made him an enduring icon for

Indonesian Islamists; *Sabili* featured him in a special issue titled 'Muslim Indonesia's Golden Era'. Yet, ironically, he was more an eccentric charismatic than an Islamist in the austere contemporary mould. He claimed to have been ordered by God to become imam of a world caliphate. He refused to allow himself to be photographed. His disciples believed that he possessed the power of invisibility, and that he could fashion amulets that made them impervious to bullets. He was said to carry two magic swords, one each for victory and prosperity. It was the sort of thing more likely to find favour with TPI than with Din Syamsuddin, let alone with Osama bin Laden.

The mosque was a large Javanese affair with a two-tiered sloping roof. A touch of Darul Islam survived in the car stickers spread out on mats outside: 'Jihad is our Way', 'Be a Good Muslim or Die as Syuhada', 'No Prestige without Jihad', 'al-Qur'an is My Way of Life'. I flipped through a book by someone named Riza Shibudi titled *Israel the Pragmatic Terrorist?* A two-CD set by one Hj. Irene Handono, a former Christian missionary, expounded on the dangers of Christianisation. I tried to haggle the price down to 20,000 rupiah, but the man selling it wouldn't budge below 70,000.

Din disappeared inside the mosque. It was a pleasant day, cool and crisp, and suddenly I couldn't bear the thought of another speech. Instead I sat outside sunning my toes and reading a Magnus Mills novel about an English foreman and his two surly Scottish underlings. Every now and then Din's voice broke my concentration. 'Muslim growth rates are lower than Christian growth rates... America doesn't want Indonesia to lead the Islamic world.'

After a while the girl with goldfish lips and a fear of secularism, who appeared to be in charge of finances for this outing, came up. I thought she had introduced herself as a student the previous night and asked what she studied.

'Women's studies,' she said.

'BA or MA?'

'DO.'

I must have looked puzzled.

'Drop Out,' she explained with a giggle. Then she added, 'Do you know that I was once Miss Jakarta? Would you believe it?'

I wouldn't, and not only on account of the jilbab. She was, to put it baldly, blimplike in proportion. The situation called for tact. 'That's really interesting,' I said solemnly, as though she had revealed a new theory on global warming.

The former Miss Jakarta wandered off and I went back to my book. After a while an older man with a beard and a skullcap came and stood beside me.

'Where are you from?' he asked.

'I'm with Din.'

'Oh, Jakarta.'

I nodded and continued reading.

'Where are you *really* from?' asked the man.

'From India.'

'From Bombay?'

'New Delhi.'

'Oh.' He nodded.

He hung back a few moments before his next question.

'There are already many Muslims in New Delhi?'

'Yes. There are many Muslims in New Delhi.'

After the sermon someone suggested a nearby Sundanese restaurant for lunch. By now Din's entourage had swelled to about a dozen people including a former actress and a former pop star. At the restaurant we sat on the floor on bamboo mats by an artificial pond and ordered fried gouramy and rice. Astri Ivo, the former actress, had renounced show business and now appeared in television spots for the hardline Islamist PKS (Prosperous Justice Party). In a severe jilbab and a loose *salwar kameez*, she looked like a cross between a Palestinian suicide bomber and a prosperous Punjabi housewife. A gold Hermes watch shaped like a lock circled one slender wrist; on the other glittered three gold bangles studded with diamonds. She sat in a corner and poked at her plate with a spoon. Everyone else used their hands.

The former pop star was a picture of youthful vigour with teeth like marble and rippling biceps beneath his grey T-shirt. He wore a knitted cap of the sort favoured by The Edge of U2 and clutched a necklace of large silver prayer beads. An Ericsson phone dangled from his belt. He looked at my notebook and struck up a conversation. He said he had belonged to the nasyid band Snada before going solo.

'I used to do Islamic a cappella and now I do Islamic R&B and rap mixed,' he said.

'What is Islamic rap and R&B?'

'It's for teenagers. They should not make love to each other, but should love God.' He stabbed at the ceiling with a fish-smeared finger. 'My plan is to make an Islamic Westlife.'

'What's that?'

'It's a boy band that will perform like Westlife, but nasyid.'

They would sing only about Allah.

After lunch we began the long drive back to Bandung. Din and I shared the back seat of a Kijang driven by one of the boys in a blazer. Next to him sat an excitable youth with shoulder-length hair. On the road from Garut to Tasikmalaya that morning he had talked about being stopped by the cops for speeding before being hurriedly waved on when he told them that the secretary general of the Council of Ulama was in the back. Now he repeated the story. Din, always eager to please, recounted a similar incident on the way to the airport in Medan.

We paused at a roadside vendor where Din treated us to rojak, guava and papaya doused in a fiery brown sauce. Then, our faces sweaty from the kick of the spices, we drove to an empty lot by the side of the road and the boys tossed our soiled plastic bags out of the window with a little laugh. Such were the perks of power: ignoring traffic regulations and littering at will. A few minutes later, back on the road again, the long-haired boy found something new to excite him. 'Look, such a long road and no churches!' he exclaimed. Din, still melting from the rojak, removed a handkerchief from a leather suitcase and dabbed his cheeks and forehead. I caught a glimpse of a purple toilet bag emblazoned with the palm tree and crossed swords of the kingdom of Saudi Arabia. The long-haired boy continued to expound triumphantly on his discovery.

'There are no churches. Every hundred metres there's a mosque. How come?'

'This is the success of artists from here in Jakarta,' explained Din. He meant dangdut singers like Inul, though she of course was from east Java. Din reeled off names of Sundanese dangdut stars. 'After they are successful they build mosques.'

6

Yogyakarta/Parangtritis

The French woman lived in a village at the foot of Mount Merapi, central Java's most sacred volcano. The village, about thirty kilometres north of Yogyakarta, was called Gito Gati; it was named after two brothers, master *dalangs*, shadow puppeteers. I had first come across Elisabeth D. Inandiak's name in a newspaper story about her translation of *Serat Centhini*, a nineteenth-century Javanese epic, into French. She called it the collective memory of 120 million Javanese. It involved cosmic sex, Sufis solving abstruse religious puzzles, and a sacred flower that blossomed at midnight with a scent so strong it awoke the sleeping.

Elisabeth lived in a cottage with concrete floors and Javanese glass paintings on the walls. It opened out on a tangled garden with purple orchids and a chorus of crickets and frogs. The day I visited, two weeks after the trip to Garut and Tasikmalaya, was pleasantly cool. From where we sat in her living room you could see rice fields stretch out in the distance. The yearly rent, I learned with a twinge of envy, was about half of what I paid each month for the dubious benefit of being 'strategically located' in Jakarta's golden triangle.

Elisabeth made coffee on a small gas burner and served it with Indonesian dairy milk chocolate. I asked her why it had taken a French woman to translate the Javanese epic. Why hadn't it been translated into Indonesian?

'Can you imagine?' she said. 'They are not interested in their own history. It's in Javanese and they can't read it. It's like a French person not being able to read Victor Hugo.'

Elisabeth had once worked as a journalist. She had come to Java for the first time in 1989 to write an article for a French magazine about *Kebatinan*, the inner science, another name for Javanism. Most followers of Kebatinan, the abangan and priyayi, were officially Muslim, though it retained a following among Javanese Christians as well. The state refused to recognise Kebatinan and over time this lack of official sanction had proven deadly. It meant that despite Suharto's own leanings towards Javanist practice its followers were the biggest losers during his rule. The New Order banned many mystical societies, especially those explicitly anti-Islamic; public support for abangan feasts and festivals vanished; in school their children were forced to study a state-approved faith, most often by-the-book Islam. Though concrete numbers were hard to come by, it was generally believed that in the 1950s the abangan made up two-thirds of Java's Muslims. This had since shrunk to well under half. If you needed a shorthand explanation for the inroads made by orthodox Islam it was this: the children of the Javanists increasingly looked to Mecca before Merapi.

After the magazine assignment, Java drew Elisabeth back again and again, and eventually she married and stayed. Now divorced, she wrote books and lived frugally with her thirteen-year-old homeschooled daughter; her one luxury was the 130,000 rupiah she paid each month for the pool at the Yogyakarta Hyatt. She took part in a procession to the sacred volcano's summit each year and had thrown herself into an effort to organise a trip to Indonesia by the Dalai Lama. These attachments, of course, came at a price. She told me about a visit to the museum in Yogyakarta. 'It's so badly kept. Outside there are beautiful Bodhisattvas. Women in jilbabs were queuing up and talking about them like they were pieces of stone. They have no idea, they talk like it's completely outside their own culture. I was so depressed. I said, "I'll never go there again."'

She said it was different here in the village of dalangs in the foothills of Merapi. Here they kept the old traditions alive. Here she felt connected with the past. She disappeared into another room and returned with a slim book, *The White Banyan*, one of her earlier works. It recalled the mythology of Merapi in three languages, English, Japanese and Indonesian; the accompanying black and white drawings brought to mind *The Little Prince*. 'To Sadanand,' she wrote. 'This small book on the foot of a big volcano.'

The rituals on Parangtritis beach were not due to begin for a few hours so, rather than linger at my mosquito-infested shack, I thought I'd pamper myself with dinner at the Queen of the South beach resort. It sat on a cliff and was by far the nicest hotel in Parangtritis. The slender palm trees in the garden were tastefully spotlit; the water in the pool was the palest blue. A thin glass sheath guarded the white candle on my table from a gentle breeze. You could smell the salt of the sea air and hear the crashing waves of the ocean below.

It began to drizzle and I took shelter inside a wide patio overlooking the garden. A woman in a pleated navy blue skirt and a blazer, her hair in tight, middle-aged curls, brought me a menu. She was from Yogyakarta, about 25 kilometres to the north. She wanted me to know that she usually worked in the sales office and was waitressing only for a change of scene.

'Will you also go to the beach later tonight?' I asked.

'No,' she said. 'I'm Muslim.'

'Aren't they Muslim too?'

She shifted her weight from one foot to the other.

'I'm Muslim,' she repeated. 'For me praying five times a day is enough.'

I had come here at Elisabeth's suggestion, after a couple of days in Yogyakarta, to experience a slice of Java that both globalisation and Islamisation were driving to extinction. The beach was sacred for followers of Kebatinan: an imaginary triangle connected it with Mount Merapi and the sultan's palace in Yogyakarta. Below the inky waters off Parangtritis lived Kanjeng Ratu Kidul, Her Royal Highness Flower of Gold, or simply the Queen of the South Seas. It was here that the Queen had emerged from the Indian Ocean and offered to share her powers with Senopati, the sixteenth-century founder of Java's Mataram dynasty.

As the story went, Ratu Kidul was born a princess in the pre-Islamic west Javanese kingdom of Galuh, the daughter of a spiritually gifted king named Prabu Sindula. Through the rigours of asceticism she transformed herself into a spirit and came to rule Java's spirit world. She reigned from an undersea palace of gold with jewel-studded halls; she looked, they said, like the Goddess of Love.

As with any good royal match the Queen's union with Senopati (who reigned during 1584–1601) was political, in this case an alliance between a heavenly queen and an earthly king. For Senopati it came with tangible temporal benefits; during a crucial battle with his foster father the Queen's troops are said to have intervened on her lover's behalf. His victory made Senopati the ruler of Java. His descendants in Solo and Yogyakarta still sent the Queen offerings: silk, bananas, flowers, bolts of fine batik, hair and toenail clippings. Some court dances were performed with nine or eleven dancers, leaving an imaginary space for the Queen. Legend had it that the sultan sometimes arrived for their trysts by a secret tunnel near his water palace in Yogyakarta. Farther down the coast stood a hotel where room 308 was permanently reserved for her. It smelled of incense and jasmine and was stocked with queenly raiment: a red gown, a traditional gold lace *kebaya*, a bolt of batik, gold high heels.

The occasional waitress returned with a plate of chicken satay. Now that she had established her Muslimness she loosened up a little. She told me about Satu Suro, Javanese New Year, when tens of thousands converged from all over the island to pray to the Queen, wading into the ocean to catch what they could of offerings from the palace. The crush of worshippers stretched several kilometres from the beach. You could only hope to approach it by abandoning your car and walking.

Had she participated?

'I watched it once. But I'm Muslim.'

I took this to mean she didn't have time for superstition.

The rain showed no sign of subsiding. 'I'm worried that it won't stop tonight,' I said.

'It will stop,' she said matter-of-factly.

'How can you tell?'

'A *pawang* will stop it for the festivities.'

A pawang was a paranormal, a kind of shaman, someone who could propitiate the rain Gods. Paranormals came in all shapes and sizes; they even had their own magazine, *Liberty*, printed cheaply and packed with classified ads and advice. In Yogyakarta I had visited a famous paranormal, Gembong Danudiningrat, popularly known as Mas Gembong. His clinic was a darkened room off a busy street; you could hear the afternoon buzz of motorcycle engines and the occasional honk of a car. The room smelled of hair oil and rose air freshener and cigarette smoke. Mas Gembong, his gut wedged behind a glass-topped desk, alternated puffs of a Davidoff in an ivory holder with bites of freshly skinned turmeric. His hair, combed back in a pompadour from a wide brow, was an unnatural shade of black. He held the middle three fingers of my right hand and smiled showing small black teeth. He said I had trouble with my back and neck. (This was true.) He assured me that my book would be translated into eleven languages. (This I hoped was true.)

A reed-thin boy came in for a consultation. Mas Gembong told him he would soon be offered a job. The offer would come from an agro-business, a finance company or the tobacco firm Sampoerna. Next came a fat woman from south Sulawesi. Mas Gembong held three fingers of her right hand; he got up and poked her shin. 'Don't eat any more Coto Makassar,' he said. The woman nodded gratefully and Mas Gembong scrawled a prescription on a yellow slip of paper.

In between patients Mas Gembong told me his story. He was born a paranormal, but only discovered his gift as a six-year-old when he looked at a neighbour, an old woman, and sensed that she was ill even though she didn't know it herself. A few days later the woman developed a high fever and started vomiting until Mas Gembong found some herbs—instinct told him which ones—and made her well again. The neighbours heard about this and before long people from far and wide were carrying their ailments to his doorstep.

Despite being born with the gift Mas Gembong had needed to work on it. Between the ages of six and seventeen he gave up all meat. At thirteen he starved himself for forty days, subsisting on water and a single thumb-sized piece of turmeric per day. At eighteen he walked from Solo to Bali, where he spent two months among the Hindu temples. He himself was a Muslim, though. He raised his eyes towards a verse from the Koran on the wall above his desk.

For the most part people came to Mas Gembong with three kinds of issues: sickness, family troubles and problems at work. For the first variety you had herbal medicine, the others weren't quite as straightforward. The family problems tended to involve women—with unfaithful or abusive husbands, or with children on drugs.

At this point Mas Gembong's assistant interrupted; in the fifteen minutes we had been talking six people had lined up in the hot sun outside. Mas Gembong apologised and returned to work. The next patient, a somewhat matronly woman, rummaged in her handbag and extracted a photograph of a boy and a girl. The boy, she explained, was her 22-year-old son; the girl was his girlfriend. The girl was materialistic, said the mother. She refused to let go of the boy. She had made him love her by using black magic. She had made him forget his parents, his school, his studies. The mother wanted Mas Gembong to counter the black magic with white.

Mas Gembong listened sympathetically. At length he said the boy must keep the Muslim fast for three days—eating only in the afternoon and evening. In the morning he was to bathe in cold water mixed with three kinds of flowers: jasmine, rose and kantil.

'Will that be enough to break her spell?' asked the mother.

'I will also pray. With flowers and using Alpha and other waves.'

After the woman had left Mas Gembong confided that he could emit four kinds of Electro-Encephalo magnetic waves from his brain—Alpha, Delta, Beta and Tetra. In this case a strong dose of Alpha would likely suffice.

Despite the waitress's assurance the drizzle only thickened. Fortunately, for a 10,000 rupiah fee a bellhop agreed to ferry me to the beach on his motorcycle. I couldn't afford to postpone things to another night for this was the eve of *Jumat-Kliwon*, when Kliwon of the five day Javanese week coincides with Friday. It occurred only every 35 days and was considered propitious for meditation, a time when the wall between the spiritual and the earthly was as thin as a sheet of paper.

The approach to the beach was dark and crowded. A stream of men on small motorcycles poured in from all directions, their tinny engines rasping, their wheels spraying fine slush on my jeans. It was only nine but about two hundred metres from the shoreline, in an open gallery blazing with light and packed with people, the night-long wayang performance had already begun. The cross-legged dalang sat with his back to the audience, the gamelan orchestra massed on the floor behind him. Arranged by the screen before him were flat wayang characters from the *Mahabharata* in red and gold, good on one side, evil on the other. Outside, wrinkled old ladies sold flowers—jasmine, rose and kantil. Something about them, the milky softness of their eyes, the tender corners of their lips, clawed at my heart.

As I made my way from the effulgent gallery towards the ocean I saw that there were younger women too amid the milling crowd, heavy and squat, with red lipstick and low centres of gravity. They stood sodden under trees. Some clutched umbrellas. They had expressionless faces, but occasionally I passed one and an ask-me look brightened her eyes. I passed by a hawker with a megaphone peddling 'generic' anti-*masuk angin* pills for 2000 rupiah each: masuk angin translated roughly as 'entered wind', and could mean anything from indigestion to the flu. The megaphone man promised relief from tiredness and smoker's cough. Nearby two chess players hunched under a tree in the light of a kerosene lamp. A vendor with a hypnotic voice chanted something over a mound of silver-coloured rings. A little farther up they were hawking energy drinks, baseball caps, cheap T-shirts. I knew that farther still, in the darkness of the surrounding caves, people were meditating, seeking out the Queen.

At the water's edge, where the ocean's frothy white tongue licked the sand, a knot of people braved the rain. A few carried flashlights. Most of them weren't wearing waterproofs; they didn't seem to

mind the wet. Nobody wore green. Green was the Queen's favourite colour and if you donned it she would drag you to her palace in
the ocean's depths. I thought I spotted a tall woman in a jilbab,
shorthand in my mind for some education and little imagination,
not the sort of person you would expect in a place both pagan and
poor. Curious, I tapped the jilbab on the shoulder. The tall figure
turned around; it was a man who had draped a tiger-striped cloth
around his head as protection from the rain. A petite woman in a
black knitted wool cap had turned around too. His name was
Wawan, hers Uut. They said they were combing the beach looking
for a flower, a red rose. They said the sultan's palace in Yogyakarta
had sent an offering to the Queen earlier that day and it would bring
them luck if they found the red rose.

The rain by now had soaked all three of us to the bone. I asked
Wawan and Uut if they would join me for a cup of tea and we
retreated to a *warung* with Formica table tops. Opposite us three
hookers sat on hard plastic chairs staring out at the rain and at the
flashlights of the remaining red rose seekers flickering like fireflies.
Another hooker, reclined on her side across a bench, shot me a wink
and a cavernous grin. At the table behind us three unshaven men,
one of them in a bright red T-shirt of Megawati's PDI-P (Indonesian
Democratic Party of Struggle), crouched over a small bottle of
Mansion House whisky.

Wawan lit his filterless Dji Sam Soe with a broken pink lighter,
then cupped his hands and lit mine, a Sampoerna Mild. Wawan and
Uut were 26 and 25 and had been married two months, they said.
He didn't have a real job; sometimes he rented a car and picked up
early morning passengers at the railway station in Yogyakarta. Uut
was pretty in a clear-skinned Sundanese way. She had a red and blue
sun tattooed on the base of her neck. She was also unemployed. She
said she wanted to work in a beauty salon, but Wawan would not
let her.

'Sometimes the girls go home with customers for extra money,' he explained.

I asked them about Jumat-Kliwon.

'You must find a woman here tonight,' said Wawan. This explained all the hookers.

'Why?'

'For success.'

'What would your wife say if *you* found one?'

'It's okay tonight,' said Uut. 'It's for success.'

What was Wawan's idea of success, I wanted to know.

'Furniture,' he said without a second's hesitation. 'I want to own a furniture store.'

They had stopped by the beach for a few hours on their way to Semarang to visit Uut's family. They hadn't eaten yet. The weather had made me hungry too and I also longed for a dry T-shirt. Wawan and Uut agreed to drive me back to my bamboo hut, about five minutes away, so I could change before we ate. We wended our way through the sodden bazaar to where they had parked. As I entered the dark of their beat-up Kijang my eyes alit on a white plastic bottle filled with petrol on the floor. A stab of fear made me pause. What was I doing with these people? Then a rush of guilt washed the fear away. Only people in rich countries, I reminded myself, murdered strangers.

We picked up lamb satay with a pungent black sauce, small purple onions and rice; we sat in the mat-floored verandah attached to my room and ate hungrily from the satay's brown paper wrapping. Wawan was a big Megawati supporter. He told me about seeing her at a rally and claimed to have shaken her hand. He said Megawati's rallies had the best dancers. He had voted for her party in parliamentary elections the previous month, and would vote for her again in the first round of the presidential election now barely five weeks away. Then he turned to the Queen and to the *Mahabharata*; he had watched it many times and could detail all the plots and subplots. All in all he seemed an impressive repository of Javanese lore.

'Tell me about *tuyuls*,' I said.

Tuyuls were magical dwarfs, clever and mischievous. According to Javanese belief, a tuyul could make a man rich by, say, stealing another man's chicken. TPI devoted an entire show to tuyuls. On television they were bald and ran around in their underwear. Lately they had been much on my mind.

Wawan became grave.

'The Javanese are not allowed to buy tuyuls,' he said. 'It's a sin.'

Did he know anyone who had acquired one?

'Yes. One person. He got rich and bought a car. But his children got smallpox. Or maybe they went crazy.'

We finished the last of the satay, then it was time for them to continue to Semarang. They offered to drive me back to the beach. In the back seat I picked up Wawan's broken lighter and placed a cigarette between my lips. 'Could you please light it a little bit away from the petrol,' said Wawan softly. There was something in his politeness that made me sad. As we nosed into the dark he asked where I lived in Jakarta. I told him. 'Is that near the furniture stores?' he asked hopefully. Uut was savvier, in a feminine way. 'It's near Mall Ambassador,' she said.

The flowers I had seen sold by the gallery were for worshippers at a shrine a few yards away that marked the spot where Senopati first communed with Ratu Kidul. It consisted of two grey stones surrounded by a low, white wall. They called it the venue of miracles. Guarded from the rain by the shrine's doorway, the priest sat ramrod straight and cross-legged, formal in his Javanese turban. His disciples huddled behind him. The stones they faced were slick and strewn with jasmine flowers and rose petals. Senopati had sat on the larger one, the Queen on the smaller; in that sense here, unlike in Islam, the spiritual was subordinate to the temporal. A woman approached the priest with a thin black plastic bag, extracted a folded banana leaf, and handed it to him. He passed the leaf over a flame and handed it back. The banana leaf contained rose petals. The woman unfurled it and poured the petals in fistfuls on the stones.

It was past midnight but the crowd showed no sign of thinning. Those who couldn't find space in the gallery watched the wayang standing three-deep in the rain. The male characters had nasal voices; the women spoke melodiously, but with the slightest hint of a squeak. I could see why this scene might upset Muhammadiyah and *Sabili*—the cult of the Goddess, the Hindu shadow play, the promise of low-budget sex. My thoughts drifted to Wawan and Uut and the waitress for whom praying five times a day was enough. It seemed as though sometimes the difference between abangan and santri wasn't belief itself as much as self-consciousness about it. Santris who couldn't quite shake old habits of mind lived with a kind of confused shame. To them one kind of belief in the supernatural (in a magical chicken-stealing dwarf) was primitive and irrational, another kind (in an angel giving God's dictation to an illiterate man in a mountain cave) refined and logical.

But how could you scrub your mind clean of spirits when they were everywhere? You did it Muhammadiyah's way and *Sabili's*, by launching a permanent war against anything touched by the past. Pressed against the crowd, the puppets dancing and darting before us, I had the sense of witnessing history in slow motion, a premonition that if I returned to this spot in ten years it would no longer be this way.

After a while, wearying of the rain, I walked over to the nearest warung, packed with plastic chairs and plastered with stickers for Sutra condoms, and asked to use the bathroom. Someone gestured towards a corridor at the back. A chunky woman, lipsticked and wet-haired, led a customer in by the arm; then a man emerged tightening his belt. On the way to the bathroom I peered inside a small room with a rickety bed. A tired fat hooker on a thin mattress rolled up a pair of eyeballs like yellow marbles before looking away. I expected the bathroom to be filthy, but even here it was clean.

When I returned to the warung and ordered a coffee the owner, perhaps hard of sight, said that I reminded her of the Indian film star Shah Rukh Khan.

'India, India,' she said.

'Mahatma Gandhi,' said a man at the next table.

'Shah Rukh Khan,' said the woman.

I picked up my coffee, sweet and chalky, and settled down at the warung's edge, smoking and watching and waiting. At four-thirty the roosters began to crow. The performance of the *Mahabharata* ended. The words *Allahu Akbar* rose from a mosque and merged with the shallow revving of motorcycle engines.

7

Jakarta/Bandung

The effort to purify Indonesian Islam, to align it with Arabia, was not in itself new. In the nineteenth century, long before the advent of Muhammadiyah, the Dutch had put down the bloody Padri rebellion (1803–1837) in west Sumatra. It was led by a preacher named Imam Bonjol, who, inspired by a pilgrimage to Mecca, sought to graft the austere Saudi version of the faith known as Wahhabism on the matrilineal culture of his people, the Minangkabau. What set similar contemporary efforts apart then was not the desired end but the means, the capacity to marry a medieval message to modern technology.

I first met the televangelist A. A. Gym in Jakarta a year and a half earlier, on new year's eve 2002. His jacket unbuttoned, his legs flung lazily forward, Gym reclined on a chair inside a brightly lit white canvas tent. Newspaper photographers and television crews fluttered around him. Behind him a stone-faced aide in a shimmering green silk batik shirt stood sentinel.

Gym glanced at my business card and then at me. 'This is the second time *Asian Wall Street Journal* is writing about me,' he said in halting English. He motioned to the man in the batik shirt to hand me a card. Then he announced, to nobody in particular, that he was tired. The words immediately rang through the tent, gathering urgency at each repetition.

'A. A. Gym is tired.'

'A. A. Gym is tired.'

'A. A. Gym is *tired*.'

Someone turned a camera crew back at the tent's mouth; reporters already inside stepped politely to one side.

Gym's delicate bones and chiselled face dusted with the faintest hint of fuzz gave him a boyish aura. I recognised his outfit from television and from roadside calendars: wire-rimmed glasses, a tailed white turban, a turtleneck under a blazer, black boots with chunky buckles. In his palm he cradled a silver phone the size of a small brick, a Nokia Communicator, the phone of choice of the wealthy. His eyes scoured the tent without pause. As midnight drew closer Jakarta's governor and police chief arrived with their retinues. Gym greeted them without the usual obsequiousness before authority you see in Asia. After a few minutes of banter he turned his back to everyone and wiped his forehead with a tissue, readying himself for the evening's climax.

The stage faced a circular fountain and a soaring column topped by statues of a waving boy and girl that had been erected forty years earlier for the 1962 Asian Games. The state-owned Hotel Indonesia, another relic of the Sukarno era, squatted to the right. Beside it loomed the Grand Hyatt, with its sweeping marble stairways and bubbling fountains, said to belong to one of General Suharto's sons. You could collapse the history of independent Indonesia in that circle: Sukarno's socialism and fixation with monuments, the excesses of the boom years under Suharto. And now, nearly five years after the financial meltdown had toppled the general, five years of violence and economic decline, thousands had gathered to welcome a new hero.

Unmindful of a light drizzle, Gym strode onto the stage, headed straight for the standing mike, and raised his palms.

'*Assalam aleikum wa rahmatullah wa barakatuh...*' he shouted.

'*WALAIKUM SALAM,*' roared the crowd.

'Hopefully this drizzle becomes a drizzle of God's mercy for us. If you, brothers and sisters, agree the year 2003 will be a year of harmony for us. No more fighting. What for? Fighting only makes us like sheep. Shame! A country this rich can only fight. Shame! Do you agree?'

'WE AGREE.'

'We need clever people who can live in harmony, and we need citizens who want harmony! Fine, *alhamdulillah*, that's enough. Now nobody is fighting. Only a few people getting into fist fights. We begin, this will be no more. Shall I continue?'

'CONTINUE!'

'We don't only commemorate the changing of the year. But in the year 2003 we must want to become people who have self-confidence. Right now, we feel shame!' He shook his fist.

I had shouldered my way onstage and could see the faces in the crowd—attentive, expectant, spellbound. A television crane swooped down above them; a half-dozen channels were broadcasting the celebrations live. The stage was also packed: rows of male Gym followers in white, rows of female Gym followers sheathed from head to toe in white, the safari-suited governor and the slack-jawed police chief basking in the preacher's reflected glory. Gym's velvet voice caressed the crowd, playing it like an instrument, carrying it with him, making it aware of its inadequacy one moment, quickly reassuring it the next.

'Indonesians are ashamed to admit that they're Indonesian...I'm a poor man, but I'm a Muslim and an Indonesian...The secret is never be inferior...Only because our country is not yet devoted enough to Allah.'

He began to murmur a prayer in his low baritone. And then everyone onstage was praying—the governor, the police chief, the men in white, the women in white, one with tears streaming down her cheeks. The crowd prayed too and the drizzle washed away the tears of the touched.

Gym broke into a song, his voice soaring above the crowd, at first a solitary voice taking up a slow and simple melody.

'Guard your heart, don't let it be dirty.

Guard your heart for the light of God's will.

If the heart is open, it's hard for life to be held up.'

Then a deep echo as thousands of voices joined in.

'GUARD YOUR HEART, DON'T LET IT BE DIRTY.

GUARD YOUR HEART FOR THE LIGHT OF GOD'S WILL.

IF THE HEART IS OPEN, IT'S HARD FOR LIFE TO BE HELD UP.'

This was a government-sponsored event. In a nod to Pancasila, priests from the country's other recognised religions—a Protestant, a Catholic, a Buddhist and a Hindu—had filed onto the stage behind Gym. Midnight crept closer. At the edge of the stage a man used a kretek to burn through the plastic twine that held together several small bamboo cages filled with white doves. Another man clutched bunches of helium-filled balloons in anticipation. The crowd continued to chant.

'GUARD YOUR HEART, DON'T LET IT BE DIRTY.

GUARD YOUR HEART FOR THE LIGHT OF GOD'S WILL.

IF THE HEART IS OPEN, IT'S HARD FOR LIFE TO BE HELD UP.'

'Happy New Life with a New Spirit!!!' shouted Gym.

Then all I could see was people shouting, people blowing on paper trumpets, waving their arms, balloons soaring into the night, the doves fluttering helplessly with their clipped wings and landing, terrified, in the crowd.

A few weeks later I visited Bandung to profile Gym for the *Far Eastern Economic Review*. He lived in a poorer part of the city, a warren of narrow streets pockmarked with potholes and lined with low shops and cramped houses, a neighbourhood of noodle vendors and bicycle rickshaws. A mosque with a tapered, tiled roof, a Javanese mosque, dominated one side of the main street. A two-storey Islamic mini-market, an Islamic bank and MQ FM, Gym's radio station, clustered nearby. Gym's turbaned, bespectacled visage was everywhere, on posters, on stickers, on calendars. The streets teemed with his white-clad followers.

On an aide's advice I squeezed into the back seat of a Toyota Kijang minivan taking Gym to a new mosque built by a state-owned telecoms company. Ahead an outrider on a sleek black Honda motorcycle with a blue flashing light cleared a passage through streets beginning to clog with rush hour's first onslaught. Gym's time was precious, I had been warned, so I launched into the inter-view with little ceremony.

'What exactly is Manajemen Qolbu?' I asked. I had seen his Manajemen Qolbu tapes and CDs for sale all over the country.

His response had a distanced quality, as though we were separated by the span of an auditorium rather than of a car seat. He said that according to the Prophet Mohammed there was something called the *qolbu*, or heart and soul, in everyone and that the whole body depended on this for its wellbeing. ('If someone can manage qolbu, everything is getting better.') He pointed out that some people were intelligent but still did bad things. ('Why? Very dangerous—clever, but no heart.') Others had good bodies but misused them by wearing immodest clothes. ('Without heart they fall down.') Only people with good qolbus were happy. ('If you have good heart, everything going better.')

The explanation in English appeared to exhaust him and he stopped abruptly. 'I beg your pardon, but I talk too much today,' he said. 'I have to take a rest. Forgive me. I try to sleep.' A beefy aide sitting behind us began rubbing Gym's slender shoulders while he tipped his head back and shut his eyes.

At the mosque sunlight poured through large double doors and stained-glass windows. Gym sat on a plump white cushion on a dais clutching a wireless mike. He reminded the gathering of the importance of a good mosque in Islam. He shared a joke about a Frenchman, an Englishman and an Indonesian marooned on a sinking ship where a djinn appears and grants each of them a wish.

'I miss my beautiful wife, my big house and my beautiful car,' says the Frenchman. 'Please send me home.' Poof! The Frenchman vanishes.

'Please let me go home,' says the Englishman. 'I miss my great job, my beautiful home and my good life.' He too disappears.

The djinn turns to the Indonesian. He says, 'My wife is asthmatic, my wages are barely enough to cover the rent and I've fallen behind on payments for my scooter. I have nothing to go home to, but I feel lonely here. Please bring back my friends.'

The audience chuckled. Gym dropped his voice and his face became grave. He talked about a massive bank bailout during the depths of the crisis; most of the money had still not been recovered by the government from crooked businessmen. This showed that it was the clever who were corrupt, he told them. Then, after reminding everyone to manage their qolbus, he launched into a familiar melody.

'Guard your heart, don't let it be dirty.

Guard your heart for the light of God's will.

If the heart is open, it's hard for life to be held up.'

A chorus rose to meet his voice, the women in the balcony crowning the voices of the men below. Gym shrugged lightly, as though to jokingly say, 'Let them sing, let them do my work for me.' Then it was time to wash and pray.

Afterwards we ambled across to the telecoms company's glass-faced office tower for lunch. Gym sat with the minister for communications, the head of the national tourism board and the president of the company. I sat at another table with a couple of men in their forties. One of them was the head of the company's internal audit division. He wore a plastic tag around his neck with his name and the letters MBA; he had earned the degree at the University of Birmingham it turned out. I asked him what someone like him, a professional, a man educated in the West, saw in Gym. 'We learn management, but we fail,' he said. 'We feel we have to be careful, not only with the brain but also with character. An MBA is not enough to make a good manager. An MBA is teaching only the brain—making people clever.'

Back in the minivan Gym elaborated on his philosophy. He said work and money were not enough to make a qolbu content, and that this was why some people ran to discotheques and others took drugs. He said he wanted Indonesians to learn self-control. Meshing his fingers, he said he wanted them to join together to defeat their problems. I must remember, he said, that Islam was three things: beautiful, universal and entrepreneurial, and that it was for everyone and everything. Indonesia's troubles stemmed from its neglect of Islam, first under three hundred and fifty years of Dutch rule and then, after independence, when schools devoted only an hour each week to religious instruction. He was playing his part in remedying this error. Just the other day a former minister had told him that his white-clad community, Daarut Tauhiid—the One God—represented the country's future.

Up close, sunlight streaming through the windows, Gym's boyishness faded. His teeth were yellowed, his face blotchy with half-concealed black marks. At the telecoms mosque he had retreated briefly to an antechamber with a powder puff. He was nearly 41; his early years had not been easy and it showed. My eyes strayed from his face to the motorcycle outrider slicing through traffic, blue light flashing.

Gym followed my gaze. 'I don't like this,' he said. 'I like going just like normal people.' Then, exhaustion apparently upon him again, he excused himself for another nap.

If anyone personified Islam's new middle-class dazzle it was Gym. A shade too short for the army, which had been his father's dream for him, he spent his youth, the story went, delivering newspapers, driving a minibus and selling meatball soup on the street before founding Daarut Tauhiid in 1990. Ten years later, in 2000, Gym had emerged from the rubble of Reformasi, a small-time religious vigilante who dressed his followers in blue and white paramilitary uniforms and used them to harass prostitutes in Bandung's red light district. But the camera had since discovered him. Now, three years later, in a toned-down avatar given more to penitential weeping than to thuggish vice control, he was the country's most influential televangelist, invited to preach to President Megawati herself and asked to pose for pictures with visiting dignitaries such as Colin Powell. Newspapers mentioned him as a potential dark horse in the 2004 presidential elections.

Gym had quickly spun his popularity into a business empire. One company churned out his CDs, booklets, comics and cassettes. Another produced dial-up sermons on 'The Art of Self-Improvement' or 'Facing Life's Questions'. MQ TV had begun work on an Islamic soap opera; MQ Radio broadcast Islamic pop and Gym sermons; MQ Travels had crammed a Boeing 747 with hajj pilgrims; MQ Fashions turned out headscarves and gloves for women. A joint-venture bottled mineral water. A line of Islamic soaps, shampoos and toothpaste was in the works.

The secret of Gym's following lay in his gift for dishing out practical advice sprinkled with scripture. In Indonesia's half-modern cities the anxious turned to his television shows with their problems. Was it okay to have sex with a colleague at work? ('Definitely not. In Islam, a woman must open herself only to her husband.') Was it permissible to fib to a neighbour who continually badgered one for loans? ('Ask yourself, is she truly needy?') Why was a kitchen infested with roaches? ('Allah made the cockroaches too, and he sent them to your house.')

The next day, intrigued by the promise of religious commerce, I visited the Daarut Tauhiid Super Mini Market. A soft Koranic melody rose from a spotlit corner devoted to Gym products: the usual CDs, tapes and books supplemented here with stickers, comic books, a row of cotton T-shirts and, for the fashion-conscious female Gym follower, gauzy gloves and an array of head coverings. A few feet away two women in shapeless robes rifled through lingerie bins.

The Super Mini Market strove to give its merchandise a religious cast: Annija pantyhose, The Quraesi Collection of women's kurtas (an apparent nod to the Quraish, the Prophet's tribe), a plastic clock with a picture of the Masjid al-Haram in Mecca, phials of strong perfume—*firdaus* (paradise) and *malaikat subah* (angel of the morning). The formula was simple enough: you could transform the profane into the sacred simply by giving it an Arab name or by slapping on a picture of a mosque. But this effort, like so much else, was uneven. The minimart sold knapsacks and apple juice, bottled tea and condensed milk, instant noodles, water dispensers, boomboxes and tracksuit bottoms. The only thing Islamic about them was their place on the shelves of the Islamic minimart.

The muezzin's cry sounded and the store's green metal shutters slammed shut as everyone shuffled across the street to the mosque. A loudspeaker boomed: 'Camera crews be ready. A. A. Gym will arrive at the mosque in ten minutes.'

Later that afternoon, concerned over my lack of face time with Gym, I staked out a place on a sofa outside his home, an ostentatiously traditional-looking affair with walls of woven bamboo. Through the open front door I could see an old white kitchen fridge, its face cluttered with magnetic fruit stickers. The fridge had been carefully covered with a green cloth, a mark of the attention paid to appliances in poor countries. But Gym was rich now and the same well-kept fridge that would have been a sign of wealth here only a few years earlier was now a symbol of holy poverty. The effect was compromised, though, by the crew at work on a half-built second floor, its concrete walls not yet dressed with bamboo, and by the gleaming black Kawasaki racing motorcycle that hulked in the driveway.

After several hours of fruitless vigil I was joined by a wizened man with a neck like a tortoise and a grey tuft of beard. Around his neck hung a plastic tag with his name, Avianto, in capitals, and the number 010238. He wore white like everyone else. With a shallow bow he introduced himself as Gym's chief personal secretary, the head of the 'secretariat'. By now dusk was almost upon us and he apologised for the wait. 'Mr Gym is very busy because his wife is pregnant and going to the hospital,' he said in English with the air of a minor court official making a pronouncement. The lie gave me face; we both knew that Gym wasn't by his wife's bed, but in the mosque taping back-to-back shows to be aired while he was on a visit to Mecca.

The appearance in the driveway of a woman in maroon robes and a snug white jilbab interrupted our small talk. She carried a baby girl with thin gold hoops in her ears. A five- or six-year-old boy walked by her side. The woman looked distraught.

'A. A. Gym is not here, *Ibu*, but I can help you,' said Avianto. He saw her hesitate and look at me. 'Sit down. Never mind him. He's a foreigner.'

She had come seeking guidance about a domestic matter. Her husband taught Islam at their home in a small town about an hour by road from Bandung. They had been married three years—the boy was from a previous marriage—and she had begun to feel neglected. About ten days earlier she had spoken sharply to her husband in public. He responded by divorcing her, by pronouncing the word *talak* three times. She and the children had had to leave home and were now wearing out their welcome with her relatives in Bandung.

'I'm not a santri, but I'm a Muslim,' the woman sobbed.

The husband, a religious teacher, was by definition a santri. After marrying him she had donned the jilbab and begun to pray five times a day, she said between sobs. But the sense of inadequacy, it looked to me, still lingered.

'Is it so wrong if a wife gets angry with her husband?' asked the woman.

'It's your right, Ibu,' said Avianto, his high voice rising higher with emotion. 'It's your right.'

'I have nowhere to go. Eric needs a father.'

Eric, who had been sitting poker-faced, grabbed a wedge of orange out of his mother's hand. He was old enough to know that something was wrong, young enough to be bored by the fuss.

Avianto's tone became expansive. 'In Islam, if someone says "talak, talak, talak" without meaning to, it is like firing a gun accidentally but not hurting anyone.'

'He told me he regretted it, but that there's nothing he can do. The divorce is already final.'

'That's because he doesn't have enough knowledge about Islam. For how many years has he studied Islam?'

'For ten years, at a pesantren.'

'That's nothing. For us, that's just beginning. You know more, Ibu. You aren't a santri, but you know more than your husband.

In my opinion, you're a better Muslim than he.'

Avianto invited her to join him in an appeal to God. They raised their palms and mumbled under their breaths. This, then, was her consolation: a pat on the back and a prayer with a famous mullah's secretary.

After the woman had departed, the baby across her shoulder, Eric's little orange-smeared palm clutched in hers, Avianto reverted to English. He had worked as an English teacher before heading the secretariat; this may have explained some of the stiffness in his manner. 'Do you remember the British comedy "Mind Your Language"?' he asked. The show hinged on the verbal gaffes of a group of immigrants learning English.

'Yes, we watched it in India too.'

'*Subhanallah*, I remember the Indian.' He mimicked an Indian accent: 'Greetings and salutations to all my friends. Long life may be always with you all.' Avianto giggled and shook his head. 'Subhanallah. "Jolly good." Subhanallah.'

I had stumbled upon a rich vein of memory. As evening shaded into night Avianto entertained me with stories of his former life. At Alabama, the school where he taught for many years, he had found 'Mind Your Language' a wonderful teaching aid, along with another British show called 'It's Your Turn to Speak'. He much preferred them to 'Switch On', which I gathered was American. Of course, the best way to learn English was to ambush tourists on the street. In his youth he had mastered the language in this way, though there were few English tourists at the time, this being the late 1970s, and Avianto often ended up conversing over coffee with Dutch backpackers instead.

It was nearly eleven when Gym reappeared in the driveway and announced that he would talk to me while he ate. His wife had just given birth to their seventh child, a baby girl, he said. As we moved indoors I detected a murmur of excitement in the servants' voices in the kitchen. We sat cross-legged on the living room floor under a framed verse from the Koran, and across from a desk where a flat-screen Samsung displayed a desert cactus screensaver. The bookshelf was devoted exclusively to religious works (multiple copies of the Koran, *Halal and Haram in Islam* by the Egyptian mullah Yusuf al-Qaradawi) and translations of American self-help bestsellers (*Living the Seven Habits*, *Principle-Centered Leadership*, *The Seven Habits of Highly Effective Families*). On a narrow maroon sink below a mirror perched small tubes of anti-acne scrub and anti-acne cream for men.

A servant placed a tray before Gym. Avianto, kneeling deferentially, appraised its contents: a clear chicken soup with carrots and potatoes, rice, vegetables and four glasses—water, orange juice, a green juice and a mud-coloured liquid.

'Mr Gym is not allowed to eat greens,' said Avianto solemnly.

'Why? Aren't greens supposed to be good for you?' I said.

'Yes, but Mr Gym is not permitted—'

Gym cut him off with a soft yet sharp, 'It's okay.'

'Greens are okay, sir?' asked Avianto, his voice rising now in appreciation tinged with wonder. 'Back to normal? Alhamdulillah.'

Gym proceeded to tell me about his life, his years as a delivery boy and a busker and a meatball seller, about a pious brother who lived long enough to find God before dying of a terrible disease, about his start as a preacher in a single room. Religion was his true calling. He said he was a businessman as well only because, 'Mohammed was an entrepreneur and a professional.' He referred me to a biography published by Daarut Tauhiid; all the details I needed were there.

Did he want to be president?

'I don't worry about that. I never think about that.' He stuffed his mouth with rice and continued to talk. 'But I have to do the best thing that I can for this country. I'm not worried about what will happen later. Did you read today's *Straits Times*? They say I'm one of the candidates. You can read it later. Is it a very famous, big magazine?'

'It's a newspaper,' I said gently. 'And it's only read in Singapore.'

8

Jakarta/Yogyakarta/Solo

Herry knew Abu Bakar Bashir well. He took credit for naming
Bashir *Sabili's* man of the year shortly after the Bali bombings. He
had pictures with the older man stored on his laptop, a black
Compaq Presario. One of them, taken in Jakarta's Salemba prison,
showed Herry and Bashir seated side-by-side against a backdrop of
large coils of shiny barbed wire. In another, taken in the prison
mosque, Herry listened intently as Bashir preached. At an appropriate distance sat a pair of policemen, their heads cocked politely to
one side. In a third picture Herry sat smiling as Bashir broke his
Ramadan fast by sipping a glass of water with a straw. They had
prayed together in the prison mosque afterwards, Bashir on Herry's
right.

A few days after I returned to Jakarta from Parangtritis I asked
Herry about seeing Bashir. He immediately whipped out his cell
phone and made a call. After speaking for a few minutes, to one of
Bashir's aides I gathered, he hung up and turned to me. 'We can see
him, but only to greet him,' he said. 'No interview.' The prospect

of a face to face encounter with a person of such notoriety set my journalistic pulse racing, but it was accompanied by a cloud of apprehension. The cloud darkened the day before the meeting when Herry called to remind me that under no circumstances could we enter the prison as reporters. 'No camera, no tape-recorder.'

If fame meant having your name spoken by strangers, then Bashir was perhaps the most famous person in Southeast Asia. Just the other day Tom Ridge, America's director of homeland security, had accused him of 'an intense and deep involvement in the planning and execution of terrorist activities.' With typical subtlety, Australia's foreign minister, Alexander Downer, had called him 'a loathsome creature'. By now the outline of his life had appeared in enough newspapers, magazines and think-tank reports to pulp a small forest. He was born in 1938 of Yemeni parents in east Java and received a modernist Islamic education. In his youth he had founded something called Islamic Proselytization Radio in Solo. After the authorities shut it down he and his closest friend, a fellow Yemeni named Abdullah Sungkar, set up a pesantren in that city in 1972. In the 1980s, at the zenith of Suharto's opposition to Islamism, Bashir and Sungkar did a stint in prison for subversion before slipping across the border to Malaysia for fourteen years of exile. They returned home only after Suharto's fall in 1998. Sungkar died the following year.

Of course, Bashir was best known as Jemaah Islamiyah's alleged spiritual head. *Sabili's* theories about Israeli agents and missiles fired from hidden American ships notwithstanding, Jemaah Islamiyah was responsible for the Bali bombings. Bashir had also been accused of masterminding the Christmas Eve 2000 bombings of 38 churches and priests—nineteen people killed, one hundred injured. He had been accused of conspiring to assassinate Megawati. About six weeks earlier, at the end of April, seven hundred of Bashir's supporters had massed in Jakarta to welcome his expected release from prison after serving a year and a half for immigration offences, but the police had rearrested him immediately, this time on terrorism charges, and whisked him away in an armoured car. Amid cries of 'Allahu Akbar', Bashir's followers battled the police with bricks, bottles and paving stones. Skulls had been fractured; there was blood on the street.

We arrived at the police complex at about ten on an unusually cool and cloudy June morning. The low, dun-coloured police buildings were spaced across a sprawling lot in the heart of the city and ringed by malls and office towers. In honour of the occasion Herry wore a tunic with a gold button and grey embroidery down the front; with the beard and the dark skin it gave him an almost Middle Eastern look.

My worries had less to do with Jemaah Islamiyah's history of violence than with my dodgy visa status. To help me stay on in Indonesia, a friend in New York had appointed me Southeast Asia correspondent of a small Indian–American magazine. I had no salary record—there was none to record—and only one clip, about a travelling Punjabi girl-band that did Madonna and Kylie Minogue covers. Though I had taken care to employ the fixer who handled documentation—fingerprinting, police booklet, entry and exit permits and so on—for virtually the entire foreign press corps this would do me little good if the government got its back up about my poking into sensitive matters. I could no longer count on the heft of an influential magazine and newspaper, and behind them a massive corporation. An Indian passport alone afforded little protection.

Herry pointed towards a shabbily clad throng shuffling across the lot ahead of us, a couple of women in shapeless robes and about a dozen nondescript skullcapped men. 'They are from Indonesian Mujahidin Council,' said Herry. The council, headed by Bashir, agitated for the implementation of sharia. As we followed the group towards Bashir's cellblock a plainclothes policewoman flanked by two uniformed subordinates raised a hand to stop us.

Where were we going?

We told her.

'May we please see your Kitas?' she asked me. A Kitas was official identification, in my case a laminated yellow card that I kept stapled in my passport for safekeeping.

'I'm sorry,' I said in my politest Indonesian. 'I forgot to bring it.'

They took down my name, address and phone number. When we resumed our way across the lot I was struck by the number of policewomen we passed—in pants, in knee-length skirts, with cropped hair. They carried themselves with square-shouldered confidence; for Bashir they were a vision of hell. The government had already shifted him from another prison because proximity to female inmates (and to Christians) caused him anxiety. After a few minutes we arrived at a dirty yellow building ringed by a chainlink fence topped with barbed wire. Waiting there was an assistant carrying a thin plastic bag stuffed with coffee, oranges and two kinds of instant noodles. Herry immediately spotted an opening. 'Have you brought your camera?' he asked. 'Maybe we can take it inside this bag.' I had played it safe and left the camera and tape-recorder at home, but in any case the assistant didn't sound too enthused. We were being allowed in as visitors, he reminded us, as family and well-wishers.

A policeman unlocked the chainlink gate with a clink. 'Identity cards out,' he barked. We crossed a short passageway, entered a shallow anteroom and approached a desk at one end where I surrendered my bag and phone and the only piece of identification on me, a Jakarta Foreign Correspondents Club card. A cleanshaven policeman, most likely a plainclothes intelligence operative, examined it for a few seconds before looking up at me.

'Journalist?' he asked.

I could hardly deny it. 'Yes,' I said. 'But I'm not here as one.'

He must have been new on the job. He examined my card carefully and wrote something in a register. Then I followed Herry to the other end of the room where Bashir sat waiting.

He wore a green sarong with a white tunic, and a white scarf tossed over a shoulder. A pair of large wire-rimmed glasses sat above a thick tuft of white beard. A beaten steel watch circled his wrist. He exuded an avuncular air; to my surprise, after all the press reports that described a foaming madman, his eyes reflected intelligence and calm.

Herry introduced me with a slight bow. 'He's from India, *ustad*.' 'Ustad' was a term of respect, Arabic for 'teacher'.

'Does he speak Indonesian?' asked Bashir. I couldn't help notice the teeth, yellowed and prominent as a camel's.

'Yes, ustad.'

Bashir signalled his approval with a slight nod.

He sat with his back to a wall, beside a barred iron door. We took places on a bench across from him, our backs against the opposite wall. A faded lace cloth covered a low glass-topped table between us. On it sat a plastic jar with sugar-dusted biscuits, a fried peanut snack and small bottles of water. The Mujahidin Council crew we had seen earlier began making its way from the police desks to our end of the room. The skullcapped men—wispy beards, prayer calluses, a few in Mujahidin Council T-shirts—filed past Bashir with great deference, each pausing to embrace his gaunt hand in a two-handed clasp. Then they shook hands with Herry and with me. Their hands were limp, a concession of sorts to Java, where a handshake too firm was considered impolite.

The jilbabs on the shapeless-robed women spilled across their chests like giant bibs. Not one revealed a wisp of hair. A mother settled down on a bench and dandled an infant, in powder blue and a white jilbab, on her knee. Another jilbabed girl, maybe four or five years old, played with the infant's leg. Even in Iran they didn't cover up girls this young. Nonetheless the women gave the scene a touch of domesticity. If you took away the iron bars and the police on the other side of the room it might have been a picnic—the children, the sugar-dusted cookies, the plastic bag with oranges and noodles.

Nobody interrupted Bashir while he spoke, evenly, and with the practised ease of a preacher. He spoke about the enemies of Islam, about America, about how some Muslim leaders supported the kafirs, supported America, the enemy of Islam. But they would all lose in the end because God had said that Islam would triumph over the kafirs, and that there would be a caliphate for all Muslims.

Bashir said he didn't want to expound upon Megawati's re-election effort; the first vote was now three weeks away. The Prophet had declared that no country under a woman could progress and that was enough, there was no need to debate the matter further. Some people thought they could discuss everything. They said Indonesia was too plural a society to implement sharia, as though they were cleverer than Allah! Iblis had also argued with Allah. Iblis was created out of fire and humans out of earth, so Iblis thought he was better than they were. (This, I later learned, was a famous story from the Koran. Iblis, a djinn made of fire, was banished from paradise after he refused to obey Allah's order to bow before Adam, who was made of clay.)

Our encounter with the cops in the courtyard had already smeared the morning with worry; all this talk about kafirs wasn't making things any better. I felt glad for my goatee: along with Herry's company, it made my kafirness less apparent. My intention was to listen quietly and write things down later, away from the prying eyes of the police, but then Herry started asking for paper. One of the women ripped a few sheets out of a diary. Herry thrust them in my hands along with a ballpoint pen. By force of habit I began to scribble, as unobtrusively as possible, my back pressed hard against the wall.

Bashir returned to America. 'Bush said that if you're not with us you're against us. I'm against them. It's a choice—like between water and fire, or between carrots and steak. I'm a Muslim. I'm a leader of Hezbollah (the party of God); he is the leader of the kafirs. He is the leader of Hizbut—'

'*Setan.*' The woman with the baby completed the sentence with the Indonesian for 'Satan'.

Bashir looked at me, his gaze level. 'Osama bin Laden is a soldier of Allah, he said. His bombings are not action, but reaction.' He paused, but continued to look at me. His followers turned to stare too. It seemed like I was expected to come up with a question.

'Do you think you will be released from prison?' I asked softly.

He responded matter-of-factly, without anger or melodrama. He had been held for a year and a half already. This was not about the law; it was about politics. He didn't know his fate. It all depended on whether or not the new president was scared of America.

The lecture must have carried to the other end of the room for the next thing I knew the aide who had met us outside was standing beside me. 'The police want to talk to you,' he whispered. I got up and approached the desk at the other end of the room. A plain-clothes man reached out and took my notes without a word. Another handed me my phone, my ID and my bag. His face was tight with anger. 'Please get out,' he hissed in English. A policeman guided me outside. As I emerged from the cellblock, I heard the metal gate slam shut.

Irfan S. Awwas had also done time in prison, nine years of a thirteen-year sentence back in the 1980s, when peddling militant Islamist literature had consequences. These days he was best known as Bashir's disciple-in-chief; he was 'executive chairman' of the

Mujahidin Council, the loose grouping of sharia advocates led by Bashir. Awwas was also the younger brother of Abu Jibril, an important figure in Jemaah Islamiyah, a preacher and leader of anti-Christian forces in the Moluccas. The brothers belonged originally to Lombok, an island once colonised by Bali that retained a large Hindu population. In the 1980s, when Amnesty International was demanding his release from prison, Awwas had been Irfan Suryahardy; Surya, of course, was the sun God. But the pagan last name had since shrunk, like a vestigial organ, to a middle initial.

He had not been among the visitors at Bashir's cell, but I had seen Awwas before, at a conference of the Mujahidin Council in Solo the previous year. A hint of violence had hung in the air. Young men in faux military costume—boots, camouflage, bandannas—were everywhere, many of them veterans of jihads in Ambon and Poso in central Sulawesi. At the conference they had 'proof' that four thousand Jews didn't go to work in the World Trade Center on 9/11, and more than one person could hold forth on an economy based on the gold dinar and the silver dirham. 'In the time of the Prophet Mohammed, a chicken cost three dirhams. Under Islam, it would still be three dirhams now.' Awwas had read out Bashir's speech about the importance of sharia, punctuated every few sentences by shouts of 'Allahu Akbar' from the audience. I hadn't interviewed him that day but now, the week following our visit to Bashir's cell, I was back in Yogyakarta to see him. I wanted to know exactly what he and the Mujahidin Council meant by sharia. I was also curious to hear what he would talk about when he wasn't being badgered for his views on terrorism, Bashir's imprisonment, and hostage beheadings in Iraq.

The Mujahidin Council's headquarters occupied a modest house next to a small Chinese restaurant and down the street from a hairdresser. Though I arrived not long after dark a thick silence covered the house. I waited for Awwas on a threadbare couch under posters of bandaged Muslim children and Palestinian men buried under rubble. After about ten minutes a young man in a white tunic and pyjamas and a skullcap ushered me into an almost bare room.

Awwas was more powerfully built than I remembered. He had a scar above his left eye and a thick diver's watch around his wrist. We shook hands and I took a straight-backed chair opposite him, under a naked bulb. A plywood desk stood between us slightly to one side. As soon as I was seated another white-clad man, his skullcap curiously complemented by Coke-bottle glasses, placed his chair, back-to-front, between me and the exit. He rested his crossed arms on the back of the chair and stared at me, more appraising than hostile, but unnerving all the same.

Awwas began by asking me where I was from. I wasn't Muslim? That was no problem, he was a gracious host. Just the other day he had entertained visitors from Australia, nine journalists. 'Their funding was from Jews,' he said. 'I said to them, "You are cool for coming to the Mujahidin Council. If Islam is how you people say it is then you cannot go home today."' He laughed. Coke bottle glasses man laughed. I tried to join in but failed.

'Sidney Jones!' he exclaimed suddenly. 'Do you know Sidney Jones?'

Jones, the leading authority on terrorism in Indonesia, headed the Jakarta office of the International Crisis Group, a think tank and advocacy organisation headquartered in Brussels. She had written a widely-cited report on Jemaah Islamiyah and its links with Bashir's boarding school, Pondok Ngruki in Solo. It was titled, 'Al Qaeda in Southeast Asia: The Case of the "Ngruki Network."'

'Yes,' I said. 'I would talk to her when I worked as a journalist.' She also lived in Puri Casablanca and we shared a part-time maid. I left that part out.

'She is with American intelligence,' he said. This time his laugh burst out of his chest like a gunshot.

This struck me as extremely unlikely, but I didn't challenge him. I let a few seconds pass before gingerly broaching the subject of the Mujahidin Council and its desire to implement sharia.

'There is no Islam without sharia,' he said. 'That's what Mohammed said. It's not just laws, but how to live. It's the rules of living that come from Allah, not just chopping hands and so on. Saying 'assalam aleikum' is sharia. If you greet your guest well, even your enemy, that is sharia. Islam teaches you how to greet your guest. Like I greeted those Jews from Australia.' He paused to gather his thoughts. 'Sidney Jones!' he exclaimed without warning. 'Sidney Jones! She sent me an SMS. She says 115 pesantren are contaminated with Pondok Ngruki. She said this at Harvard. This is an example of her lies.'

Awwas seemed fixated on Sidney Jones, apparently torn between detesting her and showing off that he knew her. Her investigations of Jemaah Islamiyah had rubbed the government the wrong way and she had recently been expelled from the country. It had been all over the papers.

'Sidney Jones, Sidney Jones,' he sighed. 'She has hopes that she can return to Indonesia.' He shook his head indulgently, as though at a senile grandmother.

I wasn't quite sure how to respond but, fortunately, he seemed to have exhausted the subject and moved on of his own accord. He was exercised by the upcoming election. A woman could not be president, he felt. To prove it he recounted a story about a queen called Bilkis and the Prophet Solomon. Bilkis was a sun-worshipper, a kafir. Solomon sent her a letter, by bird. So terrified was Bilkis of Solomon that she immediately embraced Islam. She was a woman, she didn't even need to be fought. A mere letter was enough.

Tea was placed on the plywood desk. I reached for my cup. 'Please use your right hand for tea, not your left,' said Awwas sharply. I made the necessary adjustment.

He continued. 'The president has to be commander-in-chief. Can a woman become commander-in-chief? All American presidents have been men. Are the Americans so stupid?'

A part of me thought this might be a trick question but I responded anyway.

'What if Hillary Clinton becomes president?' I said.

He laughed louder than ever. 'This could become a boomerang. If Hillary becomes president we'll look for another argument.' He thumped the desk and chuckled. Coke-bottle glasses man did the same. By now the tension had more or less drained from the room. Awwas called out to a flunky in the next room for a copy of the Islamic newspaper *Republika*. When it came he cleared his throat as though readying for an audition and read aloud from an op-ed he had written. After he had finished I nudged him back towards my original question.

'What would Indonesia look like if the Mujahidin Council had its way?'

'When there is sharia, women will have to be covered,' he said matter-of-factly.

'What about non-Muslims?'

'They will have to wear clothes that are polite. They can't wear tank tops.' He half-giggled, self-conscious about using that word. 'What will they wear? Don't worry. We'll make a good design for them.'

He went on. 'Under sharia Muslims cannot drink alcohol. Alcohol is for the consumption of kafirs. Non-Muslims can drink in a place where there are no Muslims. We'll check if it's in their religion. If their religion doesn't allow it, then we won't allow it for them either.'

'Will you stone adulterers and chop off thieves' hands?'

'In Indonesia there are too many prostitutes to stone and thieves with hands to be chopped off. We can't implement it immediately.

We must first see that people are ashamed to do things like this. The biggest obstacle to the implementation of sharia is democracy. In Islam the highest authority is Allah, in democracy it's the people. There's democracy in France and a naked woman is respected more than a covered woman. You can demonstrate naked, but you can't wear the jilbab.

'Second, in Islam what is true comes from Allah. In democracy it depends on the majority. If they say a boy can marry a boy, that's okay. Or lesbianism—a girl with a girl.'

We sipped our tea. He had obviously pondered this at length.

'Third, according to Islam people with knowledge of religion have a higher status than people without that knowledge. In democracy, the vote of a prostitute and a mullah is the same. A professor is the same as a prostitute. A Dutch professor said to me, "What if the prostitute is clever?"' He laughed. 'I replied, "Because in Holland many professors are prostitutes."'

'Fourth, Islam believes in life after death where you are responsible for your actions. There's a day of judgment. Not in a democracy. They're free to do anything because they will not have to pay. In democracy, if there's a fatwa that a woman is *haram* (forbidden) as president people will protest. They say women become second-class citizens, below men. I say, for example, look at sports. In badminton the score for men is fifteen and for women it's eleven. Why don't they reduce it? Why don't they make it the same?'

'But in golf women now play with men,' I said.

He brushed past my comment and continued; a tone of wonder crept into his voice.

'In swimming, men bare *less* than women. Their clothes are *better*. And in volleyball women are naked.' He made a bikini with his hands. 'Why don't they protest? Islam says men and women are equal. But their rights, obligations and assignments are not the same.

For example, women get pregnant and men don't. Feminism will say, "I don't want to give birth to children, you bear children."' He slapped his thigh and guffawed. Coke-bottle glasses man emitted a snort of derision.

By now Awwas's jollity filled the room like a bunch of helium balloons. He complimented my interviewing skills. 'Maybe you will enter Islam,' he said. 'You can be a very good writer in Islam.' He named two alleged converts—Karen Armstrong and someone called Roger Garaudy. 'Islam does not prevent thinkers and writers from becoming Muslim. You can be a very good writer in Islam.'

Two days later Herry and I squeezed into a *becak*, a cycle rickshaw, for the short ride from our hotel to Bashir's pesantren, the infamous Pondok Ngruki. Herry had come in from Jakarta earlier that morning and I had taken the train to Solo from Yogyakarta. It was a sunny day. Megawati was also in town, for an election rally, and the streets were flooded with posters and banners in the red of PDI-P. Our becak passed a row of small shops selling batik shirts, one with a poster of the Bollywood actress Preity Zinta on the door. A few minutes later, after winding through backstreets and alleys, we arrived at the school's tall green iron gates. A pink sign announced that we were in a jilbab zone. Another said, in English, NO PRESTIGE WITHOUT JIHAD.

Once inside we waited on sagging sofas in the visitors' room for permission to tour the school. You could smell the ripe stench of sunbaked sewage rising from a gutter just outside. A rooster crowed; flies settled on the guest register we had signed. I flicked one off my knee. A sticker on the door showed a burly, bearded man dressed in camouflage with the words: 'Most people choose a happy life on the road toward death. We prefer to choose death on the road toward life.'

'That's Shamil Basayev,' said Herry. '*Sabili* is very favourite with this guy. After Osama bin Laden he is favourite.' Basayev led the Chechen Islamists fighting Russia.

'Do you like him more than Ayman al-Zawahiri?' Bin Laden's deputy.

'First Osama bin Laden. Second Shamil Basayev. Third Abu Bakar Bashir.'

A student sitting near us perked up on hearing Bashir's name.

'What about Ahmad Yassin?' The blind sheikh of Hamas.

'He's even bigger than bin Laden,' said Herry, partly to me, partly to the boy who had asked the question. 'He's the wise guy. Not in the war field.'

I glanced out the door. A gaggle of shrouded women floated past, their eyes fixed straight ahead. One of them showed only the slits of her eyes. A child-sized burqa followed slowly on a bicycle.

Herry disappeared somewhere to consult with the authorities and when he returned I found that the boy who had asked the question about Ahmad Yassin had been appointed our guide. Zainul Awwal was twenty years old, but his narrow shoulders and callow mien made it hard to use the word man to describe him. His hairstyle was a crude facsimile of something more fashionable, longer at the front and sides than at the back. Acne scars spotted his beardless face.

Cement dust swirled and eddied in the hot schoolyard, at one end of which a new building was rising with bamboo scaffolding. Outside the featureless dormitory building next door stood a shoe rack filled with ragged sneakers. We passed through a door and came upon a garish red sign on a stairway, in English: 'Don't Speak Anymore. Except ENGLISH or ARABIC.'

This was a rule at the school, said Zainul in Indonesian as we took the stairs. Could he speak either language I asked? He shook his head. How long had he been a student here? Four years, he said.

Zainul led us down a corridor to the cubicle he shared with another boy in one corner of an airless room. A thin grey mattress lay on the floor. Arabic letters covered a shard of mirror propped against a wall; they formed the word 'Bismillah' followed by a verse from the Koran explained Zainul. On a low wooden bench he had lined up a row of books, all in Indonesian: *The Last Days of Che Guevara*, log tables (up to the fourth decimal), *Characteristics of the Lives of 60 of the Prophet's Friends, Physics 3, Fiqh Islam*. Above them he had fashioned a slogan in English with bits of coloured paper—MY BLOOD FOR ISLAM 4-EVE. (I wondered if he had run out of paper for the final R.) And above that, in a pink and yellow arc, JIHAD IS OUR @ WAY.

I picked up the Che Guevara book. Did he know when Che died?

He didn't.

'Have you ever read a novel?' I asked.

'Yes.'

'Which is your favourite?'

An uncomfortable look crossed his face.

'I forget. Over here we don't read novels.'

'What's your favourite book then?'

'I don't have one.'

'If you had to pick?'

'Books on religion. Stories of the Prophet's life.'

The lack of specificity came as no surprise. In some ways specificity was a First World talent, honed by ordering coffee at Starbucks or picking a Häagen-Dazs flavour. Herry leafed through a book while I sat on the mattress and took notes; Zainul leaned against a closet fashioned from planks and cracked his toes. Pictures of motorcycles and words like Ninja and Gauloises cut out from magazines plastered the closet's doors. The smell of unwashed clothes tickled my nostrils; every night, said Zainul, sixteen younger boys rolled out their mattresses on the floor outside the cubicle.

Hearing hushed voices, whispering and giggling, rise from the next cubicle, I stood up and discovered five boys huddled together like kittens on a dark green rug. Zainul said they were junior boys, sixteen year olds, but in a richer country, or in a better fed class in Indonesia, they might have passed for twelve. They also had slogans pasted on their plywood walls: 'We are is terrorist man' and 'Nest of Moslem Fundamentalis' and beside that a yellow and black PKS sticker.

We went around to their cubicle. Were they watching the Euro championship this year? I asked as an icebreaker. As a rule, Indonesians were crazy about football; little old grandmothers in Javanese villages could reel off the starting line-up of the Italian team. But here my query met a wall of silence. They weren't watching, explained Zainul. The school banned television. Music and cell phones were the other no-nos.

But I saw a basketball court downstairs?

They could play basketball, said Zainul. They could play basketball, though not in shorts. They were allowed to play basketball as long as their knees were hidden.

'Do you have any heroes?' I asked after a pause. Then, when that failed to elicit a response, 'Who is your favourite person?'

'My Prophet,' said a boy.

'I'm from India. Is there anything you want to know about India?'

Silence.

'Is there anything you want to know about being a journalist?'

More silence.

'About anything?'

A longer pause, then a small voice piped up.

'Are you Muslim?'

Bashir belonged to the Yemeni diaspora, descendants of teachers, merchants and mullahs from the arid Hadramawt valley who began settling in Indonesia from the mid-nineteenth century onwards. The community's fortunes had forked. Yemenis abounded in Jakarta's educated upper crust—lawyers, journalists, businessmen, army officers; many of them were among the city's fiercest defenders of secularism. But Yemenis also made up a disproportionate share of the violent Islamist leadership. Habib Rizieq head of the bar-trashing Islamic Defenders Front and Jafar Umar Thalib of Laskar Jihad both descended from Hadramawtis. Their most famous kinsman was, of course, Osama bin Laden.

After completing the campus tour we returned to the fly-ridden and sticker-strewn visitors' room to meet with 26-year-old Abdul Rahim, Bashir's youngest son. His family had maintained the bloodline's purity; Rahim resembled me more than he did Herry or any of the eight or so boys in the room. He said he remembered me from our visit to his father and from the Mujahidin Council conference the previous year.

Rahim had grown up in Malaysia during Bashir's exile, had studied there and in Pakistan, and was hoping to continue his education in Saudi Arabia. He appeared mature beyond his years and, by the way the others looked at him, used to commanding authority. His eyes were intelligent, especially so after the dullness of the dormitory. He said they were usually suspicious of journalists and shared a story about how the Western press maligned the school. Twice a week the boys were taught self-defence, a mix of kung fu and karate called Wu Tang. An American journalist had taken pictures of this innocent activity and called it military training.

'Well, then why is Ngruki considered a radical school?' I asked. Police had implicated a dozen or so of its alumni in terrorist attacks—Bali, the Marriott hotel in Jakarta, a commuter train in Manila.

'Radical is the wrong word. It means people holding on to their beliefs. We hold on to the Koran and the Sunnah. I'm a Muslim. I hold on to the Koran. What's my mistake?'

'What about all the Ngruki graduates implicated in bombings?'

'We teach them and free them. They can study or work or go overseas. They are not in our control. They can meet whoever they like—George Bush or Osama bin Laden. They can meet whoever they want. We don't teach them how to make bombs.'

'But so many are from here.'

'It's a coincidence. According to me, it's a coincidence. We only teach them what is there. We teach them about *shirik*. Like you Hindus have a God with an elephant's head.' He made a trunk with his arm. 'If we don't teach them this they can become like Hindus.' The thought clearly filled him with horror, but his tone lacked malice or intent to offend. He sounded perfectly reasonable, as though explaining a self-evident truth to a child—stealing is bad, or mammals don't lay eggs.

'We have the responsibility to teach what comes from Allah and the Prophet. We can't change the Koran and Sunnah. It's our responsibility to teach it. The English wanted to destroy Islam and now the Americans want to destroy it.'

'Are they your enemies?'

'Whoever opposes it is the enemy of Islam. Jewish, Christian, Hindu. You have your Kashmir. Muslims are enemies too, like liberals. They are part of the conspiracy. Some are stupid enough to think of the world and want to progress.'

Herry chimed in. 'How can we learn Islam from kafirs?'

'All Muslims are brothers. India is a kafir country because the state is not based on Islam. Indonesia is a kafir state, but the people are not kafir. Who is more fundamentalist, Muslims or Christians? Look at Andalucia. There are no Muslims. There are still Christians in Egypt and in Palestine.'

'What about England? They have many Muslims. They are free to worship as they please.'

'England is like Andalucia. Muslims are not allowed to practise their sharia, which is the basis of Islam. They are allowed their worship, their clothes and so on. But they can't chop off hands or have our *hudud* law. So it's still like Andalucia. Isabella killed Muslims just because they wanted to pray. It's *aqida*, a war of ideology.'

I asked him about globalisation, about the school's policies on television and music and the Internet. Did he expect to stop the world at the gates?

'We ask if globalisation is based on the Koran and Sunnah. For example, if there's a film that destroys morals we stop it. There's no Internet for the students because it has pornography and things that are not good.'

'Is Britney Spears haram or halal?'

This appeared to catch him by surprise; Abdul Rahim looked startled. The boys giggled nervously. They knew who Britney Spears was; they probably knew Westlife too. It took Rahim a few moments to collect his thoughts.

'If you hear the voice of a woman, it's a sin,' he said slowly, feeling his way through the answer.

'But what if they go somewhere else?'

'We have control. We have watchers outside. I will catch them if they watch something not good.'

'But then you'll have to go to such a place yourself.'

'No. For example, I can go and see where the movie is, but I don't have to watch the movie.' He had scored a point for the gallery and allowed himself a smile.

'What do you think of Osama? I noticed a picture of him outside.'

'He's a hero.'

'And the Bali bombing?' This was a delicate subject.

'We know the people who did it. We ask, "who was behind it?" We can't say. I can't say that it was America. I can't say that it was not America. Was there a micro-nuclear device? An investigator, an Australian, found that it was micro-nuclear. The Western media blocked it, but the Muslim media published it. Does Indonesia have nukes? Does Amrozi?'

Amrozi bin Nurhasyim was the convicted terrorist popularly known as the smiling bomber. The nuke theory, like the one about the Jews being tipped off in advance about 9/11, was an Islamist staple.

Herry chimed in again. 'The TNI (Indonesian Armed Forces) had a consultant at army headquarters in Cilangkap recreate the bombing. He used 650 kilos of potassium chlorate just like they said was used in Bali. But the damage was not like in Legian.'

How did Herry know this?

He said a secret source in the military had told him. Herry had many secret sources. One had told him that Suharto was toppled because of American concern that he was drawing too close to Islam. Then there was the mysterious class of colonels: Herry believed that an entire echelon of the army had been filled with Christians in the 1980s when the army was headed by Benny Moerdani. These Christians, like a cohort of kindergarteners, were rising inexorably. They were already colonels. One day they would occupy every top post in the army.

I asked Rahim about his time in Pakistan. Could he speak Urdu?

'Only a little,' he said. 'I was in Karachi to study sharia. We only spoke Arabic. But I can speak a little. *Abhi chai piyo* (Drink tea now). *Kyon nahin?* (Why not?) *Bhool gaya* (I've forgotten).'

He said the words with a smile that ended our conversation on a warm note. I thanked him and got up to take pictures of the room. A letter pasted on a wall, near a bin Laden sticker, talked about a

Christian conspiracy to steal the election. It claimed that SBY was a Christian puppet. While I clicked and jotted additional notes Herry chatted with Rahim. 'If we in the Islamic movement work hard we'll be at the top level by 2014,' said Herry. 'Liberal Islam has no cadres.'

Rahim agreed. 'This used to be a communist place,' he said. 'It was famous for being a communist place. My mother is from here. She told me that when she was a girl this area was full of communists.'

Rahim asked about Sidney Jones. Herry said he believed that she worked for Indonesian intelligence. Then, despite their agreement a few minutes earlier on Islam's inexorable rise, they commiserated on the lamentable state of the faith.

'In Indonesia it's proof that you're Muslim if you go on the hajj,' said Rahim.

Herry recounted a tale from his childhood. When he was a little boy they had to study Pancasila in school. Herry would always bunk the class, and he would not attend the school's flag-hoisting ceremony either. Instead he would slink away to the schoolyard or hide in the canteen. 'Now I know why Abu Bakar Bashir cannot respect *merah-putih* (the red-and-white national flag) or Pancasila,' he said. 'Though at the time I was just doing it without any concept.' Rahim nodded his approval.

As we said our goodbyes Herry kissed the younger man's hand in gratitude. He thanked him with the Arabic word *shukran* instead of the Indonesian *terima kasih*.

9

Ponorogo

The teacher had a question.

'What is the opinion of Mr John about autumn? *What* is the opinion of Mr John about autumn?' Silence.

He tried again. 'What is Mr John's idea about autumn?'

The teacher called on a boy.

'Autumn is the bad season,' he answered. The room filled with teenage titters.

'He thinks autumn is the bad season. Is it right?'

'No! No!' they shouted.

The boys, seventeen and eighteen year olds, wore dark pants and white shirts with orange name tags. They squeezed tight, shoulder-to-shoulder on hard wooden benches behind graffiti-free desks. The teacher, in blazer and tie, stood in teacherly fashion with his hands behind his back. Arabic letters from an earlier class covered the blackboard behind him, but this was English, English Five.

'Very good,' said the teacher. 'In Indonesia there is no autumn. What seasons are there?'

'Spring and winter,' said a boy. More laughter.

'There is no winter in Indonesia,' said the teacher matter-of-factly. 'How many seasons are there in Indonesia?'

'Two,' they said as one.

'What seasons are they?'

'Dry season and rainy season,' they chorused.

'But today we don't study rainy season or dry season. We study autumn. What is Mr John's idea of autumn?'

'It is a fine time to enjoy,' someone responded.

'And according to Mr Robert?'

'It's a delightful, quiet time!' said another

A heavy iron gong sounded in the distance. Class was over.

Earlier that morning we had come by road—three hours in a taxi—from Solo to Gontor, near Ponorogo in east Java. More than one thread had led us here. Bashir had studied here, as had Irfan S. Awwas briefly. Din Syamsuddin of Muhammadiyah and the Council of Ulama credited the school with instilling in him, 'the science of Islam.' Other prominent alumni included Megawati's vice-presidential running mate, Hasyim Muzadi of Nahdlatul Ulama, the PKS leader Hidayat Nur Wahid, and Nurcholish Madjid, the country's most famous Muslim intellectual. This was the Eton and Harrow, the Exeter and Andover, of modernist Islamic education in Indonesia. No other school came close to wielding as much influence on public life.

Three brothers from an old family of mullahs founded Gontor in 1926. It was inspired by Al-Azhar in Cairo and India's Anglo-Muslim college in Aligarh, and like them echoed the Egyptian Muhammad Abduh's reformist zeal. It marked a departure from traditional pesantren pedagogy with its emphasis on Koranic chanting and its haphazard organisation. At Gontor they understood words like curfew and roll call; they used classrooms; they divided students into grades by age and supplemented Islam with maths and science. The school was in the midst of a lengthy enrolment boom. As recently as 1964 it had only about a thousand students ringed by an unsympathetic pro-PKI peasantry. Now it housed twelve thousand on seven campuses and milled its own rice.

A courteous young man with neatly parted hair, in a full-sleeved white shirt and a tie, showed us around. His parents had named him Hasan al-Banna after the Egyptian founder of the Muslim Brotherhood. It seemed odd to me, this smooth-faced Javanese carrying a famous Egyptian name on his slight shoulders. Himself a recent graduate of the school, he was teaching here before continuing his education, in Saudi Arabia he hoped. Many of the boys went on to study abroad, to Saudi Arabia, Egypt, Pakistan, Malaysia. Egypt was the most popular, he said, even though Pakistan strained them less both academically and financially.

Gontor prided itself on its attention to language said the young Hasan al-Banna. Students alternated between Arabic and English—two weeks of each. (This dated to the 1920s when Indonesian Muslims couldn't locate a single delegate fluent in both languages to attend an international Islamic congress.) Signs everywhere exhorted the students to uphold this linguistic discipline. Tacked on a notice board, we came upon a message from the principal:

ANY MEETING YOU ARE IN,
EVEN IF IT IS LARGE OR SMALL,
FORMAL OR INFORMAL.
YOU HAVE TO SPEAK IN FORMAL LANGUAGE,
ARABIC OR ENGLISH.
DON'T FIND ANY EXCUSE OR REASON
NOT TO DO SO,
FOR THERE'S NO EXCUSE OR
REASON AT ALL.

IF YOU DON'T KNOW ANY WORD
OR EXPRESSION
YOU OUGHT TO 'KEEP SILENT'
OR 'GET YOUR EFFORT
TO FIND THEM'.

I asked the young Hasan al-Banna about the consequences of a student using his native tongue, say Javanese or Sundanese.

'His head is shaved and he is sent to the language office.'

Indonesian provoked milder censure. First-time offenders were given a warning and made to write ten sentences in Arabic or English, either ten sentences or a composition.

'Are they expected to speak English or Arabic all day?'

'Two weeks English. Two weeks Arabic. Until they sleep.'

'What about sleep-talking?'

'There's still no case of that,' the young Hasan al-Banna assured me.

I was 'getting my effort' to learn more about the English class from earlier that morning. The young Hasan al-Banna politely issued orders for a student to be produced before us. We waited in a sunny courtyard, across from a row of boys in ill-fitting dark blazers and pecis facing punishment for minor infractions such as forgetting a book or showing up sockless in class. The consequences, standing aimlessly in the courtyard, seemed pleasant enough. In India I had endured worse.

At length our envoy from English Five arrived, a seventeen-year-old Batak from north Sumatra with a big, broad guileless face. He was painfully shy and at first would only speak to us in Indonesian, but he relented after I pressed him to, 'speak in formal language.'

'Earlier today you learned about autumn,' I said. 'Could you tell me more about that?'

'I learned about...hmm...the situation in autumn.'

'What is it about this situation? How is it different from winter?'

'The situation between winter and autumn is in autumn we can enjoy very much. Like very much object like fishing and other. In winter we cannot fishing. We cannot fish and we cannot enjoy other object. Because it's winter. The weather is cold.'

He said they didn't only study autumn. Their book included lessons on summer and spring and winter as well. There was a chapter about a journey to the seaside, and one about a hat shop.

'A hat shop?' I wasn't sure that I had heard right. 'You mean a shop with hats?'

'Conversation at the hat shop. About the wonderful array of hats, the price of hats.'

'Where is this hat shop? Is it in Indonesia or in some other country?'

'In foreign country.'

'Which country?'

'London.'

'It's about a hat shop in London?'

'Yes.'

'The prices of these hats, are they in pounds?'

'Yes.'

We resumed our campus tour. The buildings, drab but sturdy, carried names like Saudi and Tunis in gratitude to benefactors. This I admired, the selflessness of the faith, or the selflessness it inspired, its ability to build and sustain institutions. There were notices and slogans everywhere. In Indonesian: 'The difference between Muslims and kafirs is *solat*.' (The five daily prayers.) In English: 'Be brave to speak formal language.' A whiteboard displayed two sentences translated from Indonesian into English: 'Clear your nose' and 'I don't care about that.'

In a courtyard we came upon a twelve-year-old boy standing

under a tree and emitting a stream of rapid-fire Arabic. He had committed an infraction, explained the young Hasan al-Banna, and was preaching as penitence. The boys who passed him on their way to wash before midday prayers laughed at the lonesome preacher, clownish in his crooked peci, wagging a chubby forefinger and speaking too fast from the back of his throat. But their laughter lacked scorn; it was tinged with a broad camaraderie. The azaan filled the air and Herry trundled off with our guide. He was looking forward to praying with the students in a capacious new mosque topped with a large dome. The school's original mosque with its three-tiered sloping roof appeared out of favour. A small sign outside gave it the air of a dilapidated museum.

After prayers the boys gathered in the cafeteria, an open shed filled with long tables and low wooden benches. A song by the pop group Coklat blared at top volume. Slogans in English looked down from the walls: HUNGER IS THE BEST SAUCE and TO EAT TO LIFE NOT TO LIFE TO EAT. Boys clutching pink, red or blue plastic bowls lined up behind a wire-mesh screen. They returned to the benches, their bowls piled with rice, carrot, cabbage, fried potatoes, boiled eggs and *sambal*, chili sauce.

The school had scheduled a parade of some sort in the afternoon and many of the boys had changed into brown scout uniforms with patches on their sleeves and red and white scarves knotted around their necks. Their fingers flew through the rice and vegetables and their mouths rarely closed. Debris from this onslaught—salt, eggshells, pieces of carrot, potato sides—quickly covered the tables. A blind ginger cat, its pelt ragged, climbed a bench mewling; a boy bumped it off with a swipe of his hip. The blind cat mewled and rooted halfheartedly in the spillage on the floor.

The school hugged the edge of a town called Ponorogo. On the way in our taxi driver had said that if the Ponorogo police caught you running a red light you had to bribe them 60,000 rupiah. Herry had scoffed: 'In Jakarta it's 1.2 million.' If petty corruption was the measure, this made Ponorogo one-twentieth Jakarta's size, though it looked even smaller.

Later that afternoon the young Hasan al-Banna and a former classmate named Zain drove us to town for lunch. On the way back to campus the boys agreed to take us on a spin around Ponorogo. Herry and I sat in the back. In front, the young Hasan al-Banna and Zain practised their Arabic. In a few minutes we came to a large square that dominated the centre of the town. At one end local women—heads bare, blouses in primary colours—sold throwaway dark glasses, plastic cars with shiny hubcaps and posters of a plump white baby gurgling before the Stars and Stripes. At the other end rose a platform bedecked with arches and Ionic pillars. On it stood six life-sized statues of fierce-looking men striking what appeared to be dance poses. Large stone sculptures of lions and lionesses at each corner of the square added to its pagan cast. Above us a white blimp advertising cigarettes floated in the clear blue sky. It said, 'Yesterday is gone. Clas Mild is today.'

Ponorogo's claim to fame, the one thing that found it a place in guide books and doctoral dissertations, was a dance called Reyog that dated to Hindu times. Sometimes they performed it in the square. The central figure—part beast, part human—melded the traits of a lion, a tiger and a peacock, and was played by a man in a giant mask that resembled a tiger's head crowned by hundreds of peacock feathers. The cast also included kings and clowns, demons and dwarfs and hobby horses, usually young boys dressed as women. Audience participation was part of the performance and often, it was said, chants, ululations and blood-curdling yells drowned out the gamelan orchestra backing the dancers.

Back on the road in the Kijang I asked the young Hasan al-Banna and his friend if they had ever watched Reyog Ponorogo.

'We cannot go to the square,' said the young Hasan al-Banna. We're not allowed to do bad things.'

'How is watching the best known dance from this part of Java a bad thing?'

The young Hasan al-Banna was silent.

I tried again. 'What's bad about it?'

The young Hasan al-Banna kept his eyes on the road.

Finally Herry offered a two-syllable explanation. 'Mystic,' he said.

Both boys were proud of their school, of its famous alumni; even A. A. Gym was being taught Arabic by one of them said Zain. They said the village of Gontor had been a vile place, a polluted place, before the coming of the school. In those days everyone associated it with the five 'M's—words that began in Indonesian with the letter M. They listed them for me—gambling, sex (they called it 'playing sex with women'), stealing, drunkenness and drug addiction.

My mind was still on the dance. 'What else are you not permitted to do?' I asked.

No chess. They were allowed to play football and basketball, but not chess. Chess was a waste of time. Could they read novels? Yes, Islamic novels. They mentioned a few names unfamiliar to me. 'We're allowed to read *Sabili*,' said Zain.

'What about music?'

'Music is okay. But English music is forbidden,' said the young Hasan al-Banna.

'What about Cat Stevens?'

They hadn't heard of Cat Stevens, but Herry had. He told them that Cat Stevens had converted to Islam and was called Yusuf Islam.

'I think we can listen to him then,' said the young Hasan al-Banna with the first hint of exasperation marring his unblemished politeness.

Herry told them about being interviewed by SCTV, a private television channel, for a special investigative report. They wanted his opinion on which presidential candidate was closest to America. He then launched into an elaborate theory involving human rights cases and secret backchannel military contacts while the young Hasan al-Banna and Zain listened rapt. At last, amid coconut trees and black earth thick with sugar cane, we arrived at a gleaming white mosque paid for by Kuwait. The young Hasan al-Banna and Zain perked up visibly. As soon as we emerged from the Kijang they skipped into the mosque and flopped down on the cool of a tiled floor. Herry joined them while I took a short walk by myself.

In a whitewashed verandah, under a gold ceiling fan, sat the principal, his gut bulging under his blazer. He oozed a well-groomed, moist-eyed languor. After bowing to the principal, a boy poured us tea with fairytale formality, his left hand gripping his right wrist as he tilted the teapot.

'Are you Muslim?' the principal asked.

'No,' I said.

'Non-Muslim,' he said half to himself and pursed his lips.

'What will you do with the information you gather here?'

'I'm writing a book.'

He turned to Herry.

'He will give this information to the Americans.'

The principal didn't say another word to me, but he was too polite to ask me to leave. I sipped my tea, right-handed, while he addressed himself to Herry. Dusk fell softly around us. Behind me I could hear Koranic verses pouring like honey out of loudspeakers, and below them the sound of shuffling, the shuffling of hundreds of pairs of feet either on their way to the mosque or on their way back from it. They were always either on their way to a mosque or on their way back from one.

As he had with Abdul Rahim, Herry began by sharing something agreeable. Secularists and liberals had no hope in Indonesia, he said. 'They don't have a strong base—the Koran and Sunnah—so they will lose.'

The principal was not as sanguine. 'The Americans and the English are memorising the Koran to destroy Islam,' he said. 'Their NGOs—France, Japan, Australia, America, England—are out to promote SBY. They are training nine hundred people to memorise the Koran and the science of the Hadith (compilations of the traditions of the Prophet) to influence Islam with secular ideas. And then they will send these people to the heart of the Muslim community for the secularisation of the Koran and the Hadith. There are quite a lot of people like this in Indonesia being trained by America.'

He turned to politics. What did Herry know about a possible Christian coup?

'I've seen it with my own eyes, the Christianity motor in SBY's party.'

Herry had a garage mechanic's familiarity with this particular motor, a complex piece of machinery—economic, educational, constitutional—that worked ceaselessly for the downfall of Islam. His talk with SBY's supporters, for which he had left Garut early, had done nothing to dull his suspicion.

Their conversation drifted to an assessment of which candidate prayed the most and whose wife dressed best. Herry commented on the sad fact that the wife of Amien Rais, the Muhammadiyah man, was merely jilbabed; though General Wiranto had a military background, his wife sheathed herself from head to toe in the abaya. I had heard this before, but I now learned that Wiranto's three daughters dressed like their mother and that his son had signed up with the international missionary group Tablighi Jamaat. Listening to Herry and the principal something that had been nagging me now became clear. The supposed gulf between the putatively moderate Gontor and the radical Ngruki was really not much wider than a gully. Yes, they played music in the cafeteria at Gontor, and no they displayed no pictures of bin Laden or Basayev in the hallways; one of the slogans here, curved around a shield, said of conversion to Islam, 'By Sincerity not by Sword.' Yet Ngruki, with its exhortations to speak only Arabic or English, with its reliance on the Koran and Sunnah, with its claims on the female body (jilbabs compulsory) and its mistrust of the outside world, was simply an amplification of Gontor's principles not a departure from them. The young Hasan al-Banna had boasted that over one hundred and fifty Gontor alumni had opened schools of their own. No great writers or painters or scientists, let alone chess grandmasters or orchestra conductors, could emerge from their classrooms. The school was like an amoeba, able to reproduce only itself.

Afterwards Herry and I trudged back in the dark to our rooms in a school guest house. Mine had light green walls, a prayer rug and a strangely punctuated sign. ('Have you prayed!') Herry's had a picture of the Nabawi mosque in Medina on the wall. He sat under it and told me about the city. 'When it's cold, or in the rainy season, your lips are cracked and your skin is almost bleeding. The wind hurts you. But during Ramadan season it is most beautiful. The people are like in Java, very friendly, full smile. Many people ask you to have dinner with them before *maghrib*.' (Sunset prayers.)

I asked him if he had visited the Nabawi mosque. He said he had. He paused for a few moments and when he spoke again his voice was grave.

'I'll tell you one thing,' he said. 'I will tell you if you agree or not. Don't call it mosque. Call it *mesjid*.'

'What's wrong with mosque?'

'Mosque is not a good word. It is like mosquito. It is taken from the Mexican language. You know we do not like mosquito. This is deeply propaganda, and I know that mesjid is not disturbing you.'

Part Two

Sulawesi, Borneo, Riau,
The Moluccas

10

Makassar

For the most part the Islamist version of Indonesian history was a litany of victimhood: the policies of Snouck Hurgronje, the defeat of the Jakarta Charter, Sukarno's closeness to the PKI, the ban on Masyumi, the failure to reward Muslims for cleansing the land of communists, Benny Moerdani, Tanjung Priok, Pancasila as the sole basis for all organisations. American academic orthodoxy tended to blame the New Order as well. Dissent banished from the public square had naturally found shelter in the mosque. The Islamist obsession with enemies combined with the academic distaste for military dictators created a bromide: that the Pancasila state of the 1970s and 1980s had somehow gone too far, that discouraging the jilbab and keeping mullahs on a tight political leash had midwifed Islamism rather than aborting it.

From a strictly secular perspective, however, this made little sense. Far from being oppressed, Islam had always occupied a privileged position. Too little secularism rather than too much, and nationalist timidity rather than overreach, had brought things to their present pass. To start with, the Dutch, far from suppressing Islam, had in fact aided its consolidation. Throughout their rule they interfered little with Muslim preachers, who worked tirelessly to firm their faith's shaky grip. The half-hearted Dutch proselytisation effort began relatively late, in the second half of the nineteenth century, and for the most part ignored Java to focus on animist regions such as north Sulawesi and north Sumatra that had never been Muslim. Snouck Hurgronje, the orientalist villain of Islamist legend, curbed the ambit of Christian missionaries, who didn't quite fit into his plans to starve political Islam by feeding its religious twin. Had the hands-off Dutch been more like their Spanish cousins, then by 1945 Indonesia may well have resembled a Protestant version of the Philippines.

After independence the officially non-sectarian state deepened this pattern of privilege. At orthodox Muslim insistence, 'Belief in God', originally proposed as the fifth and final pillar of Pancasila, became the first instead; and that after amendment, with the usual contempt for polytheists, to 'Belief in One God'. In 1946, partly to compensate Islamists for the failure of the Jakarta Charter, the new republic established a ministry of religion, nominally meant to represent all recognised faiths but for practical purposes a Muslim project. It would go on to house an army of bureaucrats overseeing religious instruction, the hajj pilgrimage, the distribution of *zakat*—the Islamic alms tax—and the administration of a parallel legal system of sharia courts for marriage, divorce and, eventually, inheritance as well.

The contrasting treatment of abangan communists and santri Islamists was equally telling. When the long arm of the PKI was deemed to have challenged the state it was messily amputated. By contrast a certain delicacy accompanied both the battle with Darul Islam and the ban on Masyumi for supporting the Sumatra-based rebellion against Jakarta. The army didn't touch either

Muhammadiyah, which supplied much of Masyumi's support base, or the party's student wing.

Even in the early days of Suharto, with the army in command of national life, the orthodox were never quite powerless. In 1973, for example, they beat back a secular marriage bill that would have diluted the power of sharia courts and made polygamy more difficult. Of course, had the early New Order been truly secular rather than merely piously non-sectarian, it would never have concerned itself with building mosques, administering the hajj, placing mullahs in classrooms and expanding Islamic universities. It would have actively discouraged religious education in Egypt, Pakistan and Saudi Arabia. As for the late New Order, a secular state backing a blatantly sectarian organisation such as ICMI would have been laughably absurd.

In short, there had never been a serious nationalist effort to derail the Islamist project, though naivete was probably as much to blame as lack of will. The most Islamists had had to contend with was delay. Nonetheless, to their credit, they had shown superior reserves of patience and guile. Knowing when to pause at a waystation and when to chug full steam ahead required finely tuned instincts. When you found one set of tracks blocked, you had to turn smoothly to another. One man's life illustrated this lesson perfectly.

Mohammad Natsir was born in devout west Sumatra in 1908. His grandfather was a mullah, his father a government clerk. As a boy Natsir displayed an unusual intelligence and his parents, though far from wealthy, strove to give him the best education they could. They enrolled him in a local Dutch school and, after hours, in one based on modernist Islam. Later Natsir won a scholarship to a prestigious Dutch school in Bandung, one of a handful open to Indonesians, where his schoolmates included several other future leaders of the republic. In Bandung Natsir was among the early recruits to a modernist movement called Persis, short for Persatuan

Islam, or Unity of Islam. Founded in 1923, Persis, though similar to Muhammadiyah in inspiration, tilted less towards social work and more towards promoting an arid orthodoxy and a fierce commitment to an Islamic state. On completing high school, Natsir—already touched by the writings of Abduh and his Syrian disciple, Rashid Rida—turned down law school in Batavia and the Rotterdam School of Economics to instead launch his own network of modernist schools.

Natsir was fluent in both English and Dutch, and by the 1930s had established himself as a promising intellectual. He attacked Christianity for its 'irrational' belief in the trinity and, especially, for allowing mere men to tinker with the word of God. For Islamists, worried that Sukarno's evocation of Mother Indonesia threatened monotheism, Natsir provided an alternative vision. He argued that Islam was the only basis for nationhood, that the ultimate goal was not merely independence from the Dutch, but a state governed by sharia, created to serve Muslims, and in which Muslim leaders dominated. In 1940 the ever-inclusive Sukarno, lodged at the time in a Dutch jail, reached out to the younger man in a series of letters. But the chasm between their world views proved unbridgeable. Natsir, unsurprisingly, rejected Sukarno's aversion to a literal reading of the Koran and the Hadith and his belief, inspired by Kemal Ataturk, that Muslims must ultimately be guided by reason.

In 1945 Masyumi, with Natsir at its head, made its unsuccessful push for the Jakarta Charter. Despite his differences with the dominant nationalists, Natsir was appointed minister of information in the revolutionary government that battled the returning Dutch. His exposure to office earned him what would become a lifelong reputation for probity. As the story goes, at one point his staff, concerned that their boss appear more ministerial, pooled in for a new shirt to replace the much mended one on his back.

In 1950 Natsir became prime minister briefly, for six months.

Again he clashed with Sukarno, over what Natsir felt was undue interference in foreign policy. Again he lost. Subsequently, as the president tilted leftwards and Masyumi rightwards, relations between the two men continued to sour. In 1958, along with other Masyumi leaders, Natsir joined the rebel cabinet headquartered in the west Sumatran hill station of Bukittinggi. When Sukarno banned the party two years later the army balked at arresting its leaders, but in 1962 a failed Islamist attempt on his life gave Sukarno his excuse and he had Natsir first jailed and then placed under house arrest. He remained there until released by Suharto in 1966.

It's easy to imagine Natsir's rollercoaster of hope and despair as the Old Order gave way to the New. At first, with both Sukarno and the communists out of the way, he naturally expected to come in from the cold. But the army, for whom Masyumi was tainted by both rebellion and fanaticism, quickly ruled this out. They barred Natsir and other senior leaders from the toothless replacement, Parmusi, that foundered for a few years before being folded into the equally toothless United Development Party. Natsir would remark bitterly that the New Order treated the orthodox like, 'cats with ringworm.'

His political career in tatters, a lesser man might have given up. Instead in 1967 the 59-year-old Natsir founded a new organisation, Dewan Dakwah Islamiyah Indonesia (DDII). Its goal was simple: to realise an Islamic state by minting ideal Muslim citizens. 'First we used politics for preaching,' Natsir was to remark later. 'Now we use preaching for politics. The result will be the same.'

From the start DDII occupied modernism's paranoid bleeding edge. As he had thirty years earlier, Natsir saw a grave danger to Islam from Christianity. The tiny Catholic population had doubled between 1953 and 1964; then, in the wake of santri participation in the anti-communist pogroms, about 3 percent of Javanese, almost all abangan, turned to Christianity. Under Natsir DDII kept up a shrill tattoo against 'Christianisation'. At the same time it stoutly opposed Kebatinan in all its forms, as well as the reverence of Nahdlatul Ulama-oriented santris for mullahs, and their habit of grave worship. As the economy expanded it set itself against conspicuous consumption and the wealth of the Chinese.

Following the 1973 OPEC oil boom, Natsir's international connections—he was a vice-president of the Karachi-based World Muslim Congress and a member of the Mecca-based Muslim World League—opened DDII to a gush of petrodollars. It focused its message tightly on mosques, pesantren and universities, supplying books, establishing scholarships for study in Pakistan and the Middle East, training missionaries and preachers, and promoting the jilbab. Its in-house magazine, *Media Dakwah*, became a kind of forerunner to *Sabili*, and in an ideological sense DDII itself was a forerunner to Jemaah Islamiyah. Bashir's partner and co-founder of their pesant-ren at Ngruki, Abdullah Sungkar, served as the chairman of DDII's central Java branch.

From the late 1970s onward DDII began translating seminal Muslim Brotherhood texts by the Egyptians Sayyid Qutb and Hassan al-Banna, as well as the work of the Pakistani Islamist Maududi. When the Al-Imam Muhammad bin Saud University sought to establish an Indonesian branch in 1980 it reached out to Natsir to make it a reality. Later DDII became a conduit for funding Indonesians who participated in the anti-Soviet Afghan jihad. All this while Natsir never shed his paranoid cast of mind and never stopped struggling against Pancasila. From time to time he would attack Suharto for allegedly misusing the ideology. He never stopped warning of a conspiracy to split Muslims by granting Kebatinan the same status as Islam.

On the whole Mohammad Natsir lived a life on the margins, one that merited only a paragraph or two in most history books, but in the end the dour ideologue's influence had come to match that of his two great presidential adversaries. In 1993, the year he died, Natsirism finally triumphed after a fashion when Christians, for the first time unwelcome for their faith, watched their positions in the cabinet dwindle and Benny Moerdani eased into retirement. The Islamist-friendly Habibie completed the rehabilitation five years later by declaring Natsir a leader of the nation.

Of course, the credit for Islamism's march from periphery to centre hardly belonged to Natsir alone, much less to DDII. Suharto himself, Muhammadiyah, American foreign policy, global capital flows and the price of oil had all played their part. Nonetheless Natsir's life embodied his movement's unwavering purpose. The path he charted from personal piety to political influence had largely held. His suspicions about religious minorities had bled into the mainstream. All that remained was his dream of the final destination: the sharia state.

We first visited Makassar in mid-June—the day after seeing Bashir in prison—for a 'working meeting' of the Preparatory Committee for the Implementation of Sharia Law, better known by its Indonesian acronym KPPSI. One of Herry's reporters, a gangly young man named Dani, in a long-sleeved T-shirt printed with the words 'Live by Values or Die a Martyr', received us at the airport. Taped to the windscreen of the rattletrap Kijang Dani had brought with him was a sheet of paper with the word 'Committee' written on it. It hinted at official sanction and cloaked us with a kind of self-importance. On the road Dani summarised the local situation for Herry. According to his sources the government had suppressed a poll revealing that 91 percent of south Sulawesi residents longed for sharia. Officially released figures pegged support at only 43 percent. 'The government is cheating,' he said. 'They are afraid of Islam.' Then he turned to the good news, the amazing progress of a nearby district, where the *bupati*, the district head—who was scheduled to speak at the conference—had begun to introduce sharia. He had ordered schoolgirls to wear the jilbab. We ought to visit and see it with our own eyes. They *all* had to wear the jilbab. And there was talk of replacing local taxes with zakat. In this district they served alcohol in only one place. The bupati had banned it everywhere else.

'Why would they allow alcohol in that one place?' I asked.

'Tourist area,' said Dani.

'We know foreigner always needing beer,' added Herry.

Dani didn't expect too many journalists at this year's working meeting. Since the Bali bombings, more than a year and a half earlier, the Preparatory Committee had maintained a low profile. Its armed wing, Laskar Jundullah, or Army of Allah, was keeping its head down too. Unlike previous years, the Preparatory Committee had not put it in charge of conference security.

I thought I had seen a posse of Laskar Jundullah men at the Mujahidin Council conference the previous year, though it was difficult to keep your militias straight in that sea of camouflage and jackboots. A Laskar Jundullah bombing at a McDonald's in Makassar had killed three people two years earlier, but the group's particular distinction lay in attacking Christian villages in central Sulawesi. Its founder, Agus Dwikarna, tied to both the Mujahidin Council and Jemaah Islamiyah, languished in a Philippines prison on terrorism charges.

Herry and Dani began to compare notes about Dwikarna.

'He has already memorised seventeen out of thirty chapters of the Koran,' said Herry.

'They only give him two glasses of water a day. Now he's a cripple,' said Dani.

I could see the myth taking shape. If I returned in ten years the locals would all know the story of the martyr who memorised the Koran while living on water in a Christian prison.

The conference organisers had commandeered a hostel built for hajj pilgrims on the outskirts of the city. We arrived well past nine to find it somewhat deserted. The skullcapped men in white at the registration desk shook my hand with surprising firmness, a reminder that we were no longer in Java. Most delegates would not arrive until the next morning, they said.

Herry and I stowed our bags in our room and wandered into a hall bathed in the glare of fluorescent bulbs. A gaggle of volunteers made last-minute preparations, colouring fat Styrofoam letters with felt pens and pasting them on a wall to spell out, 'Preparatory Committee for the Implementation of Sharia Law.' Koranic verses played on a portable stereo on the floor. A short distance away two skullcapped youths squatted on the ground before a TV. One of them wore a name tag that said Ade Basayev.

'Why do you have a Russian name?' I asked.

Herry corrected me. 'Chechen.'

The youth ignored my question. They adopted false names, explained Herry. You never knew, there might be intelligence agents snooping around. The fake Basayev picked up a remote control from the floor and flipped through five channels of women belting out dangdut (but not drilling) until he finally found something to his liking, a true-crime show in which they were enacting the crushing of a child's skull underfoot.

From across the room another man stared at me with sullen intensity. The mark on his forehead had been upgraded from the usual callus to a bump. His tunic accentuated a thick neck and an ape-like hunch; his skullcap sat above shrunken ears. At length he stopped staring, crossed the room, and accosted me.

'Pakistan?'

'India.'

This detail did not deter him. 'You teach me Urdu,' he demanded.

'I'm tired,' I said. 'Maybe if there's time tomorrow.'

If he was disappointed, he didn't show it; instead he told me about a friend who had studied in Pakistan. This friend knew how to make chapatis. His voice filled with pride when he said this. If I liked, he would take me to see his friend tomorrow and we could eat chapatis.

After a noncommittal response to this plan Herry and I returned to our room. It reflected the haphazardness and dilapidation I had glimpsed of the city. Coarse bedcovers with a pattern of red and yellow tulips covered three low beds arranged in a U. Here and there brown stains ate into the shiny blue curtain stretched across the window like an accordion. A battered dresser leaned against a wall. In the pink-tiled bathroom disorganisation gave way to filth. Someone had wedged the broken toilet seat beneath the flush; there was no sink. I brushed my teeth with an unfamiliar brand of bottled water—Alba not Aqua—and spat into the toilet bowl. As I poured water from a bucket my nostrils filled with the smell of stale piss.

When I returned to the room I found Herry, changed into a sarong and undershirt, sitting on his bed with his back against the wall. After Java this was like visiting a new country, I said, the stares, the loud voices. He seemed to find this amusing. 'If Javanese people come here they think Makassar people always angry.'

I asked if it was his first time too in Sulawesi.

He said, 'In 1997 I was on a ferry from Surabaya to Makassar the day Lady Diana died.'

'I remember that day. I had just arrived in Princeton.'

He mulled this over for a while before changing the subject.

'I'll ask you one thing,' he said. 'What is your religion?'

'What do you think?'

'Because you're Indian, I think Hindu. But I'm not sure.'

'Because of the Koran stand?'

On the TV cabinet in my living room sat a carved Koran stand, a gift from a Pakistani classmate in graduate school. Though surrounded by bric-a-brac it would have caught Herry's eye.

'Yes, but I'm not sure.'

'That's just something a friend gave me. I'm what you might call secular.'

'You're agnostic?'

'I used to not believe at all. But now I'm willing to look. I'm not sure what I'll find, but I don't mind looking. You see I'm older now.'

As I said this a part of me was dimly aware of deception, but the words carried just enough truth not to feel like an outright lie. My atheism, arrived at by instinct, was largely unexamined. Surrounded by the pious for the first time in my life I couldn't help but revisit my own attitudes towards God and religion. Nonetheless, if I hadn't instinctively sought to dull the edge of my unbelief to stay on Herry's right side I might have answered differently. I might have said, 'I'm an atheist and, frankly, not terribly inclined towards the spiritual.'

'I'll pray for you,' said Herry. 'I'll pray for you because you have good attitude.'

In the nineteenth century, Makassar gave the world the hair oil whose popularity led to the invention of the antimacassar, a cover to protect furniture in Victorian drawing rooms. Darul Islam secured south Sulawesi's place in more recent history. Here the rebellion was led by Kahar Muzakkar, like the better known Sekarmadji Kartosuwirjo of west Java, a charismatic militia commander who refused to demobilise his followers after independence. In 1951 Kahar Muzakkar took to the hills from where he waged a guerilla war for fourteen years before soldiers tracked him down and shot him. Blood ties tethered his legacy to the Preparatory Committee, which was headed by Abdul Azis Kahar Muzakkar, his youngest son and namesake. In forty years the family's relationship with the state had been turned upside down. South Sulawesi had recently elected Abdul Azis to the Regional Representatives Council, Indonesia's version of America's Senate.

Outside the conference hall the next morning they were hawking the usual books about threats from Christians and Jews and bank interest, as well as a range of A. A. Gym materials: Manajemen Qolbu CDs, Post-it-note sized booklets, only 2000 rupiah each, on 'Time Management' and 'Overcoming Inferiority' and tapes of the 'Guard Your Heart' song. Young men, predictably enough mostly in white or off-white and invariably skullcapped, squatted in the dust and fingered the booklets and sniffed the usual perfumes in gold-capped phials.

An announcement boomed and we made our way inside the hall, now brightened by sunlight pouring through slatted windows and left uncooled by the lethargic fans on the high ceiling. There were about a hundred men and three jilbabed women, a journalist who sat alone in the back row nervously shaking a leg and two wives who tucked themselves to a side while their husbands occupied a table on a platform by the podium. Herry watched me take this down. He said, 'Maybe in five or ten years this will be the most interesting place in the Islamisation of Indonesia.' The setting erased the unfamiliarity of the previous night. These men reminded me of participants in the Mujahidin Council conference, tightly coiled, on a hair-trigger, quick to pump their fists and shout, 'Allahu Akbar.' Only a telltale sign here and there warded off an overwhelming sense of staleness. Herry gestured with his eyes at a man a couple of rows ahead of us in a green shirt, a synthetic green brighter than anything in nature. 'A Javanese person would never wear such a colour,' he said. 'He would never dare.'

After a few minutes Abdul Azis Kahar Muzakkar took the podium under the felt-coloured Styrofoam letters assembled by the fake Basayev and friends. His bones belonged to a sparrow, his tuft of beard on a baby goat, his long tunic in a black-and-white newsreel. In contrast to the audience, he exuded a lack of vigour that bordered on self-effacement, yet his presence evoked an anticipatory hush. Abdul Azis spoke softly about the attention garnered by the Preparatory Committee—in Holland, in England, in America. Not long ago he had been visited by a delegation from Japan, Japanese Muslims. He talked of the Committee's dedication to the implementation of sharia and said that it had been unfairly labelled anarchist, as had Laskar Jundullah. It was their duty as Muslims to live by sharia; yet they lived in a society where most people did not understand its true meaning. The speech evoked the usual cries, accompanied by batteries of raised fists, but as exhortations for sharia went it was peculiar, a passionless disquisition peppered with words like 'substantive' and 'formalisation'.

Afterwards we followed Abdul Azis outside and buttonholed him for an interview. I said that not only the Dutch, the English and the Japanese, but the Indians too, were interested in the Preparatory Committee. I quickly recapped the questions driving my travels. Indonesia was at the crossroads of two larger debates: about Islam and democracy, and Islam and development. Globalisation and Islamisation were both shaping the country, and they were often in conflict with each other. What was his assessment of the future?

He chose his words carefully, in a manner that deepened his somewhat academic demeanour. He began by recapping the last 25 years—the quickening of Islamic political thought after the Iranian revolution in 1979; the dark days of Benny Moerdani when the army suppressed Islam and everyone had to swear by Pancasila; the so-called Salman Mosque movement (which encouraged strict personal piety among students) born in the prestigious Institute of Technology in Bandung before spreading to other campuses and eventually incubating the PKS leadership. He called his generation the third generation of Muslim leaders in independent Indonesia. The demands of the first, of Masyumi and Natsir were formal—that the country be declared an Islamic state. The second generation had found politics closed to it during much of Suharto's rule, so it had propagated Islam culturally—the jilbab, the Ramadan fast, the pilgrimage to Mecca. He gave the example of the Muslim intellectual Nurcholish Madjid, who in the early years of the New Order had famously declared, 'Islam yes, Islamic party no.' And now the baton had passed to his generation, which was using both culture and politics to achieve its goal. That goal, he said, had always remained the same: they all believed that the ideal society was that of Medina in the time of the Prophet. Only the methods had changed. If I wanted to learn more, the best way was to see how the Preparatory Committee's efforts were bearing fruit in the district where the bupati had introduced sharia.

I asked him what he remembered of his father.

He had no memories. The youngest of fourteen children, he was only two months old when his father died. He was born in December 1964; Kahar Muzakkar was killed in February 1965. He did not remember his father, but he had heard many stories about him and had read all the books that he left behind, as well as the books written about him by others.

Did he ever worry that he would find himself on the wrong side of the law? That his campaign for sharia would meet the same end as his father's?

Again he chose his words carefully.

'It is not possible, unless this agenda is foisted from outside. There isn't the political power in Indonesia now to turn things back. There is no one strong enough to do that.'

What about globalisation? What did he make of 'Indonesian Idol'?

'I am not worried. If you look at Malaysia you can see that two states are ruled by (the Islamist party) PAS. Why can't that happen in Indonesia as well? Modernisation is not the same as westernisation. Indonesia can progress with Islamic concepts, with science, knowledge and technology, but without the westernisation of culture.'

So he was saying he wanted Microsoft but not Britney?

'Microsoft but not Madonna.'

I told him that most people thought of sharia as chopping off thieves' hands and stoning adulterers to death. Did he agree with those punishments?

His tone remained perfectly reasonable.

'It is true that the Koran prescribes stoning for adultery and the amputation of thieves' hands, but people forget that during the ten-year rule of the Prophet only one person had his hand chopped off. One person in ten years in the entire country. I can't claim that it isn't there in the Koran or that I don't believe in it, but to label such punishments cruel is wrong. They come from God. A poll in south Sulawesi shows that 91 percent of people agree with a broad implementation of sharia—compulsory prayer five times a day, women required to wear the jilbab and so on. And 58 percent want to embrace it fully—amputation, everything.'

I shuddered inwardly, but Abdul Azis had earned my grudging admiration for not equivocating. A. A. Gym and Din Syamsuddin had both deflected the question of where exactly they stood on sharia; Gym by saying he didn't want to get into that controversy because he would be criticised no matter what position he took and Din by claiming to favour more discussion and debate. Even Irfan S. Awwas, despite his careful study of volleyball fashion and his plans to establish alcohol-free Muslim zones, had been less blunt about the bloody parts, albeit on purely practical grounds.

Abdul Azis suggested that I speak with one of his lieutenants, the secretary general of the Preparatory Committee. He had written a master's thesis on Kahar Muzakkar and had recently graduated, cum laude, from a local university.

Later that day, during a break from the program, we found the secretary general and cum laude graduate in a makeshift common room surrounded by well-wishers and sipping a cup of thick coffee. I had expected someone in his twenties, perhaps slim like Abdul Azis, but the secretary general turned out to be a jowly middle-aged man with a hail-fellow-well-met manner and the meaty forearms of a sailor. When I asked him what he thought south Sulawesi would look like in five years or ten he took my pen and drew a table in my notebook:

	1999	2004	2009
Jilbab	_	+	++
Alcohol	_	_	++
Koranic Education	_	+	++

He explained: Five years ago, many women in south Sulawesi walked around bareheaded, shops sold alcohol freely and Koranic education in the schools was substandard. Now the jilbab was common and Koran reading standards had risen, but alcohol was still sold, especially in the city. In five years, all women would be covered, every child would be able to read the Koran and nobody would sell a drop of alcohol. He too saw no threat from globalisation. Quite the contrary, there would be no borders between Muslim lands. The world was moving towards a caliphate. People were getting fed up with a 'free' lifestyle. 'Taliban, Sudan, Pakistan will be more influential,' he said. 'People will see what is right and come back to the Koran.' Then, in a bit of a non sequitur, he added, 'Net effect of HIV is back to religion.'

That evening, numbed by the repetitiveness of the speeches, I decided to skip day two of the conference and instead see something of Makassar. I got out my *Lonely Planet*, which recommended an old Dutch bungalow converted into an inn. Herry, encountering the book for the first time, called it my magic book. We found another beat-up van courtesy of Dani, who insisted on accompanying us to the hotel.

After we had been on the road a few minutes Herry began telling Dani an obviously fabricated story he had unearthed about SBY. Apparently SBY's mother had belonged to Gerwani, the allegedly orgiastic female communist torturers of New Order lore. 'SBY disowned her and now pretends that someone else was his mother,' said Herry.

For some reason this piece of gossip made my stomach turn. It was clearly a concoction. (When had *Sabili* allowed that to get in the way?) SBY's anti-communist credentials were widely known; his father was in the military; his father-in-law, a general, had played a leading role in the eradication of the PKI. Like all army officers of his generation, his family background had been carefully vetted. Nonetheless the lie revealed a sordid truth about Indonesia. In the hysteria of the 1960s you could imagine a boy denouncing his mother for her politics and then hiding this for his career. And even now you had people like Herry out there, knocking on doors, trawling gutters, turning over grave stones to find out whose mother might have held the wrong beliefs forty years ago.

'How do you know this?' I asked. I tried to keep my voice calm, but it escaped with an edge.

'I have secret information. I found out that he disowned his mother.'

'Did you check with him?'

He ignored my question. After a few minutes, Herry and Dani resumed their conversation. 'There aren't many churches here?' said Herry looking out of the window.

'There are,' said Dani. 'But not in this part of town.'

'Are Christian numbers going up or down?' I asked. 'Protestants and Catholics.' In Indonesian the word Christian referred only to Protestants.

'Going up,' said Herry. 'Catholics by education method, Protestants by economic method.'

'How do you know?'

'I have secret data not released. This shows that Muslims are only 76 percent of the population.'

Something inside me snapped. 'I'm sorry, but that's paranoia. All official figures say that between 88 percent and 90 percent of Indonesians are Muslim. I've been all over this country and haven't seen a scrap of evidence to say that 24 percent aren't Muslim.'

'It may be paranoia,' he said evenly. 'But I have information.'

We didn't speak a word during the rest of the ride to the hotel. I silently berated myself for the outburst. It betrayed both my training as a journalist and my years in Indonesia. I ought to have known better than to raise my voice at Herry, especially in front of Dani. You never raised your voice at a Javanese, even an Islamist Javanese. It meant a loss of face for him. It meant the same for me; it revealed a lack of self-control, and self-control lay at the heart of breeding.

If I had offended Herry he didn't show it; he too appeared glad to have escaped the conference and was his usual gregarious self over dinner. The next morning we squeezed into a becak—smaller here than in Java, tight transportation in a tight economy—to begin our sightseeing. It quickly confirmed my dim view of the city. At the dilapidated museum in an old Dutch fort simple factual errors and spelling mistakes riddled the labels. Dust covered the display cases. A faulty fluorescent light flickered and buzzed like a demented insect. At another well-known tourist destination, on the outskirts of the city, underwear dried on the mildewed graves of south

Sulawesi's medieval kings. There wasn't another tourist in sight. Only the mosque, the oldest in this part of the country—the original, since replaced by a newer structure, dated from 1603—boasted a fresh coat of paint. Herry disappeared inside and when he emerged posed for a picture framed against its whiteness.

We still had a few hours to kill before our flight back to Jakarta. On our way to the grave site Herry had made quite an impression on our taxi driver, who had listened awestruck to his tales about Jakarta. ('The fleets have a thousand taxis.') Our sightseeing options more or less exhausted, the driver suggested a café where we could while away what remained of the afternoon. After our experiences thus far I was expecting a pit, but Café 52 turned out to be a welcome break from the squalor. A balcony jutted into the blue-grey Indian Ocean. There were hardly any customers and we had no trouble finding a table by the water's edge.

The conversation turned to terrorism. We joked about what it was like to be bearded and brown after 9/11. I explained how these days I couldn't take a flight in America—my girlfriend was completing a doctorate in Chicago—without being pulled out of line for additional frisking. You couldn't really blame them though, I added, for the truth was that if you slipped my picture amid those of the nineteen hijackers nobody could pick me out. Herry laughed and told me about going through seven checks one time at the British Council library in Jakarta. When our waitress came by I asked for a Bintang and Herry for something called Lady in Rose after checking that it really was non-alcoholic.

'Of course it's non-alcoholic,' I said. 'They aren't going to lie about it, especially not to someone who looks like you.'

He laughed. 'I will explain to you about beard in Islam,' he said. 'Mohammed says if you have one hair, one angel will pray for you. If you have many, many hairs imagine how many angels are praying for you.'

'But that's discrimination. Not everyone can grow a beard. Look at all those guys at the conference with their wispy little beards.'

'But they have other ways to get an angel. They can smile. They can greet people. They can say, "assalam aleikum."'

A cool breeze blew across the balcony and our ears filled with the sounds of a peppy pop tune. When our drinks arrived Herry looked pleased with his Lady in Rose, pink and frothy, with a cherry and a wedge of pineapple. The breeze tousled his hair, the ghost of a smile played on his lips. By this time Herry had decided that he would also write a book about our travels. I had given him a stack of reporter's notebooks and now, in between straw sips, he scribbled away in one, raising his head every now and then to think. His letters were small, closely bunched, a hand accustomed to not wasting paper.

'What will you do with your life when you have finished this book?' he asked.

'I'm not sure. I hope I can make a living from writing, but if I can't I'll work something out. Money's not the most important thing to me. Something will work itself out. It always does.'

He pondered this and said, 'You know, you are not Muslim but your thinking is like Muslim.'

'How is that?'

'Not caring about money. Caring about ideas.' He looked at my glass. 'Except for Beer Bintang your thinking is like Muslim.'

I laughed. It was meant as a compliment and I took it in that spirit. Then I turned to my copy of Hemingway's *Men without Women*, oddly appropriate reading for Makassar. Herry continued to scribble in his notebook. After a while, he spoke again.

'You know, I'm thinking Mohammed is very visionary.'

I lowered my book, but kept it open.

'Every Muslim must teach his child three things. First, making poetry. If a child learns poetry he learns the value of brevity. Second, to ride a horse and use a bow and arrow. For war, to give you power. And third to swim.'

'Does this apply only to sons?'

'To daughters too. According to me this is unique. The Arabs don't have the sea so how can you teach them to swim? They didn't have swimming pools in those days. This is what I'm thinking. Mohammed was thinking Islam will cross the continents, will convert other peoples and if you need to cross the seas you need to be a good swimmer. For me it's quite visionary.'

'Okay,' I said, with a bluntness made possible by familiarity. 'Now let me read my book.'

11

Makassar/Bulukumba

This was the question: What is the key word in a formal letter?

The student stared blankly at the professor, who turned to me and said, 'This is the globalisation era and he can't identify the key word.' Her tone said, 'Can you believe it?' I was glad that she hadn't asked me to identify the key word. I did not want her to discover my own woeful lack of preparation for the globalisation era.

President Megawati, on the wall in her obligatory portrait, was the only un-jilbabed woman on the campus of the Muslim University of Indonesia in Makassar. A few weeks earlier hundreds of students, still enraged over the rearrest of Bashir in Jakarta, had clashed with police. Our friends at the Preparatory Committee had urged us to visit the campus for a taste of activism, but when Herry and I showed up at the end of June, en route to the sharia-friendly district of Bulukumba, we found it on break and mostly deserted. After searching in vain for rock throwers for more than an hour we stumbled upon the professor of English and her hapless student.

We sat under a lazy fan facing a picture of the Great Mosque in Mecca. A (properly punctuated) sign on the wall said, 'Have you prayed already?' The professor was fleshy like a fruit, with a face that recalled a long and losing battle with acne. She wore a colourful jilbab. Nine hairs of various lengths sprouted from a mole on her chin. She had a loud voice and a louder laugh and these made me warm to her at once.

'Key word, KEY WORD,' said the professor. The student—his name was Askar—continued to stare at her blank-faced. He sat opposite her, across the narrow width of a long table covered with green felt. A cowlick curled like a comma on his forehead. A notebook and a ballpoint pen lay in front of him. To his right, opposite me, sat Herry.

The professor turned to me again. 'There is a key word in every letter. He has to identify the key word.' She refused to be held responsible for Askar's acute deficiency in the key word department. 'His teacher before wasn't me,' she said. She was not that kind of professor she assured me. Her sister held a doctorate from Macquarie University in Australia.

At this point a girl in a severe black jilbab, tight jeans and a white T-shirt with a zip down the front breezed in. Evidently she was an hour and a half late. 'Traffic,' she explained without apology and pulled up a chair beside Askar. The professor ignored her and continued grilling the boy. She asked him what he would do if he had to ask his parents for money.

He thought this over for a few moments. 'I would call them,' he said softly.

'See, telephone!' exclaimed the professor in triumph. 'They must have a conversation with their parents on the telephone. They use the telephone!'

Askar's inquisition was the closest I'd come to a good time in Makassar, but Herry appeared distressed. He tried to intervene on the boy's behalf. 'You can't really blame technology,' he said politely. 'It's faster.'

The professor cracked a knuckle loudly. She wasn't convinced. 'Yes, they think problem can be finished. Short technology, short language.' She raised an imaginary phone to her ear and mimicked a student. 'Ok-bye-*sudah*. See you!'

I asked her if she expected them to write letters to their parents instead of calling. 'Phoning is the informal method,' she said. 'Writing is the formal method, but they don't even know how to compose a sentence.' She turned to the students sharply. 'How would you write if you wanted to ask your parents for money? Do this now. It's your assignment.'

Askar was 22; Trimurti, the girl, 24. They were both students of English and would have graduated by now, except that they had failed English Correspondence, and an English major couldn't graduate without passing English Correspondence. The grim responsibility for remedial coaching, of ensuring that Askar and Trimurti were fit to join other alumni of the Muslim University of Indonesia, Makassar, had fallen on the professor.

I didn't want Askar's suffering to end just yet. I said, 'He might not know the key word, but I bet he knows all about football.' I asked him to name the four Euro championship semi-finalists.

'Greece, Portugal, Czech Republic,' he said. He scanned his brain for a few seconds and added, 'The Netherlands.'

'He'll get an A in Euro,' I said to the professor.

Her cheeks reddened. She threw up her hands; her watch was slim and feminine with a thin leather band. 'Look at their expressions,' she said. 'Just look at their expressions.'

She had a point. Askar and Trimurti resembled cattle trapped in a car's headlights, their eyes blank, their brows perfectly unlined, the faces of innocents.

'They don't like me,' said the professor. 'I'm a killer.' She snipped the air with imaginary scissors. But the students did nothing to make their dislike evident. They seemed placid, impervious to humiliation, capable of absorbing every barb with equanimity.

Since Askar was a student of English, I asked him what he liked to read.

'I like novels,' he said.

This came as a pleasant surprise. Whose novels did he like? He pondered this. Lines formed on his smooth forehead. Finally he spoke. 'The novels of Mira W.'

I hadn't heard the name before. Could he name a few of her books?

Again silence. You could hear the ceiling fan rotating overhead.

'I forget the titles,' he said. 'There's a *sinetron* on TV.' (A soap opera.)

I thought I'd try out Herry's technique of telling people exactly what they wanted to hear. 'Kids are spoilt these days,' I said to the professor. 'I would bring back corporal punishment. These kids need a ruler wouldn't you say?'

She laughed raucously. Yes, yes, they are all so spoilt. They need a thrashing. Can't write a sentence. Don't know the key word. Only want to use the telephone.

As Askar and Trimurti hunched over their assignment, three of Trimurti's friends entered the room. They were evidently waiting for her to finish. They sidled up to Trimurti and whispered in her ear. They didn't seem to care that this was under the nose of the professor, the killer, the sister of the doctorate holder from Macquarie University. The girls whispered in Trimurti's ear. Trimurti wrote. Askar peeked at Trimurti's paper, quickly turned his sheet over, and started again.

The professor now turned to Herry, whose business card lay on the green felt before her. She looked at the card and then at him again.

She said, 'Friend of Amrozi.' The Bali bomber. 'Careful, terrorist!' She laughed.

Herry grimaced. His feeble attempt to shield Askar had failed and now he himself was under attack. The professor went on. '*Sabili* is—' She sliced the air with a make-believe sword.

'It's not only that,' said Herry, his tone both testy and plaintive. He was struggling to retain his dignity. His lack of a formal education inflated the professor's authority in his eyes and put Herry at a severe disadvantage. I found myself enjoying his discomfort as well. It seemed a small price to pay for lionising terrorists.

The professor was high on her own wit. 'Careful! Careful Osama bin Laden! Dangerous.'

'It's not like that. It's—'

'Bomb Bali! Friend of Amrozi! Dangerous!'

This went on for a while, Herry alternating between pleading and glowering, the professor, the killer, too practiced in her art to be deterred by either tactic. Eventually Herry was rescued by Trimurti and Askar. They slid their letters across the table to the professor.

Askar's first attempt had begun: 'Dear Sirs, Firstly I would to talk my condition in Makassar is very fine and hope father and mother fine also, amien.' On the other side of the paper was the letter he had written after cribbing from Trimurti and her consortium of helpers:

Makassar, 29 June 2004

Dear Father and Mother,
　　Assalamu Alaikum wr-wb.
　　Firstly I would like to talk my condition in Makassar is very fine and I hope father and mother fine also amien....!

Related with this letter your child would ask money for to pay the SPP next semester about Rp. 1000 000 I hope will send soon. I think that is all my letters. Thank you very much.

Wassalam wr wb.

Yours child,
Askar

It had taken them nearly an hour, albeit with distractions. The professor circled the words 'Related with' and wrote, 'This is more the style of formal letter.' Askar and Trimurti were free to go. They would both pass. An air of gaiety touched the room and even Herry managed a smile. It was only later that I remembered that I still didn't know the key word in a formal letter.

The next day we left Makassar for Bulukumba. Our minivan had space for eight but carried thirteen; soon the sour smell of sweat mingled thickly with kretek fumes. Two passengers got into an argument and the van filled with hot, slurry speech, the words jammed as tightly together as chickens trussed for market. Thomas Stamford Raffles, the founder of Singapore, had once said that what separated Java from Sumatra was a thousand years of civilisation. With south Sulawesi the distance seemed twice as great. At last, four cramped hours after we had begun, we pulled into a lot that appeared to double as a bus terminal. A crush of porters engulfed us as we alighted, yelling, tugging at my sleeve, grabbing my bag, touching my shoulder.

'GET AWAY!' I barked, raising my palms. The porters scattered backwards.

A few minutes later we clambered aboard the local van to Bira Beach. Even in the dimness of dusk I could see that Herry was shaken.

He waited until we were on the road again before speaking.

'You should be more calm,' he said.

'You're right. Sometimes I find it hard.'

By now I counted Herry as a friend. With the passage of time the role play that had marked our earliest interactions had eased. Herry no longer seemed compelled to underscore his Muslimness at every opportunity, to assure me, for example, that he was so sensitive to immorality that setting foot in a disco was enough to give him a splitting headache. My part as the disinterested foreign journalist had also evolved. I could laugh at his uncomfortable run-in with the killer in Makassar. He could tell me when he found my manner uncouth.

In some ways I had come to know Herry as well as I did anyone in the country. I knew, for example, that he sometimes began his meals with dessert: on the flight to Makassar he had demolished the apple crumble before turning to the chicken and potatoes. Such trivialities shielded me from my normal journalistic impulse to see Herry simply as a stand-in for something larger. After all he belonged to the first generation exposed to the New Order's systematic religious education. He was an urban youth with once uncertain prospects who had glommed on to the growth (and the glamour) of the Islamist movement. He was a Javanese who, his daughters' names notwithstanding, embodied their shrinking from their own culture. His views on Christians and communists reflected Natsir's rather than Sukarno's. But there was also the fondness for fizzy pink drinks, the appetite for apple crumble, the photocopied books toted about and shared with such zeal. These, to my mind, belonged to him alone.

At Bira Beach we checked in at a small oceanfront hotel, the kind with a heart-shaped plastic mug bobbing in a bucket in lieu of a hot water shower. The bathroom reminded me of the innate sentimentality of a country awash with heart-shaped mugs, Hello Kitty knick-knacks, Winnie the Pooh toys, the ubiquitous Westlife. The more intelligent Islamists exploited this perfectly. To each other, for instance, they praised Bashir's commitment to sharia and his aversion to kafirs. To the public at large they portrayed him as a harmless grandfather, a pious old man heartlessly persecuted by the state for the crime of believing. For the Mujahidin Council and the Preparatory Committee, Palestine and Iraq impelled rage, but in their public packaging they evoked tears.

After we had stowed our bags Herry disappeared in search of a prayer room while I headed to the empty café overlooking the beach for a beer. This was the one place in the district of Bulukumba where alcohol remained legal. The beer felt special, an almost illicit pleasure, a brave, sweating bottle of Bintang.

After dinner Herry and I decided to explore the beach. We took a flight of rough-hewn steps and at the foot slipped off our shoes. The sand felt like talcum powder, fine and cool against my soles. The moon was up and waves gently slapped the fishing boats moored in the shallows. There wasn't another soul in sight. As we strolled towards the ocean Herry said he was excited about being in Bulukumba. We had heard so much about it at the Preparatory Committee meeting and *Sabili* had already run a story lauding the bupati for his foresight. I too thought of it as a sneak preview of the future, a trailer for the film that would one day run seamlessly across the archipelago, if the bupati and Abdul Azis Kahar Muzakkar and Irfan S. Awwas and Abu Bakar Bashir and, depending on who they were talking to, perhaps Din Syamsuddin and A. A. Gym as well, had their way.

We hugged the tide's edge trailing two long, moist sets of footprints in our wake. After a few minutes we came upon a clump of large rocks and above them, on a ridge, a dark knot of trees.

'Let's go back,' said Herry abruptly.

'Let's see what's beyond these rocks.'

'No, let's go back. I don't have a good feeling here.'

We turned around.

'I have a sixth sense, they say,' said Herry.

'What did you sense?'

'Something. I no longer felt happy when we reached those stones.'

About halfway back to the stairs we plonked ourselves down in a tranquil spot, untouched by the tide, yet close enough for us to hear its ripple and wash. I buried my feet in the sand and sat mesmerised by the small fishing boats bobbing in the shallows until Herry punctured the silence.

'What if a beautiful woman suddenly appears? What will you think?'

'I'll think it's Ratu Kidul.'

'Will you go to her or run away?'

'I'd probably run away.'

'What if it's a mermaid?'

'If it's a mermaid she won't have legs. Maybe I won't need to run.'

A companionable silence fell upon us again. My thoughts drifted to Ratu Kidul in her undersea palace before returning to the beach.

'I wish I could play the guitar,' I said. 'This place is so beautiful it makes me wish I could play the guitar.'

'I can. But after I joined the Islamic movement I stopped.'

'How come?'

'It's controversial in Islam.' He thought for a few moments. 'But I don't agree with those who say in Islam music is haram.' His voice trailed off.

For the first time I felt sorry for Herry. Nobody should have to agonise about such things.

The next morning we hopped into a garishly painted *angkot*, a minibus, for Bulukumba town where Herry had unearthed an old friend to show us around. Hamka ran a small orphanage for Hidayatullah, the nation-wide Islamic NGO, and was a PKS activist. He had a broad, smooth forehead and a thick beard. He wore the sleeves of his embroidered tunic rolled up and exuded an earnestness of purpose and a no-nonsense manner. He lived in the orphanage, a simple three-room house with an unpainted door, a corrugated tin roof and children toddling and tumbling in the cramped courtyard. Some effort had gone into making the place cheerful. A poster in the front room showed a skullcapped boy and a jilbabed girl before a mosque with a bright yellow dome. It said: 'Let's go to the mosque!'

The orphanage, explained Herry, ran mostly on charity. To defray costs they sold *Suara Hidayatullah*, a magazine similar to *Sabili*, and housed a small public telephone booth. I knew that Herry had also studied at a Hidayatullah school, though not at an orphanage, and that after graduating he had worked for the organisation. At the orphanage he recalled spending three months setting up a similar no-frills operation in Solo. 'My life then was like this,' he said looking around.

About an hour after arriving at the orphanage, once Hamka had arranged for transport, we set off to see for ourselves a sharia-minded government school. Hamka led on a Honda; I rode pillion behind Herry on a Suzuki. The school occupied a low concrete building with a sloping tin roof. The red and white national flag hung limply in the hot, hot schoolyard where scrawny black chickens clucked and pecked at grass strewn with scraps of plastic and paper. Rough-hewn wooden tables and half-erased blackboards filled the classrooms. We found no students that morning. School had let out at eleven and we had arrived just in time to watch the last of them trudge their way towards home. Hamka had pointed at three girls and exclaimed, 'Look, they all wear the jilbab!'

Luckily, in a corridor by the schoolyard we bumped into a

teacher still on the premises. He had a kind face and the slow, somewhat hangdog, manner of someone who has seen life pass him by. He was 54 years old, he said. These days he taught local language and culture, but he had begun his career thirty years earlier teaching painting. The district had since scrapped the subject from the curriculum. He found this regrettable; he still believed that painting ought to be taught. It made a child 'proportional', by which he meant well-rounded.

What did he feel about it now being compulsory for schoolgirls to wear the jilbab?

The teacher's expression brightened and his words suddenly acquired animation, as though someone had surreptitiously inserted new batteries in the back of his head. He was delighted. Before the bupati intervened only about half the girls would cover up, but now they all did—100 percent. The female teachers too, they had to. (I detected a special note of triumph here.) His only complaint was that the bupati had yet to introduce a similar regulation for boys. They were discussing it in the local legislature. There would be a law soon, *inshallah*, and the boys would no longer show their knees. He had been teaching for thirty years. He remembered when the jilbab was banned in government schools. Then it became optional. Now it was required.

Across the street from the school stood a large mosque, an eyesore with a misshapen dome that looked like a piece of tin foil beaten into shape by a blind man with a hammer. The muezzin emitted a raspy call; it sounded like a cat being throttled. I winced and resisted the urge to plug my ears.

'They need a new sound system,' I muttered to Herry. He grimaced at my comment, but didn't respond.

The teacher continued. 'There's a test now. You can't enroll in primary school unless you can read and write a passage from the Koran. They open it at random and ask the child to read.' Students now spent an hour each Friday memorising the Koran. The bupati had also introduced a one-month Koran-reading camp in the holidays. In the old days teachers decided when their class would break for prayer; one might choose to finish explaining something first. No more. Now all the children in the school prayed together. All four hundred and fifty of them left class at the same time.

'What if someone doesn't want to pray?'

He looked at me as though I was daft.

'There has never been a student who doesn't want to pray.'

I believed him.

At my request, the teacher agreed to take us on a little campus tour. The school had no basketball or tennis courts, no sports field of any kind and, needless to say, no gym. It supported only two kinds of extra-curricular activity—scouting and first aid training. The solitary computer had broken down, said the teacher, and there was no one to fix it. ('You can still push the buttons, but nothing happens.') He showed us the science lab: a couple of ancient globes, a fierce looking plaster model of the human eye (a blue eye) and a handful of beakers on rusted stands. Then he led us to a corner of the school compound, not far from where we had stood by the schoolyard, to a half-built mosque. They had been at work on it for a year, said the teacher. Inshallah, it would soon be ready for use.

I pondered the large mosque across the narrow street and the smaller one coming up inside the school. While Indians learned computers and maths, Chinese crammed English, and Vietnamese ratcheted up worker productivity in factories, here they were building a little mosque right next to the big mosque. Who would dare oppose it?

Who would say, 'Excuse me, but might there be a better way to spend this money?' So they would go to the school with the little mosque inside and the big mosque outside. If they were lucky they would get a graduate of the Muslim University of Makassar to teach them how to write letters.

We thanked the teacher for his time and then Herry and Hamka stepped across the street and entered the big mosque.

Afterwards, on Hamka's recommendation, we stopped by a popular local warung for lunch. It was a rudimentary affair, a shed filled with tables and thick with customers and flies. We ordered grilled fish and rice, and when they arrived more flies came with them. I brushed away as many as I could and watched one alight on Abdul Azis's goateed face on a Preparatory Committee wall calendar. ('Fighting Corruption, Collusion and Nepotism by Maintaining Islamic Sharia.') Another settled on the round PKS sticker on our table; south Sulawesi was a party stronghold. I asked for candles to ward off the flies, but they were of little help. Against such odds there was only so much two feeble candles could achieve.

At the table behind us sat a pair of government employees in their new uniforms—full-sleeved khaki suits and jilbabs, one pink the other black. I drifted over and introduced myself.

'What do you think of the regulation requiring you to wear the jilbab?' I asked.

'It's a very good thing,' said Pink.

'Did anyone object?'

'No,' said Black.

'What if someone didn't want to wear it?'

'That has never happened.'

Hamka, who apart from his comment about the covered school-girls had said virtually nothing all morning, stopped picking his teeth with a fish bone and turned around.

'They all want it,' he said with a note of finality. 'It's better.'

'If they all want it, then why do you need a regulation?'

'We still need a regulation,' said Pink and Black.

'Why do they need a regulation?' I asked Herry.

He turned halfway around. 'They still need a regulation,' he snapped. 'I cannot explain that.' He shrugged his shoulders and returned to his meal. After a few moments he added, his tone softer, 'Regulation is for motivating the people.'

The women, all aflutter now, told me about the bupati's new plan. Any government employee caught drinking would be paraded around the district with a sign around his neck. The bupati would do this himself.

'You mean drinking on the job,' I said.

'No,' they chirped. 'Drinking anywhere. Even at home.'

I rejoined Herry and Hamka at our table.

'The villagers used to get drunk and fight,' said Herry. 'Now they don't drink. All of them go to the mesjid.'

'If the police catch someone who makes country liquor they douse him with it,' said Hamka. 'There are fewer fights now and fewer crimes.'

I paid and we got up to leave. After the shade of the warung it was like stepping into a wall of brightness. The heat fit like a wetsuit; I felt it behind my neck, behind my knees.

'In English, how do you say, almost in tears, but with happiness?' asked Herry.

'I'm not sure there's a single word for it.'

'Well that is how I am feeling right now.'

The bupati of Bulukumba had arrived at the Preparatory Committee conference in Makassar in the nicest car of all, a silver Toyota Landcruiser imported from a colder climate, with red defrosting lines across the rear window. He was a delicately built man with rheumy eyes and baby smooth skin. Those eyes and that skin didn't belong together. They created the effect of an old baby, an ancient baby with a pencil moustache and a gold watch.

Nonetheless the bupati appeared to see himself as a man of action.

At the conference he had taken the podium and raised an alarming survey according to which 30 percent of the people in his district could not recite from the Koran. Of course, he had taken immediate steps to remedy this. He assured his excitable audience that Bulukumba's Christians were thronging to Islam in large numbers. He evoked warm laughter when he shared the story of the women, government employees, who had come to him soon after he took office, begging for forgiveness, repentant for not having worn the jilbab until then. Later he told Herry and me about the simple method he had devised to deal with the recalcitrant. He had let it be known that the un-jilbabed would not be promoted.

The bupati was out of town when we visited Bulukumba, but after lunch Hamka took us by his house, an island of neatness amid the flyblown squalor. He lived in a well kept Javanese bungalow with a long portico, a roof of glazed blue tile and solid white walls. A flock of deer were penned in a corner of the manicured lawn. A gaggle of geese roamed the driveway. Next we stopped by his office. The bupati's safari-suited aides had read the *Sabili* story and escorted us, with some reverence, into his empty room. An artillery shell gleamed in a glass case. Large plastic sunflowers filled a coffee table vase. The customary portraits of President Megawati and Vice-President Hamzah Haz smiled down from wood-panelled walls, along with portraits of the governor and the deputy governor, in white bemedalled uniforms. The bupati's guests, I gathered, sat on the plump sofas and nibbled on Monde butter cookies kept in a round blue tin. The trappings of power appeared to cement the general admiration the bupati inspired. Herry and Hamka and the bupati's staff all agreed that he was a man of rare vision.

Bulukumba's wonders not quite exhausted, we hopped onto our little Suzuki and followed Hamka. In the town's centre we paused to admire a monument to recent advancements erected in the middle of a tiny roundabout. A Koran stand topped a stone and cement pillar in pink and grey. A plaque on the pillar, gold letters against a black background, listed the main points of the bupati's 'Crash Program for Religion'. (Koran recitation, compulsory jilbabs and so on.) A little while later we stopped again, opposite a nondescript white house. A flushed, barely contained joy appeared to suffuse Hamka as he pointed. 'They used to serve alcohol here. And there were naughty women.' If you looked closely you could make out where the word 'karaoke' had been whitewashed.

Had the bupati shuttered every single karaoke bar in the district?

'Except for Bira Beach,' said Hamka. 'That's a tourism area.'

'He knows that foreigner needs alcohol,' added Herry sagely.

When we resumed our tour, town quickly gave way to country and before long we were zipping past rice paddies and coconut palms, little jilbabed girls in horse drawn carts with bells, half-built mosques sprouting from the dark earth, each larger it seemed than the last. Somewhere along the way Hamka had picked up a slight man in a camouflage vest and a black baseball cap. A tattooed garland of barbed wire stretched across his neck. He had introduced himself as Anwar, a local 'commander' of Laskar Jundullah.

If Bulukumba contained a promise for the nation, then the village of Balimbo, which we rode into about half an hour later, occupied the same position in the district. The bupati had deemed it a model village. By south Sulawesi standards Balimbo was rich. Potholes marked the narrow street we rode in on and the men lounging aimlessly by its side wore thongs rather than shoes; but the houses, mounted on wooden stilts and roofed with tin or corrugated iron, were substantial. More than one sprouted a crude dish antenna and several had a motorcycle parked outside. Wreaths of bougainvillea and clumps of marigold here and there softened their rough construction.

Hamka disappeared inside a stilted house for a few minutes and emerged with a sarong-clad middle-aged man, pompadoured and paunchy as a late vintage Elvis. Muhammad Haris headed a group called 'Citizens for Sharia'. The village, he said, had first been settled by a group of Muhammadiyah families. Nature had been kind to them. There was almost no rice cultivation here; instead they grew cash crops—cloves and cocoa and a little vanilla.

By now a knot of the curious had gathered around us. At my prodding Muhammad Haris listed the qualities that made a model village model: 95 percent of the women wore the jilbab; everyone, except the very young, could recite the Koran; 100 percent of girls who had begun to menstruate wore the jilbab; there was no theft, you could leave your keys in your motorcycle; it was the only village in the district where the mosque filled to capacity five times a day.

A scrawny mongrel came up and cold-nosed my ankle. I was about to say, 'You know, there are no dogs in Saudi Arabia' before I checked myself. I wasn't prepared to live with the consequences that might entail for the dogs of Balimbo.

Haris agreed to show us around the village. Nature had indeed smiled upon them. Everywhere you looked you saw banana trees, clove trees with their white trumpet-shaped flowers, lush dieffenbachia. We walked by more houses with television dishes; a shrouded woman carrying something on her head, the bib of her jilbab halfway to the waist; more jilbabs (if anything the 95 percent claim appeared to be an understatement); more mangy dogs; a woman pounding dried coconut with a giant pestle; many motorcycles, but not one with its keys left in the ignition. The well stocked village store carried instant noodles, Pepsodent toothpaste and Lifebuoy soap. I recalled reading that during the Darul Islam rebellion Kahar Muzakkar had banned white sugar and milk powder and rolled cigarettes, but any early ambivalence here towards technological progress and consumer goods had evidently been brushed aside by the cash crop economy.

Haris said electricity had come to Balimbo a long time ago—ten years—but they were still awaiting telephones. As for politics, they had all voted to send Abdul Azis to the Regional Representatives Council in Jakarta. In the presidential vote they would do the same for the Muhammadiyah man, Amien Rais. A few minutes later we stopped in front of a nondescript green house on stilts partially obscured by a veil of shrubbery. Hamka pointed. 'That is a Jundullah house!' The tattooed commander boasted that the district was a militia stronghold; they counted six thousand volunteers. They weren't that far from central Sulawesi with its population of Torajan Christians with their fondness for pork and palm wine, I thought. They didn't have long to travel to find kafirs to battle. I asked if Balimbo had been part of Darul Islam. Kahar Muzakkar, said Haris, had once spent the night here while on the run from government troops.

'Because of him we are rich,' he added.

'But he died in 1965?' I said.

'If land was walked on by Kahar Muzakkar, it must be fertile,' said Hamka with an air of finality.

At the bus terminal they sold drinks the colour of pink dye in old bottles of mineral water. Goats rooted in rotting garbage. The call of the muezzin was never far. Here and there shrouded women hawked small tomatoes, green and red. My features and my beard seemed to send them conflicting signals. As Herry and I crossed the sun-baked lot, I heard murmuring rise like steam: 'Hindi...Saudi... Hindi...Saudi...Hindi...Saudi.'

We found seats in a minivan and waited for it to fill up for the return trip to Makassar. Two days of Bulukumba had given us, or at any rate me, enough of sharia for now. The conversation turned to the actress Dian Sastro. A couple of years earlier she had starred in a big teenage film, *Ada Apa Dengan Cinta? (What's Up With Love?)* After watching it twice I had developed a bit of a schoolboy crush on Sastro. It wasn't merely her looks, but also the stately Javanese name that unfurled like a red carpet: Diandra Paramitha Sastrowardoyo. She had recently converted from Christianity to Islam. The papers couldn't get enough of it, how she had started fasting during Ramadan, how she had found it difficult at first.

'I met her once,' said Herry. 'She has white skin and perfect teeth, and her hair is absolutely straight and black. Would you like to interview her?'

'No. That would ruin it. I'd just be tongue tied and stupid.'

A hawker appeared at the window; I declined a pink-dye drink.

I said, 'How could you want to put someone like Dian Sastro in a jilbab?'

'It depends on which side you're on.'

'I'm on no side. I'm on the side of humanity. I don't really have a problem with ugly women all covered up, but how could anyone want to do that to someone as beautiful as Dian Sastro?'

'She'll still be beautiful. Maybe she'll be more beautiful.'

'Come on. You *know* that's not true.'

'When I was in Saudi Arabia, in the supermarket I saw a woman in a black burqa. Only her eyes were showing, but I could tell that she was really beautiful.'

'That's because you have an imagination. I could show you someone's finger and you might think she's the most beautiful woman who ever lived. But that would only be your imagination.'

From Makassar we were headed to Hidayatullah headquarters near Balikpapan in Borneo. Herry said he hadn't been back in years. He told me about Hidayatullah's practice of arranging marriages for their students. Seven years earlier, when he was twenty, they had found him a bride, but he hadn't felt ready for marriage and had run away for a few months to escape. They forgave him when he returned and allowed the matter to pass.

'Do they marry you off blind?'

'No. They showed me a picture. She was very pretty.'

'Everyone there is jilbabed right?'

He nodded.

'How could you tell what she looked like if she was jilbabed?'

A note of exasperation entered his voice. 'It's not like this is the Taliban. You can still see her face.'

'But how do you know she isn't bald?'

He turned this over in his mind. 'I don't know.' He chuckled softly. 'I never thought about that.'

12

Balikpapan

Balikpapan, in east Kalimantan in Borneo, is an oil town, one of the oldest in the East; Marcus Samuel, the founder of Shell, ordered a refinery built there at the turn of the last century. But a hundred years on Balikpapan retains a flimsy quality, as though hurriedly and impermanently settled. Hidayatullah headquarters was about an hour outside the city. The macadamised road from the airport cut a ribbon of permanence through flimsy wooden shacks that looked on the verge of reclamation by the forest, and past the crocodile park where, said my magic book, for 5000 rupiah you could toss the beasts a live chicken. At last, like a mirage in the forest, rose banners fluttering on poles, and beyond them a sprawling mosque glinting in the late afternoon sun.

A squad of skullcapped and bearded youths stopped us at the gates and politely demanded identification. After we entered our names in a register they directed us to the mosque, set at a slight elevation on a grassy plateau, and distinguished by a curious egg-shaped yellow and white dome. Tucked to a side off a portico was a waiting room with a sheet of paper taped to its glass door that said, 'Committee and Discussion of Sharia.'

We settled down on a sofa and waited. After a while a man in white—skullcap, a long tunic buttoned at the collar, baggy pyjamas—perhaps about 45 years old, slipped off his sandals and entered the room followed by two identically dressed youths. Abdul Latief was built like a stevedore and radiated authority. His callus was the size of a small fist. His handshake crushed my bones and I had to make an effort not to wince. Flanked by the two smaller men, Latief sat down opposite us, across from a low table frocked in frilly pink.

'I am happy to hear that you are from India,' he said after we had explained the purpose of our visit. 'I have great regard for India. Islam came to Indonesia from India, from Gujarat. I have been to New Delhi, not long ago.' He turned to Herry. 'The buses and trains in India are very crowded,' he said. 'But India's people love nature and the rivers are very clean.'

I resisted the urge to correct him.

He looked at me again, neither friendly nor hostile, before asking the question a part of me had been dreading.

'What is your religion?'

The choices flashed through my mind. Should I tell him I'm an atheist or should I go with Hindu? Godless atheist or idol worshipper? Godless atheist. Idol worshipper. There were no good options.

'I was born a Hindu,' I said at last.

A look of pained distaste crossed Latief's face. I remembered the principal at Gontor and my heart sank. This trip would have been for nothing. He would ask us to leave. I turned to Herry and spoke in English. 'How do you say, "I'm looking for answers" in Indonesian?' Herry produced the phrase I needed.

Latief measured his words before speaking. 'Arrangements will be made for both of you to stay,' he said. Then to Herry, 'We hope you will address the congregation in the evening.'

Founded in 1976 by a self-proclaimed follower of Kahar Muzakkar—Abdul Azis ran its Makassar branch—Hidayatullah was both pesantren and commune. On paper, like Muhammadiyah, Persis and the rest of the modernist family, it preached a return to the Koran and the Sunnah. But its roots in Darul Islam and the south Sulawesi diaspora gave Hidayatullah a harsher quality. Over three decades it had spun a thick web across the archipelago. It ran 140 schools, many of them for children too poor to afford anything else. It trained mullahs and missionaries. It ran orphanages. It was setting up an Islamic business network. Hidayatullah kept men and women strictly segregated. It encouraged alumni to marry each other in mass weddings like the one Herry had escaped, and to devote their lives to spreading a pristine faith.

A reputation for violence dogged the organisation. Teachers and students had signed up for the anti-Christian jihad in Poso in central Sulawesi and Laskar Jundullah fighters on their way to battle used the sprawling campus outside Balikpapan as a pitstop. A thousand people, most of them Christians, had died in the violence. A Hidayatullah school sheltered one of the Bali bombers on the run from the police and there were persistent allegations, always denied, that militants used the secludedness of the Balikpapan campus for covert military training. *Suara Hidayatullah* (Voice of Hidayatullah), the magazine peddled out of Hamka's orphanage in Bulukumba among other places, struck the same shrill anti-American, anti-Christian and anti-Jewish tone as *Sabili*. The two publications sometimes shared reporters, among them Dani in Makassar.

With the call to evening prayer a hive-like buzz pierced the tranquillity around the egg-domed mosque. Men began streaming in from all directions. They came by foot, by bicycle, by motorbike, skull-capped and purposeful, their white clothes bleached whiter by the newly risen moon. They had about them the special urgency I now associated with Muslim gatherings, and practised an old-fashioned courtesy. I tipped my head and said 'walaikum salam' a dozen times. No women were to be seen. They had their own area hidden behind a tall wooden fence, its slats glued firmly together.

On a notice board outside the mosque someone had tacked a *Sabili* cover, 'Islam: Friend or Foe.' Though I didn't want to miss Herry's talk, this mosque made me nervous. I parked myself in the dim of the waiting room and watched the back row of worshippers rise and fall. A few minutes later two youths entered the room. One of them turned on the light and said, with a politeness I had come to expect, that Abdul Latief had sent them to keep me company. Why was I sitting alone in the dark? Latief had told them that I was 'In Process'. A person in process should not be afraid of the mosque.

My guardians ushered me inside, towards the edge of a tight knot, about two hundred men and boys on a carpet facing a wooden podium. As I sat down the words 'in process' rippled across the floor. More than one person turned around and smiled in welcome. A wilderness sound, long and piercing, filled the air. A fat, hairy spider crawled up a whitewashed wall, a reminder that we were in Borneo, that this had been rainforest less than a generation ago.

At length a nervous-looking Herry took the podium. His voice barely above a shaky whisper, he said this address had less to do with his importance than with Hidayatullah's tradition of hospitality. He recalled his years as a Hidayatullah student in Surabaya and his stint in Solo setting up the orphanage. He said he shared their values—of not living for life, but for Allah alone. Herry mentioned his friend Abdul Wahid Kadungga and a charge ran through the audience. He required no introduction: the country's first mujahidin in

Afghanistan, a son-in-law of Kahar Muzakkar, a confidante of Bashir and, they said, known to bin Laden himself. I recalled having met Kadungga once at *Sabili*—languid eyes, dense beard, quick, almost feminine, lips.

Proclaiming his friendship with Kadungga appeared to fortify Herry. His voice acquired body as he talked about visiting Abu Bakar Bashir in prison and then moved on to our trip to Ngruki. In Solo, recalled Herry, we hailed a becak to take us to the pesantren. The driver was an elderly man, more than sixty years old, and Herry hesitated before boarding a becak pedalled by someone his age. But our destination was very near, only about 5000 or 6000 rupiah away. The becak driver's name was Pak Karto. On questioning him Herry discovered that he belonged to Bashir's village. They may well also have been the same age. They were both men. So many similarities, yet one of them pedalled a becak while the other was world-famous—everyone knew Bashir, though it was true that some people looked at him with jaundiced eyes. What differentiated Abu Bakar Bashir from Pak Karto the becak driver? Why was one of them world-famous and the other a penniless nobody? The answer was faith, faith in Islam. (I had no recollection of this conversation, perhaps because I was paying more attention to PDI-P T-shirts and Preity Zinta posters.) After continuing in a similar vein for a while—more examples of the failure of the faithless and the success of the faithful—Herry introduced me, his friend from India. Heads turned again in scrutiny. 'He also doesn't like America,' said Herry by way of reassurance.

The first question came from a youth in the front row. 'Why are you travelling with a kafir?' he asked. 'What if he's an intelligence agent?'

Herry hesitated before responding. 'This is an interesting question, but why don't you ask him yourself? I can only answer that during the time I have known him he has been searching,

searching for what is good, what is true. Inshallah, in the time I have known him I have not seen any signs of his being an intelligence agent.' He looked at me for confirmation. 'Yes?' They all looked at me. I smiled weakly.

Latief asked us to dinner at the home of the vice principal of the pesantren. After the meal, delicious and eaten cross-legged on the floor, we retired for tea to a small wooden porch. Latief no longer seemed as intimidating as he had earlier that day. His posture retained its almost military bearing, but something expansive had seeped into his manner.

He expounded upon Hidayatullah's vision of a community that lived by God's laws. They had acquired 140 hectares of forest land. They were building houses for people who worked in the city but wanted to live by their faith. Half the land would be residential, the other half educational. Many employees of big state-owned companies—the telecoms company Telkom, the oil firm Pertamina—had already expressed interest in buying plots, and even a few who worked for Unocal from America. They agreed to live by the rules. All the women would wear the jilbab. The men would pray at the mosque; the women would pray at home.

I thought the women had their own mosque?

That was mainly for unmarried girls. It was better for married women to pray at home. That way they had less reason to leave the house.

I asked him to tell me a little bit about himself.

He was originally from Solo. Both his parents were devout santris and he had grown up in a religious environment. As a young man Latief had felt unhappy in Solo and began searching for a new life. He had a clear sense of what he sought—a school where the students studied for free and where the teachers were all volunteers. One day a friend told him about Hidayatullah. Latief was 24 years old when he arrived in Balikpapan in 1979. The community was new—where we sat now was wilderness—and he began work right away. In those days much of it was manual labour—draining swamps, clearing scrub, erecting the first rudimentary buildings around the mosque.

It sounded like the life of a gold prospector in the Amazon, except that here they were driven by greed for God.

'Were you ill a lot?' I asked.

He smiled indulgently. 'Never. My body was working, but my brain was at rest.' After a pause he added, 'I was the opposite of you. I can tell that you think too much.'

Latief had spent a quarter century at Hidayatullah. His wife, who had been chosen for him, was a Bugis from Sulawesi. He had only seen her photograph before they married. 'She was my girlfriend after she was my wife,' he said with a light laugh.

After a while the conversation drifted to global affairs. Latief shared his recollection of a recent trip to Israel to visit the al-Aqsa mosque in Jerusalem.

'Once I had to use the bathroom in Israel,' he said. 'Ohhh! I didn't touch anything and the water just disappeared!' He sipped his tea and continued. 'In Tel Aviv they live without cables. Everything is wireless. The tomatoes are the size of fists. And the oranges! Rows and rows of oranges with machines and no people. And the Palestinians are wearing jeans to prayer. How can we defeat the Israelis like this?'

We pondered this question. After a few moments Latief struck a more hopeful note. 'Though Israel is so small that if the Arabs all piss at the same time it will disappear.' But what about those magical Israeli toilets? I thought, though I didn't intend to push my in-process luck by bringing this up.

During the course of the day Herry had undergone one of his mini-transformations. He called Latief 'ustad', used the Arabic *Ahad* instead of the Indonesian *Minggu* for Sunday, and began punctuating his sentences with 'inshallah' and 'alhamdulillah'.

Taking advantage of a lull Herry changed the subject.

'Ustad, earlier you said Islam came to Indonesia from Gujarat. According to me, it's not true. It's from Arabia, not Gujarat. There's another theory. That in the sixth century the Prophet's companions came and looked at Java. They saw it was not yet ready for conversion. The history books say that Islam only came in the thirteenth or fourteenth century, but it's not true. The Prophet's companions had already visited Java.'

This had obviously been preying on Herry's mind all evening. Latief listened politely, but did not comment.

I asked him about television.

For years they had banned it, he said, but then they discovered that boys were sneaking out to watch football and had been forced to relent. They had recently acquired a 25-inch TV, which they had installed in the library, where they sometimes allowed the boys to watch football. It was turned off at other times, and during commercials, so that they wouldn't glimpse forbidden parts of the body.

Were they watching the Euro Cup?

They were. It was okay. The matches usually ended late at night, close to their prayer time.

How did Hidayatullah keep out Britney Spears? And Westlife?

That was not a problem. They were careful. The TV was locked in the library and a teacher guarded the remote control at all times.

Our room in the campus guest house came equipped with Japanese-sounding appliances of uncertain provenance. The Uchida airconditioner's working days were behind it, but at least the Mitochiba pedestal fan came to life with a start. When we returned from dinner, Herry, his Javanese sensibility to masuk angin apparently intact, turned the fan to face the wall.

I had trouble falling asleep. What kind of passion, I wondered, takes a man from the refinement of Solo, where even the becak drivers carried themselves with understated grace, to this wasteland? Eventually I drifted off only to be woken by a sweet nasal singing pouring out over speakers mounted outside our window. My phone display said it was past midnight. I glanced at Herry on the bed beside me, fast asleep on his side. The sounds, Koranic recordings, continued for what seemed like half an hour. They had the consistency of molasses and filled every crevice of my half-asleep mind. Then came the azaan followed by an announcement: 'Attention! Attention! All residents and students must quickly proceed towards the mosque. It is time for prayer. Ten minutes left before time for prayer.' I vaguely recalled A. A. Gym telling me about the midnight prayers of the specially devout. A few minutes later the announcement boomed again. 'Attention! Attention! Five minutes left before time for prayer.'

When I awoke it was mid-morning and Herry had already showered and changed.

'Good morning. Have you slept enough?' he asked.

'I guess so. It wasn't the best night.'

'I hope you slept enough,' he said, his voice edged with resentment. 'I've noticed that you look unfriendly when you haven't slept. Like yesterday.'

Nobody had threatened me even remotely, yet a certain disquiet had gripped me from the moment we stepped inside the gates. Perhaps it was the shadow of violence, perhaps the remoteness, perhaps the extreme segregation of the sexes, the striving to create a little Saudi Arabia in the rain forest, or the unending chatter of global Islamism—al Qaeda, America, Jerusalem. At any rate, despite my effort to hide it, my anxiety had set itself in the cast of my face. Now Herry was upset. The criticism for travelling with a kafir, their suspicions about my being a spy, would have weighed on him. He wanted me to make more of an effort to fit in.

Later that morning I suggested a walk around campus. We began at a modest office building. In an empty conference room imitation leather sofas faced each other across a row of low tables. A layer of grime darkened the white walls except for one given to a large map of the archipelago that said, somewhat confusingly, 'Proselytization Map of Pesantren Hidayatullah, SE Indonesia.' The map belonged in a military command room. A red pushpin marked Balikpapan. Gold threads connected it to five places: Denpasar in Bali, Palembang in south Sumatra, Makassar in south Sulawesi, Medan in north Sumatra and Sorong in Papua. A denser network of strings branched out from each of these places. Twelve pushpins clustered in largely Christian Papua alone.

In the heat outside a dozen volunteers with stout bamboo poles and blue plastic sheeting were erecting a makeshift booth for the first round of the presidential election in two days. One of them said to Herry that the PKS had thrown its weight behind Amien Rais. We knew this already; a text message had popped up on Herry's phone en route to the model village in Bulukumba. The word had gone out, said the man as he trussed two bamboos with twine, Hidayatullah would vote en bloc for Amien. The decision effectively ended the toss up for the committed Islamist vote and signalled the end of the road for General Wiranto. His wife's superior dress sense and the efforts of his pious children had been in vain.

We resumed our tour and a few minutes later came upon a vast artificial lake knotted with lotuses. From the other end of a path by the lake's edge approached a little girl in an Afghan-style burqa, but with a large white bib jilbab instead of a face mesh. I raised my camera and the girl flinched. As she drew closer I noticed a black plastic bag in her arms, cradled tenderly, as though it were a pet.

'What's in the bag?' asked Herry as the girl came abreast.

'Cucumbers,' she whispered, her eyes averted, and scurried away.

When we reached the end of the path Herry raised his eyes towards a sign nailed to a tree. It said, 'Special Daughter's Zone.' I tried to laugh off the error in a boy-did-we-goof way but Herry refused to smile.

At length, trudging side-by-side in silence, we arrived at a sight I had only glimpsed the previous night. Dozens of fat black tyres—I stopped counting at fifty—lay scattered across a vast clearing of baked mud and rocks. They were the largest tyres I had ever seen; a man could easily curl up and go to sleep in the middle of one. They sat there baking in the hot, hot sun—Bridgestones, Michelins—totems of an advanced industrial civilisation. Mosquito larvae wriggled and squirmed in the rain water that had collected in their rusty rims. Herry said an oil company in Balikpapan had discarded the tyres and Hidayatullah had snapped them up gratefully, to what purpose he could not say.

We ploughed on until we came upon a Hidayatullah village, rows of tin-roofed wooden shacks mounted on short stilts. Drenched with sweat, we paused in the shade of a tree beside an old oil barrel, the word 'Shell' still visible through a thin layer of rust-coloured paint. Each house boasted a handkerchief-sized garden, a rough bamboo screen and a narrow, unpainted porch with slippers and scuffed shoes resting on a plastic rack. Here and there you saw a banana tree or a palm. There were no dogs, no women and so no children and, of course, no television antennae. A shape stirred behind a screen door, but nobody came out to say hello or even simply to gawk.

Herry began to grumble. 'I think it's better if we go to the office and ask them for a car.'

'I want to walk. Some things you can only see on foot.'

'I think we should ask for a car. More comfortable that way.'

'I want to walk,' I snapped. 'Where's your work ethic? You talk of defeating America, but you can't even take half an hour of walking. Have you any idea how hard Americans work?'

Herry kept quiet. We continued to stand in the shade beside the discarded barrel. Fat dragon flies buzzed around us; somewhere a rooster crowed.

When Herry spoke again he sounded reflective. 'Look at my skin,' he said, raising his forearm. 'My colour not very good.'

'Why do you care? You're like a girl, always worrying about your skin.'

'When I'm hanging out with Amien Rais and people like that it's not good.'

'Are they white?'

'Their skin is very white. Maybe my wife will be shocked when she sees me.' He considered this. 'When I came back from Saudi Arabia I looked more light, more white.'

'How come? Isn't it sunny in Saudi Arabia?'

'I don't know. I cannot explain that. When I go, really dark. But when I come back very light, very white.'

We began the trek back to the guesthouse, stopping briefly by an empty classroom with concrete floors and chicken-coop windows and graffiti-less desks that took me back to Gontor. Their surfaces reflected the minds that sat behind them each day, wiped clean of imagination and individuality, and left only with an unquestioning obedience to faith and faith alone. If you looked hard you could spot a name (Andi, Mubarok, Dulah), an interest (Ronaldo) or an idea (*Amerika Serikat*—the United States). But there were no swear words, no covertly sketched naked girls, no expressions of love or longing, no laments to the boredom of the classroom, no rhymes or flags or faces. It was from rooms like this that they emerged from the wilderness equipped only to repeat themselves or, if opportunity arose, to battle kafirs.

Back on the sloping road near the lotus pond a man on a Vespa arced down towards us, bobbed his head, and said, 'assalam aleikum.'

'They're very polite,' I said to Herry.

'In Islam you have a rule. If one person is on a vehicle and the other is walking, then the one on the vehicle must say *salam* first.'

'What if you're both walking?'

'Then it doesn't matter who says it first.'

'What if one person is standing and the other is walking?'

'Then I think the one who is walking must say salam first.'

Herry returned to the mosque while I remained in our room with an A. S. Byatt story involving an unsuccessful writer, mutilation and murder. Herry's reading lay on the pink bedspread—a history of the conflict between Christianity, Judaism and Islam by an Indonesian veterinarian, and a Gontor graduate's account of the influence of 'Christian Orientalists' on liberal Islam. Both authors were affiliated with the International Institute of Islamic Thought and Civilization in Kuala Lumpur. The books reminded me of Herry's putative love of Gogol and Solzhenitsyn. How well did I really know him? Was Pak Karto, the faithless becak driver, fact or fiction? Early on Herry had told me his favourite movie was a toss-up between *Shadowlands* with Anthony Hopkins as C. S. Lewis and the off-beat independent film *Run Lola Run*. Later he plumped for *Ghost* with Demi Moore and Patrick Swayze. In Bandung he had flaunted the floppy hat he said he wore without fail outside Jakarta. I never saw it again. At Puspo Wardoyo's restaurant he had said he never ate sambal; he was traumatised by a childhood incident when his mother, angered by his squabbling with a sibling, rubbed fresh sambal in his eyes. Later, when I pointed out the sambal on his plate at a KFC in Makassar, he said the trauma did not extend to the factory-made kind. At least the broad contours of his story had remained consistent: the childhood in Surabaya, the six siblings, the family of slender means. I sorted and sieved its highlights. When Herry was fifteen his father lost his job at a wood company and yanked him out of the government school with the flag and the Pancasila lessons. It led to a fist-fight and then a rift that lasted until Herry's wedding. A grandmother—he described her as a fierce woman with Arab blood—had stepped in to steady his life. As a child Herry had lived with her for several years. When on leaving school he fell into bad company—he spoke of hiding in his parents' bathroom and swigging from a small bottle of gin—she enrolled him in the Hidayatullah school. With faith came the job with Hidayatullah, and finally his career in Islamic journalism beginning with the occasional piece in *Republika*.

Why then did I keep returning to Gogol and Solzhenitsyn? All journalists tailored themselves to their surroundings—my own performance was a patchwork of half-truths and evasions—but the speed and degree of Herry's metamorphosis, the clothes, the vocabulary, the stories about his childhood that made exactly the right political point, made you wonder. I knew that *Sabili* ran articles lifted from Middle Eastern websites. Now I recalled Herry telling me about a book he had written on sharia for teenagers. Though it was a slim book, about 65 pages, he claimed that it had taken him only five days. For all his quickness and curiosity, and the undeniable span of his knowledge of Islam and Islamism, this displayed a certain cut and paste quality. I could square the five-day effort, the favourite book where the American protagonist was mistaken for English, the made-up stories of SBY's mother, and the belief in Benny Moerdani's class of colonels with reading a veterinarian's account of history. But, try as I might, I couldn't square them with a serious interest in Russian literature.

A sourness had bloomed in my mouth, coating the back of my tongue and the insides of my cheeks. The squalor of the village repeated itself in the bathroom attached to our room, in the reek of wetness and ill-health. A half-spent mosquito coil and an empty bag of Rinso detergent sat atop the badly chipped flush tank cover. The broken flush handle jutted out at an improbable angle, like a snapped neck. Dirt clogged the pink shower nozzle and plump black ants in single file climbed the pink-tiled walls beside it. After brushing I rinsed my mouth with mineral water and spat in the wet drainhole that substituted for a sink. Then I began to shiver.

When he heard about my illness that evening Abdul Latief stopped by to check up on me. It was probably something in the air, he said. Many of his boys had also been sick this past week. I would feel better in the city. He arranged for a Kijang and rode into town with us. Herry was to return to Jakarta to vote early the next morning; I would remain in Balikpapan a few days.

We set out after evening prayers, stopping for directions more than once before arriving, after about an hour, at a complex of shop-houses. We had asked Latief to suggest a reasonably priced hotel near the airport, but as we stepped out of the Kijang found ourselves before a small showroom for Persian carpets. Perplexed, I followed Latief and Herry into the brightly lit showroom, past stacks of rolled-up carpets and an Indian-looking man who tipped his head in respect at the mullah, before emerging in a tiny restaurant tucked away at the back. 'I thought you might be missing Indian food,' said Latief.

Restaurant Tanduri consisted of a handful of tables along the length of a wall, each with a different coloured tablecloth and an empty glass vase. In a corner by the door to the showroom a gaggle of waitresses stood frozen before a TV turned to TPI. I was glad that Latief sat with his back to it. The waitresses were engrossed in a drama about the green underwear rapist, Kolor Hijau. A few months earlier Jakarta had been awash with tales of Kolor Hijau's exploits; no woman was safe from ravishment at his half-man, half-beast hands. The TPI version depicted Kolor Hijau as bare-chested with a pig's head and green X-ray vision. He skulked in the bushes in his green underwear eyeing three girls in mini-skirts with bare arms and plunging necklines.

We ordered chicken masala, a daal and chapatis and then Latief's voice tore me away from the on-screen action as he began to talk about his time in India. In Delhi, some years ago, he and a friend had gone to see the Jama Masjid. There the friend suddenly fell ill with a high fever. Latief knew that he needed to buy fruit to make him better, but they didn't have much money between them, only 150,000 rupiah. Though Suharto's government had already fallen, their currency still carried his likeness. Latief went to a money changer, but the Indian money changer took one look at the bills and began to shout. 'Suharto no! Suharto no!' (This was obvious embroidery. I couldn't imagine a money changer in India identifying Suharto, let alone sharing Latief's distaste for him, and besides the rupiah was not convertible.)

At any rate Latief was about to give up. There he was, alone in a strange city with a sick friend. The people did not speak his language and would not take his money. In despair he broke down on the street, fell to his knees, and began praying to Allah. 'Allah, please save my friend,' he prayed. Suddenly he felt a tap on the shoulder. He turned around and saw a stranger. The stranger smiled and offered him a bunch of fresh grapes—red, red grapes. Latief went back to his companion. He skinned the grapes and fed them to him, one by one, until he felt better again.

Our food arrived and with it my appetite; Latief had been right about the benefits of a change of scene. In the meantime Herry continued to strive to make an impression. This time he tried a different approach, opening with a jolt of blasphemy.

'Ustad, there's one thing I don't like about Mecca.'

Latief's piece of chapati, glistening with chicken masala, seemed to slow imperceptibly in mid-air. I half held my breath while Herry completed his thought. 'They sell Pepsi Cola on the streets, Pepsi everywhere. I don't like to see that in Mecca.'

I exhaled and Latief's chapati resumed its journey.

He ate with elegant restraint, somehow managing to keep three-quarters of his plate spotless while curry and daal colonised virtually all of Herry's plate and mine. As he ate he shared more stories about his travels. He had been to Pakistan too. In Lahore he had bought five kilos of mutton from a butcher and cooked it with five friends. This story appealed to me, such intimacy with a place, buying raw meat in a foreign land. I didn't know anyone who had bought five kilos of mutton in Pakistan. On the whole, despite their being expressly designed to speed up processing, I liked Latief's stories. They weren't as well crafted as A. S. Byatt's but they were simple and surprisingly sensual—red, red grapes, five kilos of mutton. Another one involved black Indian rock salt and I could taste it in the back of my throat as he told it.

Then it was time for Herry to trot out his favourite anecdote about American stupidity. A contestant on 'Who Wants to Be a Millionaire' is posed this question: What is George Walker Bush's first name? 1. Edmund 2. George 3. John or 4. Ethan. The contestant asks for fifty-fifty, the option to pick from only two choices, and Ethan and John fall away. Only two names remain. Is George Bush's first name Edmund? Or is it George? The contestant turns to the audience for help, but that only confuses him further. Finally he guesses: 'George Walker Bush's first name is Edmund.'

13

Batam

It takes a day and a night to reach Batam from Jakarta. As soon as the ship docks, the pushing and shoving, the jostling for space on the stairways, begins. The factory girls tie orange handkerchiefs on their heads and stay together. Their ears fill with sounds—the shrill whistle of a policeman, the deep honk of the ship's horn, the barks of men in uniform shouting 'ayo, ayo' as the girls wend their way through a wire mesh tunnel into a vast shed with cement floors and a corrugated ceiling.

A disembodied female voice booms through the shed: 'Remember to carry your identification papers at all times.' The orange handkerchiefs form a circle around a man with a gut and a gold ring, a kretek tilted between his lips, a megaphone in his hand. A younger man hangs in the back like a German Shepherd.

The girls sit on their bags, on which they've written their names in big white letters. They have names like Ayu and Wati, Rini and Erna. Some lug cardboard cartons bound with plastic twine. A few are shod in sandals, thick-soled or thin, but most prefer sneakers.

They wear jeans and jackets, denim or cotton, yellow or blue or brown. They are on the equator, but they are cold.

The man with the megaphone tells the girls to stand. They stand. They form a less than perfectly straight line, shuffling sideways with their too heavy bags. They clutch pieces of white paper in their hands. The man speaks again and they divide themselves into two (less than perfectly straight) rows. Then they shuffle into the sunlight of Batam, their bodies closer to each other than they need be.

In Batam the First World and the Third World collide. Per capita income in Indonesia (2004) is $1200; it's $25,000 in Singapore, a sixty-minute ferry ride away. (The *Straits Times* once ran this headline: 68-Year-Old Man, 17-Year-Old Girlfriend.) Singaporeans have opened factories here and their imprint is everywhere. Restaurants allow you to pay in Singapore dollars; Tiger beer is as ubiquitous as Bintang. Once upon a time, before such comparisons acquired the odour of a joke in poor taste, Batam was Indonesia's answer to Shanghai. Foreigners would provide the capital, Indonesians the labour. Everyone would prosper.

On their days off you see the girls at the Ramayana department store. You see them hold up two-dollar T-shirts, thin blue denim skirts, jeans with names they find appealing—American Classic, Jean Perrie, Giosport. They compare small knapsacks that say Cute Beary or Sweet Dance or Baby Cathy or Hello My Friend. They linger among the stuffed toys—a teddy bear in a bow tie, a pink bunny rabbit with a baby on her back, a koala bear clutching a pink heart.

When night falls you can find another kind of Batam girl in a club such as Pacific Discotheque and KTV. They play video games at the karaoke lounge on the second floor. They sit at the bar and practise exhaling thin jets of smoke from their nostrils. They dress in sailor suits and serve chilled beers or lukewarm Scotch. On the dance floor they form a circle, somehow managing to dance with each other even when they are dancing with men from Singapore. They dance better than men from Singapore.

You see them at Planet Ozon too. They like to wear black in the evenings, but they retain their love of denim as well. They put their hands by their mouths when they whisper in each other's ears, which is all the time. They have eyebrows plucked thin; they wear broad belts. They walk to the bathroom with short, quick steps to buy mints (Hexos or Polo) or gum (Wrigley's, in white and green, but not Juicy Fruit.) When they return they sway to the beat of a UB40 song: 'Here I Am (Come and Take Me)'.

Batam Girls may not carry handbags, but they always carry phones—Ericsson and Motorola and most of all Nokia. If they see you scribbling they'll light up your pad with these phones. As screen savers they choose pink hearts, a teddy bear, a rabbit in a basket. For some reason this can break your heart.

Batam Girls seem happiest when with each other. They laugh when one of them sticks a cigarette into a plastic straw and smokes it like a pipe. They offer to share their drinks with each other. They share their drinks with each other.

At Planet Ozon they will dance until dawn, until the floor is sticky with beer and Coke and ash. Many will end up in strange rooms, the lucky ones in a hotel like the Novotel—black Calloway golf bags in the lobby and five languages on the Do Not Disturb sign on the door. The less fortunate will awake at a place with a sign outside that says '24 Hours' or 'Special Midnite Rate', or one with no sign at all, just a bed and a window and a narrow sink beneath a naked bulb.

Batamindo Industrial Park had more of Singapore's tidy discipline about it than Indonesia's disarray. Mounted cameras overlooked the gates. Yellow diagonal stripes marked the speed breakers on the well-tarred roads. Signs warned you not to ride pillion on a motorbike without a helmet and not to dump garbage on the street. The identical factory buildings looked like they had been pulled out of a Lego set—low white rectangular blocks, each with a corrugated roof, a wire-mesh fence and a neat patch of lawn. The company names blended the familiar—Philips, Panasonic, Sanyo Precision—and the strange—Shin-Etsu Magnetics, Sinactrans Adi Sacti, Panatec Mechatronics. Together they conveyed a picture of softly thrumming efficiency.

I arrived at the park on an *ojek*, a motorcycle taxi, early one evening about three weeks after the trip to Hidayatullah. A shift had just given over and little blue and yellow Suzuki buses hummed outside the factories, quickly filling with workers ready to be ferried home. Most of them were women in blue or green half-sleeved shirts in thick cotton. The number of jilbabs appeared to have doubled since my last visit two years earlier.

Beyond the factories stretched a long row of dormitories, low pink barracks with sloping tin roofs penned behind barbed wire fencing. You saw no guards and the atmosphere was orderly rather than oppressive. I picked one at random—Block G—passed through a narrow gate and introduced myself to three girls standing in a corridor outside their room. I was an Indian writing a book about Indonesia. Would they talk to me? I had already spoken to all kinds of people. I had interviewed A. A. Gym; I had interviewed Inul.

On hearing Inul's name their faces brightened. 'We're part of FBI,' said a girl with puppy fat and thick wavy hair. FBI or Fans Berat Inul translated roughly as 'Heavy Fans of Inul.' 'All of us can drill.' Four more girls emerged from inside and attached themselves to the conversation.

They worked on the floor of a factory that made parts for elevator sensors. Singaporean and Japanese firms dominated the park but theirs, Schneider Component, was French. Fourteen of them bunked together; the youngest was eighteen, the oldest 24. They had all completed the vocational equivalent of high school and had found their jobs through the department of manpower in their hometowns—Solo, Malang, Palembang, Yogyakarta. At Schneider they worked seven hours a day, six days a week, with twelve days of vacation each year, usually during Ramadan. They would spend three years in Batam, at most four. Permanent jobs were scarce and on the factory floor you were old at 23. 'They prefer them fresh,' someone said matter-of-factly. When their contracts ran out they would return home to become wives and mothers.

Batamindo, they said, regulated its workers' lives more than most parks. There was no smoking in the dormitory. Monday through Friday visitors were allowed only between 8 a.m. and 10 p.m. and only in the living room. On weekends they could stay until 11 p.m. Curfew mirrored visiting hours. No water or lights after eleven. At midnight a supervisor did the rounds to confirm that the lights were out and the girls in.

What was it like for them to live on this island so far from home?

They liked it. Sometimes a girl would become homesick and leave the factory after a week, but for the most part they liked Batam, the independence, the friends from all over the country, the chance to send money home.

What did they miss the most?

'HOME,' came a chorus. For all of them this was the first time away from family.

All this while we had stood in the corridor, but now they invited me inside. They shared four rooms—living room, kitchen, bedroom, bathroom. In the living room a blue-rimmed Hello Kitty clock hung on the wall above a small Aiwa TV. Beside it a red and brown stuffed toy, Pluto, dangled from one long ear from a fridge with a door like a broken wing. One of the girls, a Batak I presumed, had hung a large wooden fork and spoon on a wall. The fork said 'Lake' the spoon said 'Toba'.

These girls were all un-jilbabed. I asked if there was an undercurrent of tension between the uncovered and the covered. Did they resent the jilbabs?

No, of course not, nothing like that. Everyone was friends with each other. They could understand the jilbabed girls, who were only trying to be good people. 'We don't wear the jilbab, but we're also good people,' said someone.

By now darkness had fallen and the streetlights had come on. A fat brown cockroach crawled into the living room from the corridor outside setting off a flutter of gasps and exclamations. Someone ran into the bedroom to fetch a slipper. I waited for her to flatten the cockroach, but instead she gently brushed it back outside.

Reluctant to leave just yet I invited them to join me for dinner. Could they recommend a place close by? 'Yes, yes, the food court.' They retreated to the bedroom in a blur and ten minutes later nine of us, including the ojek driver, who had waited outside the dormitory gate, piled into a minibus.

BIP Foodcourt was in Plaza Batamindo, the local minimall. We took the stairs to the fourth floor and passed a video game parlour bursting with the sounds of cars crashing and punches landing. Stalls from all over the country lined the food court and the air throbbed with the strains of dangdut. Not counting vendors, the ojek driver and I were the only men in a room of factory girls, many still in their blue or green uniforms.

After ordering at the stalls we arranged ourselves on plastic stools at adjacent tables. The girls dipped their fingers in blue plastic bowls. 'Wash your hands. Wash your hands,' they said. 'Won't you wash your hands?' I washed my hands. Five of them had ordered roast chicken; the other two, both from Palembang, had chosen something fishy and soupy that took them home. They had all asked for orange juice. 'To stay slim,' they said.

They ate fast and talked with their mouths full, their tongues white with rice and red with sambal. But they sipped their orange juice with great delicacy, through straws. You saw the same contrast of roughness and refinement in their speech, carelessly loquacious yet also painfully polite, captive to a certain etiquette. Though I had ordered far too much, they would not at first share my fried tempeh. I offered once, twice, but both times met a wall of diffidence. Only towards the end, when it became obvious that I hadn't merely been going through the motions, that I really couldn't finish, was the remaining tempeh divvied up. Afterwards a girl with a foreman's air of authority led me to the cash register to pay. The entire meal cost less than a soup and a sandwich at the New York Deli in Puri Casablanca.

On our way out of Plaza Batamindo we passed a department store.

'Souvenir, souvenir.'

'Doll, doll, doll.'

'*Kuch kuch hota hai.*'

'I love you. I love you.'

'I love your money.'

Laughter.

'Souvenir, souvenir.'

They were talking to me and yet they weren't. Their words rose like a beach ball kept collectively aloft, tossed from one girl to the next.

What did they mean by souvenir?

A souvenir could be anything—a key chain, a small statue, a stuffed toy. Only one girl, the chubby Inul fan, hinted at extravagance in a Samsung MP3 player and Bollywood DVDs. There would be no souvenirs from me. A combination of tight-fistedness and a strain of morality that I couldn't quite decipher made me balk at the thought.

'I can't buy you souvenirs,' I said. 'But we can go out again. How about a movie?' When the chatter had died down we agreed that I would return the next day.

You could think of Batam as a sort of anti-Hidayatullah. If Hidayatullah represented a shrinking from the world, or at any rate from the non-Islamic world, Batam represented its embrace. The organising principle here was global capitalism, the same get-rich-quick strain that, for all its ugliness, the brothels and massage parlours and karaoke bars, had lifted much of Asia out of poverty in two generations. Batam belonged in Southeast Asia. In the factories women vastly outnumbered men; and there were massage girls who could say 'I Love You' in ten languages.

During the boom years the island came under the watch of Habibie, then minister for research and technology, who had famously advocated that Indonesia 'leapfrog' directly from rice cultivation to aircraft manufacturing. Over three decades Batam had gone from a handful of fishing villages to half a million people living amid a hodge-podge of development. It boasted highways and suspension bridges, KFC and McDonald's, even a handful of well-watered golf courses. But, as in the rest of the country, the engine of prosperity had stalled. You saw it in the half-built office towers rotting in the rain, read it in the newspaper stories about girls making their way from the factory floor to the dance floor. Occasionally you would glimpse a Jaguar or a Mercedes glide past a mound of uncollected garbage.

I wondered what it would look like here in ten years. For how long could a poor country contain such contradictions? For how long could Batam and Hidayatullah coexist? Batam Girls and Hidayatullah Girls were the inverse of each other. Batam Girls made money; Hidayatullah Girls made babies. Batam Girls looked to the mall, Hidayatullah Girls to the mosque. Batam Girls were quick to return a smile; Hidayatullah Girls averted their eyes. In ten years would there still be Batam Girls in Batam? Or by then would this be a nation of Hidayatullah Girls with sour milk faces and the cheaply earned moral smugness of the jilbab?

When I arrived for my date the next afternoon I found the door to Block G-1 1 closed and wondered if this meant that the French factory had extended a shift without warning. I rapped on the door. No response. I knocked again. Finally I dug into a pocket, retrieved the scrap of paper on which I'd scribbled a cell phone number, and dialled. A sleepy voice answered.

A few moments later I heard footsteps, and then the door flew open. A girl stood there in shorts and a T-shirt, her eyes still puffy with sleep. 'We didn't think you were coming,' she said. They had tried calling, but had got someone else, a wrong number. They had assumed that I had been having them on about the movie—for the Javanese lying was a form of politeness—and had decided to fill the afternoon with a nap instead.

Fifteen minutes later—there was something to be said for assembly line efficiency—eight girls emerged, hair brushed, faces scrubbed, in jeans or capri pants, bright T-shirts, denim jackets, open-toed sandals or thongs. We posed for a picture outside the dorm before setting off in two taxis, an Indian and eight Indonesians from the French factory that made parts for elevator sensors. A sunny sense of adventure had settled upon our party. In the taxi the chubby Inul fan handed me a Mentos. 'Keep fresh,' she said in English.

Harry Potter and the Prisoner of Azkaban was showing at Batam's Century 21 multiplex. Armed with Cokes and large bags of popcorn we claimed a row to ourselves. The hall wasn't long in filling—with adults. The girls squealed and giggled and gasped through the movie. During the scary parts they grabbed each other's arms. They laughed loudest when Hermione slapped Harry for fumbling with her special time travel chain.

When the lights came on and we got up to leave all of a sudden another giggling fit gripped the girls. Someone pointed at a seat and the giggles deepened and travelled to their shoulders. It wasn't clear whether sloppiness or excitement were to blame, but the red chair was white with popcorn. The offender blushed. It was a girlish moment broken only when someone said, with ungirlish bluntness, 'I need to take a piss.'

It was still light when we emerged from the theatre. We hailed a taxi; with a little squeezing it would take all eight, and asked the driver to wait while we regrouped for a picture in the parking lot. One of the girls carried a simple instamatic camera in a carefully embroidered pouch. While we arranged ourselves she gingerly handed the taxi driver the camera, showed him which button to press, and ran back to join us. We unfurled our smiles. The driver squinted through the viewfinder. Then he fumbled and dropped the camera with a clatter on the asphalt parking lot. The back flew open exposing the film to the evening light. The girl's face crumbled, but she didn't utter a word of reproach and neither did anyone else. They piled into the taxi for the ride back to Batamindo. I waved until the tail lights merged with the fast-descending dusk.

From the moment she set eyes on me Ela seemed to conclude that I needed educating. 'Do you know Samuel Huntington? He talked about international politics. After the fall of the Soviet Union he saw Islam as a potential competitor and successful compared to the United States. It's a threat to the United States.'

It was night and we were in the open-air café on the top deck of a ship returning to Jakarta. I had joined Ela at a table with two factory girls with whom I had struck up an acquaintance earlier while waiting at the terminal. Ela, I gathered, had met them on board. The factory girls wore jeans and hummed along with the karaoke song on the TV. Ela was in a shapeless green robe with embroidered sleeves and a matching jilbab. She sat facing me with her back to the TV.

Nobody said anything for a few moments. Finally I spoke. 'How is it a threat?'

She pounced on this with a prizefighter's reflexes. 'Islam is rising. For example, in Indonesia you couldn't talk about politics in the mosque and now you can. It's just a small example. Although America is big, the Jews of Israel push buttons. They can control America. The Jews have a tactic to control the world. They use America.'

She spoke without pause and with pent up passion. 'If we see the whole world, the Chinese are rising. They are like the Jews. If we see terrorism, there are connections with Palestine. So it's the main cause. WTC (World Trade Center) was predicted. Osama bin Laden said the world is silent about Palestine. We're not sure who did WTC. It's possible the Jews controlled the US to do WTC to tarnish the image of Islam. It's a provocation.' She balled a tiny fist.

Were there no militant Muslims in the world?

'There are militant Muslims but they are controlled by the Jews. They are only at the bottom. Islam is not like this. There's a Hadith. Islam cannot do violence. Bomb Bali is connected to WTC. You can see the connection with Iraq. George Bush said there are chemical weapons and still there's no proof. Who is that man who committed suicide in England? I forget his name.'

The other two girls looked bored. They excused themselves and left me alone with Ela.

I asked her how the World Trade Center was connected to Bali?

'It's all to ruin Islam's image.'

Why did Jews and Americans want to ruin Islam's image?

'Because they know that Islam is a competitor to rule the world.'

And the Chinese?

'In capitalism, China is using the tactics of the Jews in economics and politics. Look at Singapore and Malaysia. Malaysia was one
with Singapore. Singapore became independent in 1975.' (She was
off by a decade, but I didn't point this out.) 'Who did this? The
Chinese. Batam is also majority Chinese. (Nowhere near.) Batam
will become independent from Indonesia. They are speaking
Hokkien. (Only a smattering.) The Chinese are like Jews. Most
people in the world are what?'

I kept quiet.

'Chinese!'

She went on.

'Who are the most genius?'

I said nothing.

'Jews!'

I had heard this from Herry too. Apparently the Koran said the
Jews were the most intelligent people in the world.

'So Jews are smarter than Muslims then?' I asked.

She was silent for a few seconds. 'No,' she said a little too firmly.
'Muslims invented medicine and mathematics but others used it.'

'But you said the Jews were geniuses?'

She thought for a moment. 'They are geniuses at stealing other
people's ideas. They are geniuses at stealing! Thirteen centuries ago
Muslims controlled the world. There was a caliphate.'

I was curious. How did she know all this?

'From books, magazines, newspapers.'

Which books?

'Books of politics of the world.'

And which magazines? I expected her to say *Sabili* or *Suara
Hidayatullah*.

'*Tempo*.' A mainstream news weekly modelled on *Time*.

She went on. Osama bin Laden ran an international network of terrorists. He had become an icon because they, the Americans, needed one. Bin Laden was a child of George W. Bush.

Why did she think that?

'Because without him they couldn't have an international scenario like this.'

Was she optimistic about the elections? It had come down to a race between SBY and Megawati, who between them had drawn about 60 percent of the first round vote. Wiranto, the Islamist-friendly general and Golkar candidate, had come a close third with 22 percent; Amien Rais, despite being backed by the PKS, had finished fourth.

She was pessimistic. She didn't trust either of the two candidates left in the fray. SBY would work with George Bush she feared. President Megawati too, if she won. Ela was a former PKS activist, but she had quit the party in disillusionment. She felt that they had compromised by not demanding the immediate implementation of sharia.

'According to me, sharia is the best for all people,' she said.

'What if someone chooses not to practise? What if someone likes beer?'

'There's no such thing in Islam. There's no such thing as you like or you don't like. In Singapore there are rules against chewing gum.' She paused. 'But I can't force people.'

'But you would like rules that force people.'

'In Islam there are rules. I believe you need rules from the top, otherwise it will take too long to convince one person at a time.'

If you took away the karaoke we might have been in a Joseph Conrad book—a ship cutting through dark waters somewhere off the coast of Sumatra. The starry night too added something theatrical to our conversation. By now the café was more than half empty. A squad of bearded men in white robes and turbans occupied the table farthest from the TV. They were from the international missionary group Tablighi Jamaat.

Ela saw me look at them. 'Their wives only show their eyes,' she said. She curled her tiny fingers into circles and brought them to her face. Apparently a handful of Tablighi Jamaat wives were also on board, safely deposited somewhere in the muggy hold. I was reminded of a headline in the *Onion*: 'Woman in Burqa Condemns Woman in Chador.' By Tablighi Jamaat standards Ela was a harlot.

I asked Ela if I could get her a cup of tea. She hesitated before saying yes. After I returned with two plastic cups—clear, sweet tea for her and a milky coffee for myself—I looked at her more closely. Angry acne scars marked her face, but it retained a certain openness. Generations of emaciation showed in her bones. The screen of the red cell phone on the table between us, gently vibrating with the thrum of the ship's engines, displayed her formal name: Nur Elisa. She had gussied it up: Nür E£isa.

'What do you think?' asked Ela for the first time.

I gathered my thoughts before responding. I said she and I could never have a real conversation, that someone like me could never really be understood by someone whose life was regulated by faith.

'I don't know how to argue with people who cannot question themselves, who can't say the words, "I was wrong." It's like playing football with someone who says, "Only I can score goals." There's no basis for conversation. To me ideas are subjective. One person may want sharia; another may think it's a disaster. It's like a painting, or a book by D. H. Lawrence. We can disagree on their merits, but what I can't understand is why you can't see that it's all subjective. I'm afraid your brain will burst and springs will pop out of your eyes if you start questioning your belief. It's what holds you together.'

She hadn't heard of D. H. Lawrence, but she liked Agatha Christie. Her voice softened; she began to talk about her life.

Ela was born in south Sulawesi. She lost her father when she was six years old and her mother subsequently remarried. 'My family was primitive,' she said. By this she meant they didn't believe in education. I admired her for having the courage to use that word.

When she was fourteen Ela ran away to Jakarta. She stayed with a relative and secretly did all the paperwork herself to move to a school there. But then her parents said they would not pay beyond middle school. She had to threaten suicide before they allowed her to continue studying. Later she won a scholarship from the Habibie Foundation in Jakarta to complete high school. After graduating she found a job working mornings in an electronics factory; at night she attended university. But then her contract at the electronics factory expired and she had no money to finish the degree. She dropped out and took a job as a reporter. That's what she was now, a reporter at some obscure publication.

When did she start dressing this way?

She had begun wearing the jilbab at fourteen when she came to Jakarta. She had become religious at about that time. 'I needed a filter for the world,' she said. 'Otherwise I might have become too free.'

I couldn't dislike her then. In her own way she was struggling to understand things. It wasn't her fault that this mish-mash about Jews and Chinese and world domination was all that her family and faith and country had to offer.

14

Jakarta

I hadn't seen Herry in almost a month, a fact that couldn't be ascribed merely to conflicting schedules. Hidayatullah had added a note of recrimination to our friendship. After we parted in Balikpapan I had spent two weeks crisscrossing Borneo by bus before visiting Batam. While I was on the road a text message from Herry had popped up on my phone. He had developed a urinary problem. A doctor had warned him to watch his diet; his wife blamed our travels. I resented the implied accusation, which seemed to illustrate an inability to deal with a setback without immediately assigning blame. At the back of my mind lurked the added worry that Herry would demand more money, or worse, abandon me altogether. My reporting was almost complete and I was looking forward to wrapping up before the election and moving back to America.

For the moment though I was back in Puri Casablanca trying to choose between two text message invitations. Din Syamsuddin had asked me to attend a 'political retreat' in Bogor outside Jakarta. Richard Oh dangled a talk by Ziauddin Sardar, a 'progressive

Muslim writer from England.' The reading, sponsored by the British Council at QB World Pondok Indah, sounded more promising than a rehash of Din's pornografi and pornoaksi speech. In the end a text message from Herry decided the matter. He was going to the QB World talk. Would I be there?

Of all QB World bookstores the one in Pondok Indah—a neighbourhood of retired generals and business tycoons and home to Inul's fabled 8 billion rupiah mansion—stood apart. Here you could recline on a plump couch and stare at a purple ceiling while washed over by the soothing strains of Dido or Andrea Bocelli. QB stood for Quality Buyers and the shelves reflected Richard's attempt to live up to the name: Stendhal's *The Red and the Black* and *The Charterhouse of Parma*, the Penguin Classics edition of *The Life and Opinions of Tristram Shandy*, the complete correspondence of Gustave Flaubert and George Sand. True to his time in Wisconsin, Richard also kept up to date with American literary fiction. This was the place to pick up a Jonathan Franzen or Jonathan Safran Foer or Jeffrey Eugenides. That most Jakartans had no time for Stendhal or Flaubert and not much more for Franzen or Foer was mere detail. Moammar Emka's *Jakarta Undercover* series kept the cash registers ringing.

A café—cappuccino on the menu, an Apple iMac in a corner—took up one side of the bookstore. The walls were given to large black and white portraits of Indonesian writers, many of them glamorous women in their thirties, the vanguard of a movement called *sastra wangi*, or 'fragrant literature'. An earlier generation of Indonesian writers had concerned themselves with landless peasants and the evils of colonialism. Foremost among them was Pramoedya—beaten, imprisoned and exiled for years on a penal island for supporting the PKI's artists and writers organisation, Lekra. The sastra wangi set, coming of age amid the market economy's dazzle, and for the most part studiously apolitical, chronicled a world of jacuzzis, wife swapping and Victoria's Secret thong underwear. Pramoedya aimed his outrage at Dutch sugar plantations, Fira Basuki at the high crime of a visible panty line.

The most glamorous of the sastra wangi set was, of course, Djenar. Her portrait captured her in a pensive mood: barefoot on a leather chair, her arms clasped around her knees, the inevitable cigarette smouldering between slender fingers. The caption said, 'Djenar Maesa Ayu was born in Jakarta on January 14, 1973. She has started writing only in the last few years, learning from authors that she has always admired: Seno Gumira Aji Darma, Budi Darma and the great poet Sutardji Calzoum Bachri. Her stories have appeared in *Kompas* and various newspapers and magazines. *They Call Me a Monkey* is her first collection of short stories.'

Traffic making it impossible to time such things with any certainty, I arrived at QB World half an hour early. As I drifted towards the back of the store, Herry suddenly emerged from behind a shelf grinning. 'Hey you,' I said, as we shook hands two-handed. 'Why are you skulking in the shadows like a ghost?' Whatever resentment lingered from Hidayatullah seemed to melt in my gladness to see him. Herry said something vaguely apologetic about having been out of touch. With the final showdown between SBY and Megawati barely a month away, work was keeping him busier than usual. We promised to catch up over lunch the next day, a Saturday, when Richard appeared. 'Why are you standing here?' he said ushering me away. 'Come on, our table's over there.' I followed Richard to where Djenar sat beneath her portrait with the obligatory pack of Dunhill Menthols and a frothy glass of Bintang.

By now a pattern had emerged to my days: when I wasn't inhabiting Herry's world you would most likely find me in Richard and Djenar's. Needless to say, they overlapped little. The Islamists possessed a general, and not entirely exaggerated, idea of sinful

Jakarta elites; every now and then a vigilante group such as the Islamic Defenders Front would attack a bar or shutter a nightclub. As for the Chivas sipping crowd, they were the same as the rich anywhere, but especially anywhere poor. The whole point of privilege was the wall it built between you and the sweaty masses.

I remained somewhat star-struck by Djenar, but over time this narrow band of emotion had widened to include a genuine fondness. In some circles they snidely referred to her simply as FFDB, short for 'Fucking fucking *dari belakang*' (Fucking fucking from behind), an immortal Djenar response to a polite cocktail party question about where she had been. To me her screw-the-world attitude defied the encroaching drabness, like lipstick in a concentration camp. In the months since the book launch at the Borobudur I felt that I had come to occupy a space in her life somewhere between a friend and a fan. My fascination with her brashness and her finely honed instinct for publicity gave our friendship a non-verbal, almost purely visual, quality, as though my voyeurism and her exhibitionism had entered a compact to feed each other.

A week earlier Djenar had asked me to a Balinese artist's exhibition at a small gallery in Kelapa Gading in east Jakarta. With its towering construction cranes and the bright lights of Dunkin' Donuts, ABN Amro Bank and Ace Hardware, the neighbourhood exuded a brassy, arriviste quality. The gallery was in a strip mall, off a drag soupy with exhaust, tucked between a café and a beautician. Kijangs, Isuzu minivans and the odd BMW crowded outside the glass doors. Inside a girl in a sleeveless red dress welcomed you with a plastic cup of Bintang. Beside her guests lined up for bowls of soup rich with chopped liver and boiled eggs. The entertainment media, the sweatered horde of Djenar's birthday party, had turned out in strength. Word had spread that the famous Balinese artist would use the shocking young writer's body as a canvas.

The famous artist had begun his career as a humble realist before a European scholarship quickly terminated that path. No more Ubud rice paddies or Legong dancers in green and gold for him. His recent work, spotlit on the walls, consisted of mauve or electric blue or canary yellow canvases crowded with indecipherable squiggles. A few people in the audience, more MBA than art academy, sipped their Bintangs and stared uncomfortably at the paintings, but most gathered in the middle of the room and killed the wait with chit-chat.

At last the lights dimmed, the chatter hushed, and the audience congealed along the length of a space near the staircase. As the opening strains of a Nora Jones song filled the gallery, Djenar wafted down the stairs in a long brown dress. Near the foot she paused and crooked a finger. The famous Balinese artist, a portly man with the bearing of an insurance salesman, hurried over and took her in his arms. Cheek to cheek, they danced for a few slow minutes to Nora Jones. Then the artist, with less finesse than he might have hoped, began to tug at the shoulder straps of Djenar's dress.

As the dress came off the room filled with scattered applause and the whirring and clicking of cameras. Underneath Djenar wore a cream-coloured body stocking, not quite matching her skin tone, but close enough. The artist dabbed yellow paint from a small bowl on Djenar's face. She kicked off her shoes and lay down on her back on the wooden floor, one knee propped up. The artist squatted beside her and, with quick jerky movements, dabbed more yellow on her belly and breasts. She rolled over and he applied some red. After five or ten minutes of this Djenar rose from the floor. A lock of jet black hair fell across her forehead contrasting with the yellow on her cheeks. They danced in place some more, this time at arm's length, and then they kissed. It was a chaste kiss, quick and close-mouthed, but it ran through the audience like a tremor. 'Ooh kissing,' exclaimed the woman in a pin-striped shirt next to me raising her camera phone.

Djenar returned upstairs to change. A few minutes later my phone rang. It was Djenar.

'Where are you?' I asked.

'Here. In the dressing room.'

'Okay, I'm downstairs.'

'I need your help. I left my shoes downstairs.'

'Why can't you come and get them?'

'I can't. I can't come down without my shoes.'

At first this struck me as absurd, but when I thought about it, it made sense. You could have no qualms about disrobing before a hundred people and half the city's tabloid press, but the idea of being glimpsed shoeless might fill you with dread. Such were the complexities of celebrity. I asked Djenar to describe her shoes. Then, with an Indian fastidiousness about such matters, I found a gallery employee to carry them upstairs.

I still had pictures from that evening on my camera, though most were smudged and blurry. Djenar and I scrolled through them while we waited for the progressive Muslim writer from England. After a while I felt a pair of eyes on us and looked up to see Herry hovering near the edge of the café looking somewhat lost. I got up and brought him to our table.

'Djenar, this is my friend Herry Nurdi. Herry, this is Djenar Maesa Ayu.'

They didn't shake hands. 'I have met you before,' said Herry.

Djenar's eyes glazed with a half-hearted effort to place him.

'I read the article about you in *Foreign Policy*,' he added. I had recently reviewed *Don't Fool Around (With Your Genitals)*.

Djenar said she had read it too. For a few minutes we argued halfheartedly about whether you could find the article on the Internet. Then Richard returned from playing host in another part of the room. 'What will you have?' he asked Djenar and me.

The café was nearly full by now. I greeted the correspondent from the *Guardian* and a former Nieman fellow at Harvard who had started a magazine in Indonesian modelled on the *New Yorker*. (It had quickly folded.) It occurred to me that this was the first time that Herry and I were in a place where I knew more people than he did. Herry had remained standing all this while. He seemed fidgety and uncomfortable. His gaze turned to a small man sitting across from us with the only jilbabed woman in the room. 'That's my friend from Mizan Press,' he said. Mizan, an Islamic publisher based in Bandung, was bringing out Herry's guide to sharia for teenagers. He hurried off to join his friend.

Zia Sardar, the progressive Muslim writer from England, wore a ratty ponytail and carried himself with a certain swagger. He read with a surprisingly strong Punjabi accent from his book, *Desperately Seeking Paradise: Journeys of a Skeptical Muslim*. A passage about an encounter with a fundamentalist in Pakistan struck a chord with the audience. The fundamentalist asks Sardar why he shaves even though he is a Muslim. Doesn't he know that the Prophet never shaved? Sardar responds by asking the fundamentalist why he doesn't ride a camel. They didn't have cars or motorcycles either in the Prophet's time. The punch line: 'The Prophet would have shaved if he had razor blades.' The café filled with laughter.

Sardar had little patience with a literal reading of the Koran. When someone asked him about 'looking for specific answers to life's questions', he responded that there were no specific answers worth looking for, that confusion was healthy. It was good to be sceptical of anyone who claimed to know it all. He mocked the Iranians, the Sudanese and the Saudis and their experiments with Islamic government.

Herry was standing by himself again, his arms crossed, directly opposite the low platform at the other end of the café from Sardar. At last he raised his hand.

'First, are you happy being sceptic?' His tone said, I know you can't be happy. 'Second, I've read your book *Why We Hate America*. Can you see America going down?'

Herry's accent eluded Sardar. 'Could you repeat the second part?' he asked.

Herry repeated, 'Can you see America going down?'

Sardar still couldn't understand him. The café had fallen silent; people shifted in their seats.

Herry began a third time. 'Can you—' I interrupted and completed the question.

'In answer to your first question,' said Sardar. 'Do I *look* unhappy?' More laughter. Then he talked about the rise of China and India and the changing world. If you looked at the World Trade Organization, for example, you saw that India and China were resisting, refusing to allow America to set the terms of the debate. There was no question, America was in decline.

After the talk I introduced myself to Sardar. Within a few minutes a knot grew around him and Herry attached himself to its edge. 'This is my friend Herry Nurdi,' I said. 'He works for a magazine that believes Osama bin Laden is the solution to the world's problems.'

Herry bristled.

I said, 'Sorry, I'm not trying to embarrass you. It's the truth.'

'I'm not embarrassed,' he said hotly.

In fact I was trying to embarrass him. I wanted him held account-able for his views, to squirm a little. The hypocrisy of this didn't strike me until later. I didn't tom-tom my atheism in Hidayatullah, but in QB World I expected Herry to wear his admiration for bin Laden and Basayev on his sleeve. After a few minutes Richard came up and handed Sardar a copy of his most recent novel. The bookstore was closing, he said, but we could continue our conversation at a wine bar in a mall called Citos that stayed open late.

As we pulled out of the parking lot I saw Herry framed in the doorway talking to his friends from Mizan press. I felt a stab of guilt for not having asked him to join us, but it wasn't my party, and as far as the others were concerned he was a bearded guy who worked for a hick magazine. At some level the distance between him and Richard was too vast to be bridged. It should not have come as a surprise to me, but in a way it did. As an outsider I could see class distinctions but I couldn't feel them. I was equally foreign watching a movie with factory girls or sipping Merlot at a south Jakarta wine bar. The normal rules didn't apply. Class only mattered when you felt it, and for the most part you only ever really felt it at home.

Though I had been glad to see Herry at QB World by now our early bonhomie seemed irretrievably lost. I sensed that there would be no more callow jousting about Dian Sastro or jokes about flying while brown and bearded. My initial rush of gratitude towards him had faded, as such things do. My effort to defer judgment, I had to admit, had failed. The more I saw of the Islamist movement the more its totalitarian cast became obvious. As it spread it would grind what remained of a once proud culture to a hollow imitation Arabness. If by democracy you meant not merely elections but also minority rights, women's rights, and the freedom of speech, conscience and inquiry taken for granted in the West, then Indonesia's prospects were not bright. You couldn't meet Islamists halfway because ultimately for them there was no such thing as halfway to God. It was as Abdul Azis had said: The goal remained fixed. They all believed that the ideal society was Medina's in the time of the Prophet.

The economic implications were almost as grim. Indonesia had prospered partly from the blind luck of resources—tin and gold and silver, timber and oil and natural gas. Its volcanic earth was fertile and water abundant. But these would not have added up to much without New Order pragmatism, without policies that encouraged female education and workforce participation, and family planning. For all its corruption, the New Order had allowed the entrepreneurial ethnic Chinese (mostly Buddhist or Christian) to flourish, and had wooed the foreign investors the Old Order had shunned. Except for natural resource extraction, which thrived under despotism, the Islamist movement threatened to reverse thirty years of effort. Unlike Hanoi or Bangkok, Jakarta could now be paralysed by events in the Middle East. The stark division of the world into Muslim and Non-Muslim encouraged talented minorities to build their futures elsewhere. Even if they were exaggerated, the spate of negative images—burnt churches, ransacked bars—reinforced the perception of Indonesia as a fundamentally unstable place. There was little danger of Indonesia sliding backwards into African- or Bangladesh-style poverty. It was too resource rich and not badly enough governed for that. But even without seizing formal power Islamists could ensure—as they had in Egypt and Pakistan—that the country, starved of innovation and investment, stagnated while its neighbours forged ahead.

My own duplicity towards Herry added to the strain. Paradoxically, the American journalist Janet Malcolm's famous assertion, still talked about when I was in journalism school in New York in the mid-nineties—that 'every journalist who is not too stupid or too full of himself to notice what is going on knows that what he does is morally indefensible'—had only made it easier for me to become what she would have called 'a kind of confidence man'. We all did it; it was what we did. Right from the start I had dealt in convenient half truths. I had (truthfully enough) pooh-poohed Naipaul's Indonesia work while neglecting to mention how much I admired him. I had (truthfully enough) advertised the revulsion I felt for the American backed anti-communist massacres of 1965–66; I had omitted, for the most part, my admiration of

American enterprise. I had disguised the depth of my disquiet about Hidayatullah and instead played up the respect I felt for the considerate and self-assured Abdul Latief. Most of all I had cloaked my atheism in greys. It was only in disapproval of the jilbab and approval of SBY, despite a latent fondness for Megawati, that I had come completely clean.

And yet I had no trouble justifying any of this to myself: the ends mattered so much more than the means. Indonesia was Southeast Asia's pivotal country and no single issue mattered more to its future than the movement Herry had helped me unlock. It wasn't remorse that lay at the heart of my discomfort—my only shame was in downplaying my Godlessness—but the fact that week by week the deception had grown heavier. The contradiction between liking the Herry who longed to once more strum the guitar and loathing the one who dug dirt on SBY's mother could not be settled. The latter made me broadcast his love of bin Laden where it was least welcome; the former made me feel guilty for not asking him to join us at Citos.

The next day I awoke late and lightly hungover. Just when I had decided that Herry had forgotten about our lunch the concierge called to say I had a guest. A moment later the phone rang again.

'I'm here with my family,' said Herry. 'Shall I bring them up also?'

'As long as they promise not to mind the mess.'

A few minutes later they were standing in my living room. Herry's wife, Tias, was plain as a post. Her ankle-length smock brushed her white-socked feet and a severe white jilbab policed her hair. A slim pair of wire rim glasses constituted her only concession to style. She carried an infant with a thick mop of hair; this was Rahma Jekar Drupadi. Irhamni Jekar Andjani, the three year old, clutched her free hand.

Small children were never terribly interesting, but here they made me feel especially awkward, self-conscious about my broken Indonesian. An adult would make allowances, was often pleased to see a foreigner try, but children were unforgiving.

'Is this the PowerPuff Girl?' I asked and smiled. My voice sounded fake and smarmy even to me. The child took a small step backward.

'This is the PowerPuff T-shirt,' said Herry.

She wore a pink T-shirt with her nickname, Eros, in widely spaced letters beneath the cartoon figure of a girl with blonde pigtails. I remembered Herry calling home from Gontor while we sat under the picture of the Nabawi mosque in his room, and Eros asking him for the T-shirt. That was the first I had heard of the PowerPuff girls on TV. Eros had wanted a black T-shirt but, in his parental wisdom, Herry had chosen bubblegum pink instead. (The pig-tailed blonde was Bubbles, the sweet talker, not Blossom, the natural leader, or Buttercup, the fierce fighter.)

'Say hello to uncle,' said Herry. If anything his voice sounded even stranger than mine. It had the thick sweetness of bad marmalade. Eros stepped forward, kissed my right hand, and then rested her cheek on it in the Muslim way. Despite myself I felt my heartstrings tugged.

Downstairs we piled into Herry's father-in-law's car—they lived with Tias's parents—an ancient fire-engine red Volkswagen the size of a small bus. I sat in front with Herry. In the back sat Tias, the two daughters and a maid, a teenager fresh from the village who had waited downstairs.

Tias was seven years older than Herry. As we pulled out of the parking lot I asked them how they had met. Herry said they had worked together at an Islamic family magazine called *Sakinah* before it went bust and he moved to *Sabili*. 'We were enemies at the magazine,' said Herry with a laugh. 'Her opinions would make me angry.'

Herry had married up, I thought. Tias had a degree in mathematics and apparently, though she said little, a thicker smattering of English than his. Her father owned a car. She had given up journalism and now taught at a private Islamic school. As we crawled through traffic I rotated in my seat and tried, without luck, to spark a conversation.

Herry turned to Eros and said gaily, 'This is the uncle who made your father sick.'

'That's not possible,' I said. 'But I guess you'll have to drink carrot juice while the rest of us gorge on ribs.'

Daeng Tata, the place Herry had picked for lunch, stood approximately halfway between his office and my apartment. The tabletops were rough aluminium sheeting and the noise and fumes of Jakarta traffic poured through the restaurant's open sides. You warded off the flies with a battery of corked candle wicks floating in small glasses of water. But they served the most delicious ribs, dripping with grease and coated in a nutty sauce. That, and the modest prices, brought us back again and again.

As often as not we would eat too much. Then Herry would lean back in his chair, pat his belly, and say with a self-admonishing laugh, 'Mohammed says every Muslim must stop eating before he's full, but I can't.'

We parked in front of the restaurant and Herry and I went ahead with Eros to claim a table; the maid stayed in the car with Tias while she fed the baby. Herry asked if Sardar and I had talked about him at the wine bar. We hadn't. He said he knew that Djenar had joined us later at night; someone had told him, one of his sources.

'I think Djenar is deeply unhappy,' said Herry.

'Why do you say that?'

'She is deeply unhappy. I can tell.'

I didn't respond.

'She said bye to me,' said Herry. 'My friend from Mizan Press was jealous. He said, "You know Djenar Maesa Ayu." He was very jealous.'

Tias and the maid joined us and we ordered the famous ribs. It seemed a peculiar way for Herry to be watching his diet, but I didn't say anything.

'You know, last night I realised that I'll miss Indonesia a lot,' I said. You spend four years in a place and get to know people and then it becomes hard to leave.'

'You'll miss *Djenar*,' said Herry. His voice dripped with innuendo.

I could see how it must have looked to him, the beers on the table, Djenar's head lolling on my shoulder as we went over the blurry pictures. A few months earlier I might have explained that the friendship was neither carnal nor romantic, but now I found the idea too exhausting. He wouldn't understand.

'Yes, I'll miss her,' I said simply and truthfully.

I asked him what he thought of Sardar's response to his question about being happy as a sceptic. Happiness was a big preoccupation with Herry, right up there with the inevitable triumph of Islam, the evil designs of Christianity and the decline and fall of America. He had even worked out a mathematical formula of sorts. Watching television for an hour reduced your happiness by 4 percent. Playing a sport increased it by 8 percent. Eating fruit, lots of it, could boost your happiness by as much as 25 percent.

'Zia Sardar is not happy,' said Herry flatly.

'He looks perfectly happy to me. He writes books. He travels the world. What more could a man ask for?'

'He does not look happy like Abdul Latief. Look at Abdul Latief—no money, but still happy.'

15

Jakarta

Through much of our travels I had been struck by the correlation between devoutness and support for the Prosperous Justice Party (PKS). At Gontor they had talked of lining up to vote for the party en masse, as they had at Hidayatullah. Party stickers and posters flooded south Sulawesi and surfaced in the dormitories of Ngruki. In its supporters, Herry among them, ran the conviction that the PKS was the country's only authentic political representative of Islam. In six short years it had emerged as the most disciplined political force in the country. In 1999 it attracted less than 1.5 percent of the vote and won a meager seven seats in parliament. Five years later its vote share had soared to nearly 7.5 percent; with 45 seats it was the seventh largest party in the 550 member parliament.

If you plotted the politics of religion on a continuum, then at one end stood PDI-P and SBY's Democratic Party, formally secular and supported by people of all faiths. Then came Golkar, again officially secular, but with its nationalist wing marginalised by

Muslim-first politicians who supported such measures as a law to place mullahs in Christian schools. Then you had Abdurrahman Wahid's PKB and Amien Rais's PAN, nominally secular parties, albeit with roots in Nahdlatul Ulama and Muhammadiyah respectively. The overtly Islamic included Vice-President Hamzah Haz's New Order relic, the United Development Party, and a clutch of personality cults such as the Crescent Star Party.

The PKS stood apart from the herd. Many of its top leaders had studied Islam in the Middle East and the rank and file swelled with engineers and doctors. (The first president had a degree in food technology from Texas.) Party cadres paid dues. They shunned cigarettes and alcohol. The women, immaculately jilbabed needless to say, stood behind the men at meetings. After a fire or a flood or a riot PKS cadres were among the first to arrive, setting up free clinics or distributing food and clothes. In a country where the idea of public service had been reduced to a Volvo limousine and shopping junkets in Singapore, many regarded PKS legislators as incorruptible. This reputation had ballooned the party's following. Less well known was its international pedigree. The PKS drew its ideology and organisational structure from the Muslim Brotherhood, whose thought had also spawned, among others, Hamas, Sudan's National Islamic Front and, most famously, al Qaeda. The Brotherhood worldview is captured in its slogan: 'Allah is our objective. The Prophet is our leader. Koran is our law. Jihad is our way. Dying in the way of Allah is our highest hope.'

Like all Islamists, Hassan al-Banna, the 22-year-old school teacher who founded the Brotherhood in Egypt in 1928, believed that Islam was not merely a religion but a way of life. (Herry spoke mistily of al-Banna, a lonely preacher trudging from café to café in Cairo with his message.) But it was his compatriot, the literary critic and writer Sayyid Qutb, whose experiences and thoughts most shaped the movement. In 1948 Qutb, then a middle-aged official in the ministry of education, was sent to America for a master's degree in education. In Greeley, Colorado there were no bars, and hemlines fell well below the knee. Nonetheless Qutb was revolted. He later wrote: 'The American girl is well acquainted with her body's seductive capacity. She knows it lies in the face, and in expressive eyes, and thirsty lips. She knows seductiveness lies in the round breasts, the full buttocks, and in the shapely thighs, sleek legs—and she shows all this and does not hide it.' In the manicured lawns of Greeley, Qutb saw neither order nor civic sense, only the insatiable greed of a country as soulless as it was depraved. As for Jews, Qutb regarded them as a craven and slavish people incapable of grasping the idea of a dignified life. He blamed them for materialism (Marx), for sexual permissiveness (Freud), and for being the sworn enemies of Muslims. 'History has recorded the wicked opposition of the Jews to Islam right from its first day in Medina.'

After returning home in 1950 Qutb quickly became the Brotherhood's principal ideologue; police had assassinated al-Banna the previous year. (In Herry's version the CIA was to blame, a crime paradoxically compounded by the meager attention he claimed the death received in American newspapers.) For Qutb, as for all Islamists, God's law, sharia, stood above man's law. The answer to all of society's problems lay in Islam. It belonged not merely in the mosque, but in the classroom and the boardroom, in banks, in courts, in movie theatres. Qutb reinterpreted the Arabic word *jahiliyya*, traditionally used to describe the ignorance of pre-Islamic Arabs, to attack Nasserite Egypt. His most influential book *Milestones*, sometimes called *Signposts on the Road*, targets a vanguard of men imbued with the spirit of the Prophet and his seventh century companions and committed to the establishment of an Islamic state. Jihad for this cause is noble and, since their actions outlive them, those who die in its pursuit are immortal.

Under Qutb, the Brotherhood's conflict with the Egyptian

government intensified. Police regularly rounded up supporters in mass arrests and in 1966, accused of plotting to assassinate Nasser, Qutb was hanged. (Herry's eyes misted when he spoke of Qutb's suffering, the four-metre-by-six-metre cell he shared with forty men, recordings of the strongman's speeches blaring in their ears sixteen hours a day.) But the assault on the Brotherhood ended up giving it an unintended boost. Many of Qutb's followers, including his younger brother, Muhammad Qutb, fled to Saudi Arabia where they were welcomed by a monarchy flush with petrodollars and eager to add intellectual muscle to its own austere vision of Islamic purity. Muslim Brothers founded the University of Medina and swelled the faculties of other Saudi universities. Muhammad Qutb's most famous student was bin Laden, another of whose teachers was Abdullah Azzam, a Jordanian Brother later widely revered as the Peshawar-based pointman of the anti-Soviet jihad in Afghanistan in the 1980s. Saudi money also secured an international platform for Sayyid Qutb's ideas. Students from South and Southeast Asia, many on scholarship, poured into its universities. At the same time, as part of a broader effort to promote Wahhabism, Saudis and other like-minded Arabs bankrolled mosques, madrassas and universities throughout the world. By one estimate between 1975 and 2002 the Saudis alone spent $70 billion on such 'overseas aid'. About fifteen hundred mosques worldwide owed their existence to Saudi generosity.

Qutb rejected democracy, but the Brotherhood's position had since evolved. The most prominent contemporary Brother, the Egyptian-born mullah Yusuf al-Qaradawi, encouraged the use of democratic means to pursue Islamist ends. Al-Qaradawi, barred from America for his espousal of violence, hosted a popular talk show on the Qatar-based television network Al Jazeera and ran the heavily trafficked website www.Islamonline.net. By an Islamist yardstick he was deemed a moderate, which is to say he backed suicide bombings against civilians in Israel and attacks on Americans in Iraq, but condemned 9/11. He recommended female genital mutilation, but didn't demand it, and he wasn't quite certain if the prescribed punishment for a homosexual was burning him alive or tossing him off a tall building.

The expense of cable television and the scarcity of Arabic speakers made Al Jazeera's Indonesian footprint faint, but al-Qaradawi's writings circulated widely in translation. He had visited Jakarta several times over the last twenty years, and was quoted in the party's founding manifesto. (Herry said he had met al-Qaradawi at a dinner in his honour.)

The top rung of the PKS was steeped in Brotherhood ideology. Hidayat Nur Wahid, who had recently resigned from the party chairmanship to take over as the leader of Indonesia's highest legislative body, the People's Consultative Assembly, held a bachelor's and master's degree and a doctorate from the University of Medina. Party Secretary General Anis Matta graduated from another Brotherhood-linked institution, the Jakarta branch of Riyadh's Al-Imam Muhammad bin Saud University, established with Mohammad Natsir's assistance. The classes were in Arabic and between 80 and 90 percent of the faculty imported from the Middle East. Herry looked upon Matta, only 35 years old but already secretary general and a member of parliament, with awe. For a PKS leader he also possessed a certain bad boy flair. A former classmate of his at a pesantren in south Sulawesi once told me that the young Matta would cut classes. ('The most clever is always the naughtiest.') They whispered about how he sometimes wore jeans.

I first encountered the party's ability to mobilise a crowd at the start of the war in Iraq, in March 2003, when several thousand people answered a call for a 'million person march' from Jakarta's Hotel Indonesia circle to the American embassy nearby. That morning a squad of volunteers with blown-up pictures of wounded children around their necks carried bright orange pillowcases in which passersby dropped cash. Others wielded hand drawn placards, many in English: 'VIVA EURO', 'BUSH LIKE MONSTER', 'BUSH IS RETARDED', 'BUSH BLAIR=ARE INSANE', 'LIKE FATHER LIKE SON, BOTH RACIST' and my favourite, 'BUSH, BLAIR AND AZNAR ARE MORE CANNIBAL THAN SUMANTO', a reference to a Javanese man convicted of digging up and eating parts of an 81-year-old woman's corpse to boost his spiritual power. Stalls had sprung up outside the barricaded and heavily guarded embassy in anticipation and the air filled with the smells of meatball soup and chicken satay. As the placard wavers approached, a woman selling Teh Botol, a sweet bottled tea, hastily draped her head in a hand towel; another made do with a scrap of cloth.

Not all the protestors were men. I tagged a troop of female cadres marching in formation—seven wide, twenty deep—led by a floppy-hatted man with a megaphone.

'America, America,' bellowed the man.

'Terrorist! Terrorist!' responded the women.

They were middle class and of course immaculately jilbabed, though only a handful took the statement a step further by adding a handkerchief across nose and mouth. Several clutched black and white flags with the party's symbol, two crescent moons flanking a stalk of rice. THE NEW FACE OF ISLAM, said a shiny green badge on a marcher's black knapsack. Another carried an infant.

'America, America,' yelled the man with the megaphone.

'Terrorist! Terrorist!' The woman shook the baby's chubby arm.

An emaciated man puffing on a filterless kretek and carrying a white case with a picture of a cartoon woodpecker tried to interest them in some Woody Super Ice Cream.

'Ice cream Muslim, Ice cream Muslim,' he shouted walking down the line.

'Terrorist! Terrorist!' they went on untempted.

A year later, shortly before I met Herry, I spent an evening at party headquarters in Mampang Prapatan, a neighbourhood of small shops and broken sidewalks. The street, usually thick with traffic, was deserted that day, but the PKS office, wedged beside a bakery that sold ball shaped candies and spongecakes in a chemical shade of green, thrummed with life. I had showed up without an appointment just as results of parliamentary elections earlier in the day had begun trickling in. It took twenty minutes of badgering and cajoling in a cramped waiting room before a young party activist instructed me to wear a badge that said *wartawan* (journalist) in large letters and led me up a narrow flight of stairs to a conference room of sorts.

The first thing that struck me about Anis Matta was his boyishness. He was chipmunk-cheeked and dressed like an undergraduate, in a black corduroy jacket over a black T-shirt printed with the word 'Yogyakarta'. The dog-eared paperback novel—*Belantara Ibu Kota* (*Capital Jungle*)—in his left hand accentuated the effect. Had you passed him in the street you would not have guessed that he wielded power or, for that matter, that he was the father of seven. Though here the ardent gatekeeper and a silver Nokia Communicator on the conference table beside him made his consequence obvious.

Matta seemed to warm immediately to my idea. He pulled up a chair at the head of the table. I sat to his left facing the room: a harsh white fluorescent bulb on the ceiling, orange plastic flowers on the walls, a frilly blue cloth on the TV tuned to the election results. About a dozen party faithful, all men, crowded around it, their expressions taut with excitement. Several wore black jackets with the party logo. Every few minutes the air filled with shouts of 'Allahu Akbar.' Something about the smell, a blend of stale potato chips and freshly skinned oranges, seemed odd but it took me a few minutes to figure it out. The absent scent of kretek made it feel like a new country.

To break the ice we began by talking about books, and the breadth of Matta's reading immediately became evident. He flitted from Arundhati Roy and Jhumpa Lahiri to Pramoedya's novels and the poetry of Muhammad Iqbal and Rabindranath Tagore. When I remarked on how rare it was to encounter a well-read politician he revealed that he had written several non-fiction books himself. One of them, titled *Mencari Pahlawan Indonesia* (*Looking for an Indonesian Hero*), had sold fifty thousand copies in just three weeks. (About five times what Djenar could expect in a year.) He was well-travelled too. Indonesian students abroad often invited him to speak on campus; in America alone he had seen San Francisco, Los Angeles, Chicago and New York.

Someone placed two cups of milky coffee before us and Matta outlined his Dick Whittingtonesque tale. He was born the fifth of seven children in a village in south Sulawesi. His parents owned a small clothes and general supplies store. ('Like an Indian shop.') They were not particularly religious; their mosque attendance was patchy and neither his sisters nor his mother were jilbabed at the time though, of course, that had since changed. In 1973, when Matta was five, the family moved to Ambon, where he lived for four years before returning to south Sulawesi. Two years later he applied to a pesantren run by a Gontor alumnus and prominent Muhammadiyah man in the region. As a modernist institution it offered secular subjects in addition to Islam. Matta had to take an entrance test and his parents had to agree to pay the fees.

The pesantren opened up prospects for bright boys and even as an eleven-year-old Matta knew that if he worked hard he might go as far as Cairo's Al-Azhar. He stood first in his class every year. He developed a fondness for history and psychology. As a teenager he began supplementing the school curriculum with his own reading, mostly politics and sociology, and began to see himself as an autodidact. On graduating Matta asked the head of the pesantren, who had become a mentor, for advice. Nobody in his family had attended university and he questioned its utility. ('I felt that you don't need to go to university to be an intellectual.') But his mentor had other plans. After a month's deliberation and prayer he summoned Matta. 'You must go to Jakarta,' he said. Matta had been awarded a scholarship to the Saudi University.

This was in 1986. In those days there were no big malls in Jakarta, not even a McDonald's, but before Matta left Sulawesi his mentor took him aside. 'Jakarta is like hell,' he said. 'Your university is like a heaven in the middle of this hell. You must stay there.'

In Jakarta he continued to excel academically. He earned a bachelor's degree in sharia in 1992. He enrolled in a master's degree in development studies at the University of Indonesia but dropped out after a while. He was also offered a scholarship to Saudi Arabia for a master's but declined. By then he had decided that if he were to study more it would only be in America. In the meantime he lectured on the Islamic economy at the University of Indonesia. The people behind the scholarship then offered to send him to Los Angeles, but by then it was 1998 and the situation in the country had changed. He decided to remain in Jakarta.

And now, I thought, eighteen years after arriving a penniless pesantren graduate, Matta was on the verge of representing the city he was taught to see as hell in parliament.

While sharing his story Matta, one eye on the TV, had kept up a playful banter with the other men in the room. 'That's not fair,' he had protested when a Megawati speechwriter appeared on TV as an independent analyst. 'He's a PDI-P candidate.' When a text message arrived demanding the immediate implementation of sharia and the unconditional release of Bashir (the PKS was among his most steadfast supporters) Matta read it aloud to hoots of approbation. I asked him to explain what differentiated the PKS from other parties.

Matta asked someone to fetch some paper. Then he began drawing a series of diagrams with a ballpoint pen. He drew smooth curved lines and shaded beneath them neatly as he spoke, crisply and without hesitation. He said Islam shared characteristics with both capitalism and communism, but was not identical to either because it was a complete system in itself. The clash between communism and capitalism was trivial; the Cold War had simply been a contest between imperialist countries fighting for resources such as oil. As a pure ideology Islam offered an alternative to both systems. The purity came not only from its holiness, but also from its inherent rationality.

A flash of scepticism must have crossed my face. 'This is subjective, I know,' he said.

I asked him which model, Saudi or Iranian, was the best example of this alternative?

'Neither. It has not yet been applied correctly anywhere.'

Unlike Sukarno and Natsir, he continued, the PKS didn't distinguish between nationalism and Islam in its message; they didn't use the words as antonyms. The main trouble with Indonesia was that people did not understand their faith. For example, the Council of Ulama had issued a fatwa against Megawati in the last election and it had barely made a difference. Islam in Indonesia was full of distortions, so change had to come from the top. The rich tended to be more religious than the poor, which was why the PKS was strongest in the cities and on college campuses. 'So we have to think of ways to make the poor rich,' he said with a laugh.

Someone brought us two hot bowls of soupy noodles with fishballs. I asked him about sharia.

'Indonesia is not ready,' he said. 'All laws should be applied only after society is ready to accept them. I can't say "cut off a thief's hand" if people are poor and there is no food. We have to remove obstacles in society before implementing it. If you have laws without conditioning the people first, it will fail.'

As the whoops of 'Allahu Akbar' increased in volume and frequency, Matta drew more diagrams in his smooth, unhurried hand while he ranged over undecided swing voters, Marhaenism and Sukarno's skill as a communicator, the role of money in politics, Clifford Geertz's typology of Indonesian Islam, Abdurrahman Wahid's remarkable mind and unstable personality, A. A. Gym's unfortunate tendency to mix religion with show business. In between he answered congratulatory phone calls, wisecracked more with the other men in the room, asked someone to change the channel when a performance by a troupe of women in sequins and feathers spiced up the vote count on Metro TV. It was past eleven before Matta politely let me know that he had another appointment.

On the way out I stopped by the bathroom. It had an unpainted aluminium door and a squat-style toilet. A plastic holder on the wall held half a dozen closely bunched toothbrushes, several of them flattened with age, and a tube of Nazhif toothpaste with Arabic letters. That bathroom captured the essence of the party—the sense of community, the overwhelming maleness, the mistrust of the West, the membership for the most part only one generation removed from poverty.

Early in August, three days after our lunch at Daeng Tata, Herry and I took a Silver Bird to Utan Kayu, an unfashionable part of east Jakarta—no Ace Hardware, no ABN Amro—and alighted by an alley too narrow for the taxi to pass. I followed Herry along the length of a shallow gutter clogged with grey-green water and fallen leaves. 'That's Anis Matta's house,' he said gesturing towards a bungalow larger and brighter than most on the street. A shiny black Honda minivan, a silver Kijang and a third car, partially obscured, stood in the driveway.

Matta had scheduled the interview at a nearby Islamic centre he headed, a concrete box that brought to mind a government school. A faded and tattered pullout from *National Geographic* pasted on a wooden board outside announced 'The Making of America.' It showed an old black and white photo of an Indian brave, the Miniconjou warrior Red Horse.

We waited an hour before Matta opened the door and invited us into a sparsely furnished room. On a glass-topped desk sat an Indonesian-English dictionary and a translation of *Don't Sweat the Small Stuff for Women*. An empty carton on the floor said www.summer-umrah.com. Matta had put on weight since the last time I saw him. He resembled a snowman in summer clothes—a round face, a round body, curious eyes behind the round rims of his glasses.

He had less time to spare than on election night and the conversation hewed closely to the party. Matta outlined its growth over the past five years, from thirty thousand cadres to between four hundred thousand and five hundred thousand. By 2009 they planned to command 1.6 million cadres and have planted a representative in each of the country's sixty thousand villages. By 2014 they would be in a position to rule.

What did he make of the run-off election for the presidency between SBY and Megawati?

Both were high risk for the PKS. At this stage it was too dangerous for them to challenge larger parties directly. Indonesians lacked the stamina for a long fight, so the PKS had to pick one of them, probably SBY's Democratic Party, to ensure that it was at the heart of power while it grew. It could not afford to be seen as too far from the mainstream.

Why did he feel they needed protection? If anything the press tended to fawn all over them.

Yes, but he wasn't sure that they could take this support for granted. The clean image would not last permanently. In the next election he would not be able to use the slogan 'clean and caring' that had worked so well this time.

The last time Matta had talked about the party's campus strength. I had been struck by the number of technical graduates drawn to the party. Why was this so?

It wasn't only graduates of Indonesian universities. The party counted between two hundred and three hundred cadres with doctorates from Europe, America and Japan. They even included a handful of nuclear scientists among them.

But what attracted men of science to a party whose ultimate goal was the imposition of sharia?

He traced it to the beginning of their movement in the 1980s, when Islam was on a leash and the government still meddled in politics. In those days the future founders of the party met in small Koranic study groups. The only places not 'contaminated' by the state were the technical and scientific schools. The movement had reached out to these students through mosques on campus. This also boosted their image; it kept with a perceived hierarchy in higher education. The technical sciences, architecture and the natural sciences stood at the pinnacle. Then came the social sciences. Last were languages and literature; you studied them only if you weren't good enough for anything else.

In Egypt, of course, the Brotherhood had been banned, its leaders imprisoned and tortured. Did he ever worry about a similar backlash here?

For the first time he hesitated before answering. The situation here was different, he said choosing his words carefully. When Nasser had wanted to destroy the Brotherhood after World War Two the Muslim world was ruled by dictators. Now there were anti-military movements in Muslim countries. The army in Indonesia did not command the moral authority of the Egyptian army under Nasser.

If the army was no longer a danger then what was?

There were only two dangers: that America would widen the war on terror, and that capitalists would oppose the party. They had recently emerged as the largest party in Jakarta, but their attempt to form a government in the city was being opposed by owners of bars and discos.

Did this mean he planned to shut down Jakarta's night-life?

'It's not yet the finals,' said Matta evenly. 'It's only the quarter-finals right now.'

The small Koranic study groups that Matta had talked about belonged to a movement called *tarbiyah*, Arabic for 'education'. Tarbiyah formed the party backbone. It supplied the legions of motivated cadres and explained the ability to flood the streets at short notice with tens of thousands. The movement was born in the late 1970s, in the leafy Dutch-built campus of the Institute of Technology in Bandung, Sukarno's alma mater, when two activists linked to the Saudi-sponsored World Assembly of Muslim Youth began indoctrinating students with Brotherhood materials. Following the Brotherhood blueprint, they organised in secret cells called *usroh*, 'family' in Arabic, each with a leader and between five and fifteen members. They met once a week to discuss Islam, to learn how to develop a proper 'Islamic personality', and to study the works of Qutb and al-Banna, often in DDII translations. In *Among the Believers* Naipaul describes one of these early 'mental training' sessions led by Imaduddin Abdulrahim, the Iowa State University graduate generally credited as tarbiyah's Indonesian progenitor.

Imaduddin could not have chosen a better time. Many of his students had already received a religious grounding in school. Many were also the first in their families to enter university or, for that matter, to live in a city. Politics on campus was sharply curtailed under the Orwellian-sounding policy of *normalisasi*, but religion was another matter. Called the Salman Mosque movement in common parlance, after the campus mosque at ITB, tarbiyah quickly caught on. It gave its members a sense of purpose and dignity, simple ideas of right and wrong, a framework for understanding the dizzying changes around them, dreams of a better future. Those who showed promise were encouraged to start tarbiyah groups of their own. By the early 1990s, when Suharto made his famous tilt towards Islam, tarbiyah already controlled student movements in virtually all the largest and most prestigious public universities.

Over two decades the first generation of tarbiyah activists rose to positions of influence in the bureaucracy, in universities, in state-owned corporations, in short wherever Muslimness itself was emerging as a form of merit. With the New Order's collapse in 1998 they announced their political ambitions with the birth of the Justice Party. The following year, after the party polled below the 2 percent threshold to participate in the 2004 election, it simply sidestepped the law by changing its name to the Prosperous Justice Party. The PKS then was simply tarbiyah as politics, just as *Sabili* was tarbiyah as journalism. They carried the remarkably resilient ideological DNA of the Egyptian schoolteacher and his literary colleague.

Though identified with college campuses, the movement was not confined to them. Herry belonged to a tarbiyah group that met on Saturdays. I had gathered this in south Sulawesi during a conversation with a local PKS leader, but when I broached this with Herry at first he denied it. Its membership was secret, he finally said. His voice took on a note of pleading. He felt uncomfortable talking about it. I had to understand, this was something he could not share. I agreed not to press him about his own group; he agreed to take me to a college cell in action.

The New Order built the University of Indonesia's sprawling Depok campus, south of Jakarta, to keep pesky students at a safe distance from the city. A few days after our meeting with Matta our Silver Bird glided past a tall row of palm trees rooted in red earth and a fluttering banner welcoming visiting students from Austria. Tall Javanese buildings, their sloping roofs a dull glazed brown rather than the usual ochre, clad the campus in sturdy dignity.

The sun seemed less severe here among the tall trees and high buildings and Herry didn't object to exploring the campus on foot. He had worn his Friday outfit, a crisp white tunic with blue embroidery. He carried a rope-handled paper bag from *Sabili* that displayed portraits of twelve Islamist heroes, among them bin Laden, Abdullah Azzam, Shamil Basayev, Ayatollah Khomeini and Ahmad Yassin. The bag imbued Herry with a kind of charisma, the aura of the Kalashnikov. In another time and another place it might have been a Che Guevara beret.

After a few minutes we came across a poster for the Miss Indonesia competition on a notice board. The contestants, one from each province, flaunted almost identical glossy black tresses, except for the girl from Aceh, where a bare-headed woman might be dragged off the street and shorn, who wore a black jilbab.

'This is all free sex life,' said Herry. He told me about an unmarried college girl, four months pregnant, who had recently been murdered by her boyfriend.

'Was she a beauty pageant contestant?' I asked.

'No, but this is all free sex lifestyle.'

The story had popped into his mind when he looked at the poster. It illustrated the speed of thought, the seamlessness between a swimsuit and a sex-soaked murder.

The domeless campus mosque, which we arrived at a few minutes later, was an example of what Herry referred to derisively as a 'mesjid Suharto'. Paid for by one of his foundations, Suharto mosques dotted the country, though usually topped these days by a hastily added ready-made dome. This one overlooked an artificial lake beaten to a metallic sheen by the sun. On a mat near the entrance crowded books by Hassan al-Banna, a slim volume on the jilbab, a translation of Karen Armstrong's *Holy War*.

I waited for midday prayers to pass before following Herry inside the mosque. The cool came as a refuge and I rested my back on a marble pillar and closed my eyes while we waited for a tarbiyah group to gather. Someone sitting nearby, a lecturer newly befriended by Herry, suggested I take a nap.

'I can't sleep in public,' I said. 'Though I read somewhere that Napoleon could sleep anywhere. He could sleep under a booming cannon.'

'I read that Napoleon converted to Islam,' said Herry.

'That's the first I've heard of that.'

'I read it. After Waterloo Napoleon became a Muslim.'

We didn't have long to wait before seven gangly boys formed a cross-legged circle in a corner of the mosque, their toes pointed instinctively inwards in the Islamic manner. I was worried that they would clam up, but they all knew *Sabili* and appeared flattered to have its managing editor among them. They were undergraduate geography students, which, by Matta's typology, made them dumber than doctors but a lot cleverer than English majors. They were in their early twenties, though somehow made more youthful by acne. Their postures would have driven a chiropractor to despair. They said they had been meeting for two years.

A mentor, an older boy, a maths student who spoke in a hoarse whisper, flagged off the session. The topic that day: education. The biggest problem with Indonesia, said the mentor, was a low stand-ard of education. Hassan al-Banna had understood its importance, which was why he founded the Ikhwan ul-Muslimeen in 1928. (The mentor used the Arabic for the Muslim Brotherhood.) Because al-Banna believed in education, the Brotherhood had grown to become one of the top three organisations in the world. (He didn't name the other two.)

The mentor then turned to Al-Azhar in Cairo. If they could provide free education to people from all over the world, then why did Indonesia, with its wealth of natural resources, charge students such high fees? The others nodded in agreement.

The mentor continued. According to Islam every person had to be a role model. You had to start with yourself, start with small things, start right now. I recalled A. A. Gym using exactly the same words with the telecoms company executives in Bandung. The mentor talked about Japan and Germany after World War Two. Both countries had made education their priority. Meanwhile Indonesia had built showy monuments like the Monas tower. The boys nodded sagely, not noticing the obvious bait and switch. They apparently saw no contradiction between following the laws and customs of seventh century Arabia and building an advanced industrial society.

The mentor brought up more errors of the past. How under Sukarno they allowed communists to become teachers. These teachers would tell children to close their eyes and ask God for a ballpoint pen. The children would open their eyes and of course find nothing. Then the teacher would tell them to repeat the exercise and this time ask the teacher instead. The pens that appeared on their tables brainwashed the children into believing that there was no God, but there was a teacher. According to the mentor, society could be changed one person at a time. If nine out of ten persons in a room were good, then the lone bad person was strange; but if nine out of ten were bad, then it was the good one among them who felt odd. Islam had all the solutions to society's problems. There was only one obstacle: Muslims weren't willing to use them. A country's leader was nothing but a mirror of society. If people were happy watching mystical and criminal programs, then their leader would be that kind of person as well, someone with a mystical and criminal way of thinking. The dig was aimed at Megawati with her Balinese Hindu grandmother.

After about twenty minutes the mentor bid farewell to each of the boys individually and left. The rest of the meeting continued in a similar vein. They talked about the Prophet, about the national budget for education, about a Koranic injunction to read. They circled back to a recent fee hike. Nobody cracked a joke or even smiled. It was all earnest and well-meaning and clearly heart-felt. Tarbiyah had tailored global content to local conditions, Brotherhood teachings yoked to economic anxiety.

In the Silver Bird on our way back Herry said the story about the teacher and the ballpoint pen was a staple. Years ago he had heard it in his tarbiyah group as well, though with the example of a pencil rather than a pen. It was designed as a goad to anger. 'You need them to feel there is injustice when they are new.'

A little while later Herry announced that he would like to share a 'serious joke' about himself.

'From Monday to Friday I'm a fundamentalist. From Friday evening to Sunday I'm a liberal.'

'How can you possibly call yourself a liberal?'

'I hang out at QB. I listen to music, not just Islamic music. Strange music. I'm watching movies. Cannes movies.' This was true. He had watched not only *Run Lola Run*, but *Fahrenheit 911* and *Bowling for Columbine* and *The Fog of War*, a documentary about Robert McNamara. He knew all about the PowerPuff girls and could identify a Missy Elliott tune from a few stray bars.

'If you were a liberal you wouldn't want to force women to wear the jilbab.'

'Not everything that is forbidden is violating your rights,' he shot back. 'Some things are trying to save you. I will explain to you.

Allah said you must protect your family from hell. From the Islamic point of view the reason is religious as well as sexual. A woman wearing a jilbab is more safe than those with mini-skirt. You can do a survey. In no rape is there a woman in jilbab.' He paused before continuing. 'I want to explain. I'll take the accusation of human rights violation to protect my children from hell.'

'I guess that's the difference between us. I don't believe in heaven or hell.'

'I don't just believe in hell, I'm *scared* of it. My grandmother told me a story when I was a little boy. After you're buried, there's a black snake. He will ask you if you solat or not. If not, he will beat you until your body enters deep into the earth. Just for one question, solat or not. I was five or seven years old when she told me that story.'

He went on. 'There's another story about *neraka*. If you're telling a lie, your tongue will be pulled out and cut with hot scissors. There are lots of stories like this. So in my head I'm very scared of hell.'

It was odd for me to hear the word 'neraka', the Sanskrit word for 'hell', so improbably stretched.

Herry continued. 'My grandmother also told me about heaven. (Here he used the word *surga*, also familiar to me.) There's a river of milk. You can drink any time. There's a river of honey. There are delicious fruits that taste like honey. There are beautiful angels.'

'Are they virgins?'

'No. Angels.'

We were silent for a few minutes, then I responded.

'I sometimes think we're like buildings, like a skyscraper. On the top floor is what we do—put a girl in a jilbab, or call Osama bin Laden a hero. But at the very bottom, in the basement, is what we believe. In your basement there's this vision of heaven and hell—the black snake, the river of milk. In mine there's none of that stuff.'

'Then what is there?'

'Not much. Just a washing machine and a dryer.'

16

Ambon

Getting Herry to accompany me to Ambon took a certain amount of coaxing. Tias had long soured on our travels; *Sabili* needed him during the countdown to the election. But more than that, Ambon was the place of Herry's nightmares, the place where he had seen fighters hurl Molotov cocktails, and shoulder bazookas made from sawed-off electricity poles, the place that had made him vomit every day for three weeks on his return. A peace deal brokered two years earlier had largely held, but violence bubbled close to the surface and erupted every now and then. What little news from Ambon trickled into Jakarta painted a picture of stray riots, police firing, pedestrians picked off by snipers.

The week following our visit with the tarbiyah group we left Jakarta early in the morning and arrived in Ambon, two hours ahead of western Indonesia time, in the afternoon. Our escort, a local PKS legislator named Suhfi, an unsmiling man with a waxy pallor that looked borrowed from a fish, was waiting at the airport. He led us at once to a Kijang, but as I opened the door someone tapped my shoulder.

'Foreigner?' he asked.

'From India.'

'Please come with me.'

We went back inside and followed the man down a corridor into a chamber. There, behind two desks, sat a pair of burly government officials, coffee-coloured and curly haired and in identical dark safari suits.

'Christians,' whispered Suhfi to Herry.

The Christians asked for my passport. I was glad for having carried it; you didn't require photo ID for domestic flights.

'What are you here for?' asked the first man as he thumbed through the pages slowly.

Herry had warned me not to mention journalism. 'I've heard so much about Ambon *manise*,' I said. 'I wanted to see it before I leave Indonesia.' I had read that 'Ambon manise', 'sweet Ambon', was how locals affectionately referred to the island.

'Where is your letter of permission?' he asked. 'Foreigners need permission.'

A Canadian who had come in after me extracted a folded sheet of paper from his passport. 'Look at him,' said my interrogator. 'Look, he has brought a letter of permission.'

'It's my mistake,' I answered. 'I did not know about the letter of permission.'

'He did not know,' he repeated to his colleague, who was getting ready to return the Canadian's passport. 'He says he did not know.' They chuckled exaggeratedly, like gangsters in a Bollywood film.

'I only want to see Ambon manise,' I said. 'I've lived in Indonesia for four years. I've travelled all over and this has never happened.'

'This is not all over the country. This is Ambon.' Then to his colleague, 'He speaks Indonesian.'

My interrogator turned to Suhfi and asked for his national identity card. Without a word Suhfi extracted it from a thin wallet in his back pocket. The man noted something in a register.

'We'll let you go,' he said handing back my passport. 'But you must report to the police no later than tomorrow.'

'Thank you *very* much,' I said knowing that I would do no such thing.

The city was about an hour away from the airport. Though the petrol drum and flaming tyre checkpoints of the conflict had disappeared, their shadows remained in the razed schools and charred houses that lined our route. We passed a wall-sized poster of a blond Jesus weeping into his fists guarding the entrance to a village. 'Christian area,' said Suhfi. Then, a little later, 'Muslim area.' Then again, 'Christian area.' In between Herry and Suhfi exchanged names of mutual acquaintances, spinning the first tentative strands of friendship. Herry mentioned Anis Matta and Suhfi repeated the name softly, as though there were something talismanic in those four syllables.

Suhfi had made a reservation at the Hotel Wijaya, the best hotel in Muslim Ambon ever since a Christian mob razed the previous claimant to that position. Even by my declining standards it was a pit. A bucket in the hallway outside our room caught a steady drip from the ceiling. A wet film covered our bathroom floor and the unclad aluminium door had trouble closing.

Herry had carried two heavy packages from Jakarta and now he and Suhfi wasted no time ripping off the brown paper wrapping. The first contained ten boxes of white envelopes: Jaya brand, No. 90, Peel and Seal. They bore the letters PKPU, a PKS NGO, printed in blue with thin white lines running through the last two letters to give them a sense of motion. The other package contained PKPU letterheads.

Suhfi looked at the stationery admiringly. 'Envelopes are very expensive in Ambon,' he explained.

Then it was time for prayers. Herry tore a stained brown blanket off a bed and laid it on the floor. I slouched on the other bed deleting pictures from my camera, knowing that the low beeps would not bother such robust worshippers. It occurred to me that I felt mildly jealous of their Islamic intimacy, of the chatter it offered to overcome the awkwardness of a first meeting. 'Which way is the *kiblat*?' (The direction of prayer.) 'What time is maghrib?' 'Are the Maldives Muslim?'

It had taken five hundred years for the Moluccas, the spice islands of lore, to go from an economic prize akin to modern-day Kuwait to a tragedy with shades of Lebanon. Christianity first came here in the early 1500s—around the same time as Islam—in pursuit of commerce that turned on a geographical quirk. You could buy pepper, cinnamon and cardamom in India, Java or Sumatra, but the forested and volcano-studded Moluccas claimed a monopoly over nutmeg and cloves, once costlier than gold. The first Europeans to stake a claim to the islands were the Portuguese. Then, from the early 1600s, they passed to the Dutch. In one measure of their worth, in 1667 the Dutch swapped New York's Manhattan island with the English for the tiny nutmeg rich island of Ran.

For 350 years Ambon—the most important Moluccan island as well as its principal town—was a cornerstone of the Dutch East Indies. Ambonese formed the backbone of the colonial army that kept the peace in Java and subdued Aceh and Bali. In turn they were favoured in schools and in the colonial government. Intermarriage with Europeans was more widespread than on the larger islands and Ambonese made up a chunk of the relatively privileged mestizo class known as Indos.

In 1950, concerned by Sukarno's decision to scrap a loose federal system agreed to with the departing Dutch, rebels backed by demobbed soldiers raised the red, green, white and blue flag of the South Moluccan Republic in Ambon. Government troops moved in and the republic's leaders fled to exile in the Netherlands where, except for the occasional hostage taking in the mid-to-late 1970s, their cause faded into obscurity.

Their fears, however, slowly came to pass. To ease population pressures independent Indonesia adopted a resettlement policy, eerily named *transmigrasi*. In the 1970s and 1980s it quickened. Tens of thousands of migrants from south Sulawesi and Java poured into the Moluccas. On Ambon island the vast Christian majority of the late nineteenth century had become a minority a hundred years later. Christians remained the traditional ruling elite and retained a sense of entitlement in government and the university. Below them seethed a growing pool of migrants touched by the new Muslim assertiveness.

In 1999, with the economy in a freefall and politics in turmoil, the region tripped into civil war. It began with a squabble between a Christian bus driver and a Muslim passenger. Though the driver was a local and the passenger a settler from south Sulawesi the battle lines that quickly hardened split along religion rather than ethnicity. At first the two sides were evenly matched; by some accounts Muslims suffered more in early skirmishes. But then the fighting became less haphazard and the weight of numbers began to bear. (*Sabili's* contribution included such helpful touches as listing every jihad verse in the Koran.) Well-armed militias poured into the island. The largest of them, Laskar Jihad, trained openly in the hills outside Jakarta aided by sympathisers in the army. Its volunteers, in red and white kaffiyehs and loose white robes, gathered funds on street corners in major cities. In battle some carried military-issue weapons.

Laskar Jihad was Wahhabist, or to use their preferred term, Salafist; its leader, Jafar Umar Thalib, once complained to me that the Taliban wasn't quite Islamic enough. For two years Thalib's men played out their desert fantasy. Here and there they converted Christian villages by force. They stoned to death a 'volunteer' who confessed to adultery. (*Suara Hidayatullah* later gave the man's family a sharia award and a 10 million rupiah purse.) A third of the region's 2.1 million people were displaced and between five thousand and ten thousand killed before Jakarta stepped in and brokered a cease-fire.

The next morning Suhfi joined us for breakfast at the formerly second best hotel in Muslim Ambon. His neatly parted hair, groomed goatish beard and round-rimmed glasses conspired to give him a likeable earnestness. 'I'm using email facility in my house,' he had announced in English shortly after we met. Predictably, he was a man of science. 'I'm a marine engineer,' he had said. 'But I have respect to industrial engineering.'

Wary of the buffet display of fried rice in an industrial shade of red and an unidentified limp yellow vegetable I ordered papaya. The pale, hard and acidic fruit that appeared on the table 45 minutes later barely seemed related to the deep orange variety you found in Jakarta.

'I wonder if it's like this because we've crossed the Wallace Line,' I said to Herry. The imaginary line divides Indonesian flora and fauna into zones: primarily Asian and primarily Australian.

'What is the Wallace Line?' asked Suhfi.

Herry, who had discovered the nineteenth-century English naturalist Alfred Russel Wallace via my copy of his classic, *The Malay Archipelago*, sprung to his feet. He went up to a map on the wall above the limp vegetables and with his thumb traced a vertical line east of Bali. 'This is the Wallace Line. Plants and animals are different on either side.'

'Oh wow!' exclaimed Suhfi.

'Wallace collected twenty thousand beetles and butterflies,' said Herry returning to his chair. He spoke with a touch of condescension, the tone of a city boy, privy to bigger experiences, bigger thoughts.

'Oh wow!' said Suhfi.

Wallace's achievements appeared to make quite an impression on Suhfi. For a moment, before I inadvertently ruined things, it looked as though his esteem for the naturalist might even catch up with his regard for industrial engineering.

'Wallace was a close friend of Charles Darwin,' I said. 'He co-discovered the theory of evolution.'

Suhfi's face became solemn. 'I don't believe that man can evolve,' he said flatly.

He continued after a pause.

'It's too hard. If man could have evolved in the past, then why can't we predict what he will look like in a few decades? It's too hard. Evolution is false.' He brought up Harun Yahya, a Turkish writer who had apparently proved that it was all a hoax.

I turned to Herry. 'Do you agree with this?'

'Absolutely. The most danger from Darwin's theory is survival of the fittest.' He turned to Suhfi. 'This means the strongest will win.' To me he said, 'This theory is against humanity!'

'How?'

'Because Darwin doesn't appreciate the weak. In the history of political power, Hitler, Mussolini, communists made this theory as a fundamental theory for their movement. And this is very danger-ous. It even enters communist China—Ma.' Ma Junren, a famously harsh Chinese coach, had reared a clutch of world-beating female long-distance runners on, it was said, turtle blood, caterpillar fungus and a regimen of high-altitude training in Tibet.

Herry's voice dropped a notch. 'Maybe Darwin has no theory for political concept. He was just doing his job in the scientific field. But it was used by other people to combine with politics. That's the main root of terror.'

'What does any of this have to do with terrorism?'

'The survival of the fittest. He must always be strong.' Herry punched the air with his fist like a hammer. 'And for that he must kill the weak.'

After breakfast Herry went upstairs to our room to fetch something while Suhfi and I moved to a pair of threadbare couches in the lobby. Suhfi was 29 and hailed from the neighbouring island of Seram. (In and around whose beetled and butterflied forests Wallace had passed nine months some 145 years earlier.) He said he had always been religious and had developed an interest in Islamic politics while still in high school. To devote himself to party work he had forsaken an opportunity to pursue a master's degree in Malaysia. He read both *Sabili* and *Suara Hidayatullah*. He knew all about Bulukumba and longed to see the bupati's reforms first hand.

Elections earlier in the year had boosted the PKS's strength in the provincial legislature from one member to five. It now formed the third largest bloc, behind only PDI-P and Golkar. Suhfi's newness to power—he was one of the four PKS freshmen—might have explained his diffidence with the airport officials the previous day, but I also detected a well-spring of idealism. Suhfi said he wanted to eliminate corruption. He wanted to transform the country.

I asked him why he thought his party could change Indonesia for the better.

Pat came the reply, 'Good people will create a good family. Good families will make a good neighbourhood. Good neighbourhoods will make a good region. Good regions will make a good country.'

'I know that,' I said. 'I heard it at a tarbiyah session.'

Suhfi froze. His voice rose to a girlish pitch. 'Tarbiyah? You know tarbiyah?'

'Come on. You're a PKS legislator and you're telling me you don't know tarbiyah.'

A part of me felt bad for him. He was earnest and provincial and torn between being a terrible liar and a natural follower of orders.

I turned the knife some more. 'When did you become a member?'

He said nothing. He just sat there frozen, his teeth bared in a rictus.

'In Surabaya?' Where he had studied marine engineering.

He refused to speak. His eyes looked past me searchingly at the staircase.

I softened. 'Are you uncomfortable talking about this?'

Suhfi glimpsed Herry on the stairs. 'What about Herry?' he croaked. 'Why don't you ask Herry about tarbiyah?'

The rest of the day passed in a parade of images.

In the hills above town, in a house of broken plaster and tilted corrugated sheets, lived a posse of Laskar Jihad stay-behinds, their Taliban wives sequestered behind blue plastic curtains. 'The Kharajites failed because they did not follow Islam,' intoned their leader, a high school graduate who now peddled Muslim clothes and books for a living.

Beside the still imposing 428-year-old Portuguese fort stood the ruins of Ambon's oldest church, a low span of wall and three slim pillars rising like fingers above a tangle of brush and long grass. Our driver slowed down and purred: 'We burnt this.'

At a cash crop village—cocoa, cloves, vanilla—cleansed of Christians the headman, or 'raja' as he preferred, plied us with multi-coloured spongecake and sweet tea. 'Yessss,' said Suhfi punching his thigh as the raja relived wiping out the village that had stood beside the ruined church.

As dusk settled we headed towards the Masjid Raya, the big mosque in town, for evening prayers. Herry sat in front with the church-burning driver. I shared the back seat with Suhfi and went over my notes. The violence had shredded the fabric of daily life.

You could ask a newspaper boy for a Christian newspaper or a Muslim one. Christians paid their electricity bills in one place, Muslims in another. The largest public hospital, the national radio and television stations, the smaller of two ports and the ferry terminal remained in Christian hands. The main port and the bus terminal belonged to Muslims, as did the mall, emptied of Chinese shopkeepers. Banks maintained two branches: Christian guards, tellers, managers and customers in one, Muslims in the other. Ambon once boasted two movie theatres, the Victoria and the Amboina, both in Muslim neighbourhoods, both razed. Suhfi was about to move to a compound exclusively for Muslim legislators.

This religious apartheid didn't bother him. 'My concept is that Ambon is for both communities,' he had said when I questioned him. 'We must have two hospitals—one for Muslims, one for Christians. We cannot have just one.' Suhfi didn't count a single Christian friend and found the idea of sharing a meal with one absurd. 'Oh no! Impossible!'

I felt Suhfi's eyes on my notebook before his voice pierced the hum of the Kijang.

'J. K. Rowling has extraordinary imagination.'

I looked up surprised. 'Do you like her books?'

'No, I haven't seen the films or read the books.' He paused. 'I don't like reading literature.'

'What do you read then?'

'I like books about success.'

I assumed he meant self-help books. At Jakarta's annual book fair self-help books and manuals for Microsoft Windows offered the only competition to Islam.

'Like what?'

'Like books about people who have successful lives.'

'Like who?' I thought he might say Bill Gates, or perhaps name an industrial engineer.

'Mohammad Natsir.'

'Have you read *Milestones* by Sayyid Qutb?'

'Not the whole thing, but I have read many of Hassan al-Banna's speeches.'

Herry piped up from in front. 'Sayyid Qutb was the most important. More important even than Maududi of Pakistan. But Hassan al-Banna is extraordinary too.'

'What about Osama bin Laden?' I had seen three men in Ambon in bin Laden T-shirts.

'As a thinker or as a fighter?' asked Herry. 'He's important as a thinker too. He is close to Abdullah Azzam, the creator of concept Afghanistan.'

After a few minutes I circled back to the PKS.

Suhfi said he had devoted most of his twenties to the party— distributing rice and sugar to hurricane victims in east Java, setting up a refugee camp in central Sulawesi, battling an outbreak of dysentery among Muslim Moluccans. Before running for office he had signed a public pledge to fight corruption. Each month he placed half his legislative salary in party coffers. As per policy, he would serve no more than two terms.

When I remarked on the number of rules, he ticked off all the things forbidden to a party member: alcohol, cigarettes, gold, silk clothes.

The last item came as a surprise. A full-sleeved silk batik shirt was considered formal wear at government and diplomatic functions.

'In Islam men can wear silk only in a medical emergency,' he explained. Gold was similarly proscribed; only PKS women wore wedding bands.

I broached the subject of economic development.

'We want Indonesia to be strong and prosperous.'

In that case what were his views on family planning?

'I don't agree with this.'

He didn't believe in birth control?

'I believe in natural.'

But if he looked around, at countries that had grown and lifted millions out of poverty—China, Korea, Vietnam—he'd see that they had all encouraged small families.

He wouldn't budge. His voice took on the same flatness he had used to dismiss evolution. 'Every country chooses its own ideology. I believe in Islam. I believe in natural.'

The Laskar Jihad men had been somewhat defensive about their role in the conflict. They said they had battled Christians only for their politics, their alleged desire to secede from the republic. Back in our room that night Herry expressed disappointment. 'They are not true mujahidin,' he said. 'They should not have regrets about what happened in 1999, 2000 and 2001. If it's right, if it's jihad, then just go. You don't need to have a political point of view.'

We sat face to face on our brown blanketed beds. You could hear the drip-drip in the corridor outside and the faint warble of fat girls from Surabaya in the karaoke lounge upstairs. Herry's suitcase lay open by the foot of his bed; he would return to Jakarta the next day while I remained in Ambon.

I couldn't quite shake the conversation with Suhfi about birth control from my mind. The consequences of the PKS's growth, of activism harnessed to atavism, were clear. You couldn't burn churches and expect the Chinese, or at least those who could afford it, not to park their money in Singapore and their children in Australia. You couldn't have your leaders line up to vouch for Bashir, and to dispute the very existence of Jemaah Islamiyah, and expect Nike or Sony to place a factory in Surabaya rather than in Hanoi. You couldn't have your premier engineering college turn out graduates better known for their piety than for their science and expect to emulate India or China, let alone Japan and Germany.

I asked Herry what he thought of Suhfi's views on family planning.

'I believe in the same,' he said. 'I reject birth control. They say the 1980s were good economically, but it couldn't be because of family planning because those children have grown up only now. So how could family planning have made a difference in the 1980s?'

'Children aren't like trees. It always makes a difference.'

I launched into a sermon about savings rates and investment rates, Singapore and China. I tried to boil it down to a simple example. 'Let's say there are two families, each with 100 rupiah to spend. One child costs ten rupiah. The family with two children spends 60 rupiah a month and puts the rest in a bank. A businessman borrows money from the bank. The businessman then builds a factory. The other family has six children. They don't save anything. No money in the bank and so no factory. Now multiply this by millions of people.'

Herry scribbled furiously in his notebook. At length he stopped and looked up.

'I have two feelings,' he said. 'Half of my brain, as a Muslim, I want to argue with you and reject what you say. But another part of me wants to understand.'

'That's why I sometimes think you're not *really* a fundamentalist.'

'Remember it's Saturday.'

The teacher, an Arab by blood, had studied in Medina. His perfectly ironed black tunic set off the pure white of his skullcap. His callus, a tight upside down triangle, announced itself in the middle of his forehead, as though placed there by a cartographer. As such things went, it belonged in a different league from anything Herry or Suhfi could muster. Though if you thought about it perhaps

Herry's callus didn't really count at all. It edged too close to his hairline, easily disguised with a baseball cap, the mark of someone who wanted it both ways—bin Laden Monday through Friday, Demi Moore on the weekends.

'*Marhaba*,' said the teacher.

'*Marhaba*,' repeated the class.

'*Kitab ul Waqqalam*,' said the teacher.

'*Kitab ul Waqqalam*.'

'*Shukran*.'

'*Shukran*.'

The room smelled faintly of sweat. A red paper fish and two shiny gold stars dangled from the ceiling, swaying and twirling in the night breeze that entered from a wire mesh ventilator. About fifty of us, all men, all but me PKS cadres, sat on tiny chairs at low, bright tables. Suhfi, in the row ahead of me, leaned back and smiled. 'Sorry we learn in kindergarten,' he said in English.

The teacher, in his twenties like most of his students, ran a relaxed and lively class. He led them through an exchange about how to politely borrow a book. First he said both parts of the dialogue aloud and the class repeated after him. Then he said only one part and the class responded with the other. Finally he stood to one side and had students come up in twos and enact the exchange by the blackboard. The first three pairs made hardly any mistakes. The fourth included a Papuan looking boy wearing a baseball cap who mangled nearly every word. The teacher corrected him patiently. The laughter that rang through the room contained no derision.

They moved on to a vocabulary exercise.

'*Dajaj*,' said the teacher.

'*Ayam* (chicken),' said the class.

'*Ayam Goreng* (fried chicken),' said someone in the middle of the room.

'*Dajaj*,' said the teacher.

'Ayam Goreng,' repeated the wit.

The teacher walked up to him and playfully tugged his goatee. I found myself laughing with the rest of the class.

You had to admire the discipline. At nine on a Monday night they might have been home watching a Mira W. sinetron instead of poring over photocopied textbooks and repeating foreign phrases from the backs of their throats. Of course only Arabic could induce this effort just as only God inspired their idealism. Herry had once declared himself certain that you couldn't bribe a PKS legislator with a Rolex or a Mercedes Benz, but that he might have trouble turning down a trip to Mecca.

The Saudi textbook contained a chapter on nationalities. The teacher read aloud in Arabic and then translated each sentence to Indonesian.

'This is the new nurse from Malaysia.'

'I am an engineer from Pakistan.'

'I am an Egyptian.'

No non-Muslims tainted their lesson, only Malaysians and Pakistanis and Egyptians, and even here you could see the hierarchy. For the Egyptian, the Arab, it was enough to simply be an Egyptian. Their jobs defined the Pakistani and the Malaysian; though Malaysia was by far the richer country, the Pakistani, an engineer, stood above the Malaysian nurse.

My thoughts turned to Herry and his tale of the Arabs who had scouted Java in the seventh century. Perhaps I had judged him too harshly for it. Perhaps I had judged him too harshly in general. How could I even begin to understand what it was like for your grandmother to warn you about a God who took hot scissors to your tongue? What did I know about marriage or a family to support? Herry would have realised early on that intelligence alone promised little in Indonesia. Islam had offered him a ladder and he had ascended it gratefully, rung by rung. I couldn't honestly say that in his circumstances I would have turned out much different.

Peripheral people always feel a greater need for authenticity; they live with a special anxiety about a shrinking world in which they play so little part. Britney Spears, Harry Potter, Colonel Sanders, Manchester United—all a part of their lives, yet (rice at KFC notwithstanding) impervious to their desires. I sensed a similar anxiety in India, in the hysterical outpouring of pride at the slightest achievement, an Indian winning a beauty pageant or becoming dean of a business school in the Midwest. Yet on the whole Indians had it easier. We could at least claim Nobel-winning economists and Booker-winning writers and legions of engineers with stock options at Microsoft and Oracle. In Indonesia you had nothing, no accomplishment on the world stage to speak of, and only Islam to fill the void. It gave you a glorious history, a great cause, a worthy adversary. Most of all it gave you order: Avoid silk and gold. Teach your daughter how to swim. Stop eating before you're full. If on a motorcycle be sure to greet a walking man first.

In the class the teacher paid special attention to the letter Z. Indonesians had trouble with that letter, he said. The Buginese tended to pronounce it as S, the Sundanese as J. Again he led them patiently.

'*Zaman...*'
'*Zafar...*'
'*Zafeer...*'
'*Zilzal...*'
'*Zilaal...*'
'*Zilzaal...*'
'*Zamzam...*'

Three sides of the large rectangular field bordered Christian Ambon, one Muslim. The previous night's lessons still ringing in my ears, I claimed a square of dusty concrete step in a sea of schoolchildren directly opposite the governor and other assembled dignitaries. The children had been bussed in earlier that morning to celebrate the nation's 59th Independence Day, August 17 2004. They wore school uniforms, white shirts and long navy blue skirts or white shirts and blue shorts, and clutched small red and white flags. My stand was given to second graders. The girls sat with their legs primly together; the boys slouched raffishly on each other's shoulders.

A conductor, the edge of his smart green jacket flapping in the breeze, raised a thin steel baton in a white-gloved hand. The band struck up a tune—the national anthem. The children began to sing, waving their plastic flags. 'Indonesia, *tanah airku…*' they sang. (Indonesia, my native land…)

They swayed from side to side in their black sneakers and white socks, their high voices rising, rising. '*Indonesia, kebangsaanku, bangsa dan tanah airku.*' (Indonesia my nationality, my nation and my native land…)

Behind them lay the razed buildings and the mall rid of Chinese. In the hills beyond lived the sullen Laskar Jihad men and their Taliban wives and earnest Suhfi memorising Arabic in the evenings. And farther still A. A. Gym in his studio, Din Syamsuddin and the Council of Ulama, Abu Bakar Bashir fulminating in his prison cell about Iblis, the young Hasan al-Banna keeping his distance from dances, the bupati with his dress code for women, that eerie music in a Borneo forest. I looked at the children with their flags and their small voices. I wished I could be some place else.

Epilogue

In February 2007, more than two years after moving back to America, I returned to Jakarta for a visit. Much remained reassuringly familiar: Silver Birds at the airport, fire floss buns at the BreadTalk bakery in Plaza Indonesia mall, the red-roofed view from the Deutsche Bank building where I once worked. The mood in Jakarta was cautiously upbeat. On the surface at least the country appeared headed in the right direction. That democracy had taken root was unquestionable: after winning the 2004 election SBY had assumed the presidency without incident. Terrorism was under control. Densus 88, an elite police counter-terrorism unit trained and funded by the US and Australia, had arrested scores of suspected Jemaah Islamiyah operatives. The last major terrorist attack, a second round of bombings in Bali that killed twenty people and injured about 130, had taken place more than a year earlier, in October 2005.

The economy too had largely recovered. Businessmen still complained about red tape and corruption, but large-scale capital flight had abated and foreign investment was on an upswing. SBY had deepened an openness towards the ethnic Chinese begun by Abdurrahman Wahid. The government now recognised Confucianism as the country's sixth official faith. You saw the Chinese community's long march to acceptance commemorated in the red paper lanterns and strips of red and gold decorations with Chinese letters in shopping malls, and in the billboards celebrating the lunar New Year that dotted Jakarta.

And yet one couldn't escape the irony that on the whole the deepening of democracy had gone hand in hand with a darkening intolerance. The twin engines of Islamic orthodoxy and Islamist politics continued to batter heterodox Muslims, non-Muslims and women, and to undermine such bedrock democratic values as freedom of speech and freedom of conscience. The old cliché about Indonesia's inherent moderation remained alive, but it had acquired an increasingly desperate ring, as though if you invoked it loudly enough you could somehow ensure that it remained true.

Heterodox Muslims—the abangan as well as followers of non-mainstream sects—continued to bear the brunt of orthodox rage, often fomented by the Council of Indonesian Ulama, the quasi-official grouping of mullahs that had once targeted Inul. In 2005 the Council dusted off a 25-year-old fatwa declaring a tiny Muslim sect, the Ahmadis, to be heretics for their belief that their founder, Mirza Ghulam Ahmad (1835–1908) had received divine revelations. (This challenges the mainstream assertion that Mohammed was God's final prophet.) Mobs attacked Ahmadi homes in Java and shut down at least seven of the sect's mosques, at times with the police looking on. Ignoring Jakarta's jurisdiction over religion, local governments in several districts had simply banned Ahmadi worship.

The mullahs' exertions gave 21st-century Indonesian justice a medieval flavour. In east Java authorities had jailed a former boxer and convert from Christianity for leading Muslim prayers in

Indonesian; the Council claimed bilingual prayers tarnished the purity of Arabic. Another east Java court sentenced a group of paranormals to eight years in prison after the Council accused them of claiming to treat cancer and drug addiction with 'heretical' methods. In Jakarta, Lia Eden, the sixty-year-old leader of Jamaah Alamulla, an eccentric blend of Christianity and Islam, found herself jailed for 'denigrating religion'. The Council's south Sulawesi branch had a man imprisoned for the 'deviant' act of whistling during prayers.

Although richer and better organised than Ahmadis, Lia Eden followers, or paranormals, Christians faced a similar climate of intimidation. In strife-torn central Sulawesi, in 2005, militants waylaid and beheaded three teenage Christian girls walking to school; the militants' leader called the beheadings a Ramadan trophy. Across Java mobs, sometimes abetted by police, continued to shut down 'illegal' churches that operated in homes or shopfronts without official permission. (In many places obtaining such permission had become virtually impossible.) A court in west Java had sentenced three women to three years in jail for allowing Muslim children to attend their Christian kindergarten.

Meanwhile the campaign for sharia had acquired a new urgency. Aceh had become the first province to introduce public canings and Taliban-inspired vice squads. Missing Friday prayers three times earned a person three strokes of a four-foot-long rattan cane. Being caught alone with an unrelated member of the opposite sex merited between three and nine strokes. Shopkeepers faced six strokes for failing to down their shutters for midday prayers during Ramadan. The punishment for betting on a game of cards or an informal lottery: between six and ten strokes. The punishment for drinking a beer or a glass of wine: forty strokes.

In Bulukumba the 100 percent jilbab record of the bupati's model village had been extended to the entire district; in all, eighteen of 22 districts in south Sulawesi had adopted some form of sharia. In Padang in west Sumatra the bupati had ordered all Muslim women to wear the jilbab; non-Muslim schoolgirls had to obey the ruling as well. The Jakarta suburb of Tangerang had begun arresting women for being alone after dark. In one celebrated case, a married mother of two, picked up by a vice squad while waiting for a bus, was convicted of prostitution after a judge found a tube of lipstick and a small compact in her purse. In parliament the PKS had proposed a law, cleverly called the anti-pornography bill, that mandated prison terms for women in short skirts or couples caught kissing in public. Opinion polls, though far from perfect, had begun to capture the broad shift in the country's attitudes. In 2006 the Indonesian Survey Institute found that one in three Indonesians opposed electing another female president; four out of ten approved of stoning adulterers to death.

Why, then, did the myth of Indonesia's moderation persist?

For one, Indonesia had changed dramatically, but only when compared to its own easygoing past. Benchmarked against most Muslim-majority countries it remained a beacon of tolerance and pluralism. Unlike Pakistan it had not ethnically cleansed itself of non-Muslims; some minority enclaves—notably Christian north Sumatra and north Sulawesi—had largely escaped the demographic pressures and jihadist violence that marked the experience of Ambon and central Sulawesi. Unlike in Saudi Arabia—where sharia determined that a woman's testimony in court was worth half that of a man's, and a Hindu life was valued at one-sixteenth that of a Muslim—in Indonesia all citizens remained equal before the law. Unlike Malaysia, where non-Muslims were encouraged to embrace Islam but Muslims were forbidden by law from converting out of it, Indonesia had not formally abandoned freedom of conscience.

Indonesia's Islamists also benefited from the world's muddled effort to distinguish between radical and moderate Muslims. Was a moderate Indonesian Muslim someone whose views on women, minority rights and human rights were broadly akin to those of a moderate Korean Christian, a moderate Indian Hindu or a moderate Singaporean Buddhist? In other words were you a moderate only if you showed a long-term commitment to democracy, accepted secular laws, respected the rights of women and minorities, and actively opposed terrorism and mob violence? Or was a moderate Muslim simply anyone against settling religious and political grievances by flying an aeroplane into a skyscraper or blowing himself up in a bar full of tourists?

Furthermore, was moderation measured by a movement's goals, or by the means used to achieve them? If you believed that Muslims ought to be held to different standards than the rest of humanity, or that means mattered more than ends, then a party like the PKS could reasonably be deemed moderate. After all, its cadres marched in disciplined formation outside Western embassies instead of detonating suicide vests in restaurants in Bali. If, on the other hand, you believed that the Universal Declaration of Human Rights applied to all cultures, and that sharia, no matter how it was achieved, was intrinsically discriminatory towards women, secular Muslims and non-Muslims, then the PKS was at least as dangerous as Jemaah Islamiyah. Like Jemaah Islamiyah, in its founding manifesto the PKS had called for the creation of an Islamic caliphate. Like Jemaah Islamiyah, it placed secrecy—the cell structure both groups borrowed from the Muslim Brotherhood—at the heart of its organisation. Both groups drew on the violent writings of Sayyid Qutb and offered a selective vision of modernity, one in which global science and technology were welcome but universal values were shunned.

Most of the people I had known or interviewed during my travels had stayed in the news.

Richard Oh had transitioned from writing novels to writing and directing films. His first, *Koper* or *The Lost Suitcase*, starred Djenar Maesa Ayu in the female lead and told the story of a man who stumbles upon a mysterious suitcase, packed with symbolic existential meaning, that changes his life. It had fared poorly at the box office, but was set for a second life on the international film festival circuit.

Djenar had acquired a butterfly tattoo above her left shoulder blade, was in the midst of directing her first film, and had written a novel, *Nayla*, based on the main character from the short story she had read aloud at her birthday more than three years earlier. The *Jakarta Post* called *Nayla* 'a testament to her [Djenar's] unchanging courage in defending women's sexuality and rejecting taboos.' The review also counted the number of times she used the word 'vagina'. (At least fifteen.)

Inul Daratista's drilling continued to generate wealth and outrage in equal measure. She had acquired a chain of karaoke lounges and had built a mansion in her home village. But the Islamic Defenders Front had called her 'human trash' and barred her from performing in the Jakarta suburb of Depok. The previous year she had drilled at the Hotel Indonesia circle in defiance of the anti-pornography bill prompting a mob to show up at her Jakarta home and demand that she return to east Java.

As expected, Din Syamsuddin had been elected chairman of Muhammadiyah in 2005. As head of the Council of Ulama he was credited with a fatwa issued that year against pluralism, liberalism and secularism. He helped scupper a proposal to drop religious identification from national ID cards. He was at the forefront of protests against the Danish Mohammed cartoons and the launch of a mild (no nudity) local edition of *Playboy*. As an alternative to the Miss Indonesia pageant he backed a Miss Muslim Indonesia. Contestants would be judged on 'moral and spiritual qualities', 'healthy values', 'excellent habits' and 'strong faith'.

A. A. Gym had shocked much of his middle-class female

following by taking a second wife, a 37-year-old former model, and justifying it on the grounds that men and women ran different 'software'. His first wife, and mother of his seven children, described her new status as 'wonderful' and 'nothing like what people fear'.

Abu Bakar Bashir had been released from prison in 2006 after serving 26 months; the Supreme Court subsequently quashed his conviction. He had resumed bemoaning the defeat of the Taliban, railing publicly against infidels and calling for democracy to be replaced by 'Allah-cracy'.

Abdul Azis Kahar Muzakkar was preparing to run for governor of south Sulawesi. (He would lose but not before drawing 20 percent of the popular vote.)

Anis Matta was in the thick of both power politics and Indonesia's culture wars. When not wrangling for greater PKS representation in SBY's cabinet, he spoke out in support of polygamy and its benefits for widows and orphans.

Herry and I had kept in touch sporadically via email. A few shreds of the personal bond between us remained—he emailed me news of Djenar's career as an actress and an essay encapsulating his views on the end of the world—but our political differences had grown starker.

In 2005 I wrote an essay in the *Far Eastern Economic Review* arguing that the PKS was a greater threat than Jemaah Islamiyah to Indonesia's fragile democracy. Herry responded by questioning my 'negative motivation'. He said he worried about the essay's impact on the party, which for him remained a force for good. Santi Soekanto, the *Jakarta Post* journalist who had introduced us, criticised Herry in an article for helping me enter 'places that might not have been as easily accessed otherwise.' Herry had been stung by the accusation, but it was hard for me to sympathise entirely with him when his own work maintained its paranoid cast. He had graduated from writing articles in *Sabili* to writing books on, as he put it, 'the tentacles of zionism in Indonesia.'

As it happened, my visit coincided with Jakarta's sixth annual Islamic book fair (official slogan: beauty of sharia in life) where Herry was to launch two of his books—*Signs of Freemasons and Zionists in Indonesia* and *Resurgence of Freemasons and Zionists in Indonesia*. When we met for dinner at my hotel the night before the book launch I found him changed, heavier in the face, his goatee blunter and more emphatic, the callus on his forehead more pronounced. He and Tias had had another daughter—Ziyadilma Sekar Marimbi—and it seemed to me that the weight of responsibility had erased the boyish quality that had marked him the first time we met three years earlier. He was no longer with *Sabili*; his business card described him simply as a writer.

The book fair, inaugurated by Vice-President Jusuf Kalla, had taken over Senayan stadium in the heart of Jakarta. The jilbabs in the audience were overwhelmingly black or white. Many of the books displayed the usual Islamist preoccupations with Jews and Christians. The cover of *The Lady Di Conspiracy* depicted the late princess with a Star of David on her neck. *Knights Templar Knights of Christ*, which warned of a dangerous conspiracy hatched by priests with an eye on Armageddon, showed a knight in chainmail with a red cross across his chest. Herry's books were slender enough to slide into the back pocket of a pair of jeans; they were embellished with verses from the Koran and illustrated with dozens of black and white photographs. Bashir had penned the foreword for both.

For dinner Herry had worn jeans and a T-shirt but for the book fair he chose more appropriate garb—a black peci, a white tunic whose sleeves ended just below the elbow, a shin-length checked sarong, black open-toed sandals. He shared the stage with a moderator and with the author of *Knights Templar*, who, it turned out, had also co-authored *Facts and Data on Jews in Indonesia*. (A considerable feat considering that the community consisted of a handful of expatriates.) The audience—more than one hundred people—occupied several rows of chairs in front of the stage and spilled over to the bleachers behind them. Behind Herry was a dark banner advertising his books. On display beside it sat a biography of Hassan al-Banna, a book by A. A. Gym on wealth management, a slim volume on the Holocaust that showed a fattened fly with a Star of David on its back.

Herry had grown in confidence as a public speaker since the last time I heard him, at the Hidayatullah mosque outside Balikpapan. He talked about the Dutch East India Company and the Theosophist Madame Blavatsky. He warned against drinking Aqua brand mineral water, owned by the French firm Danone. He ranged over the Jewish characteristics of the Chinese, the inherent inferiority of man-worshipping Christianity and race-worshipping Judaism, the religious perfidy of Sukarno, Pancasila, pyramids on US dollar bills, Karl Marx, Henry Kissinger. The crowd was attentive and several questions, invariably asked by young men, took the form of exhortations for sharia. Then it was time for Herry to autograph books for his fans. That was how I left him, my Javanese friend, seated amid a throng of admirers signing copies of a book about Zionists, Freemasons and the coming end of the world.

Organisations

Center for Information and Development Studies
Center for Strategic and International Studies
Consultative Assembly of Indonesian Muslims (Masyumi)
Council of Indonesian Ulama
Crescent Star Party
Darul Islam: House of Islam
Democratic Party
Golkar (Golongan Karya): Functional Groups
Hidayatullah
Indonesian Armed Forces (TNI)
Indonesian Communist Party (PKI)
Indonesian Council for Islamic Predication (DDII)
Indonesian Democratic Party of Struggle (PDI-P)
Indonesian Mujahidin Council
Indonesian Muslim Intellectuals Association (ICMI)
Islamic Defenders Front
Jemaah Islamiyah
Laskar Jihad
Laskar Jundullah
Laskar Mujahidin
Muhammadiyah
Nahdlatul Ulama
National Awakening Party (PKB)
National Humanitarian Foundation (PKPU)
National Mandate Party (PAN)
Pan-Malaysian Islamic Party (PAS)
Parmusi: Indonesian Muslims' Party
People's Consultative Assembly
Preparatory Committee for the Implementation of Sharia Law (KPPSI)
Prosperous Justice Party (PKS)
Regional Representatives Council
Strategic Reserve Command
Tarbiyah/Salman Mosque Movement
United Development Party
Unity of Islam (Persis)

Acknowledgments

I have drawn on the work of the following authors: Cindy Adams, Pramoedya Ananta Toer, Benedict Anderson, Greg Barton, Paul Berman, Paul Bresnan, Martin van Bruinessen, Giora Eliraz, R. E. Elson, Donald Emmerson, John Esposito, Greg Fealy, Andree Feillard, Louis Fischer, Theodore Friend, Nancy K. Florida, Clifford Geertz, Robert W. Hefner, Hal Hill, Howard Palfrey Jones, George McT. Kahin, John Keay, Gilles Kepel, Christopher Koch, Bernard Lewis, Norman Lewis, Keith Loveard, Hamish McDonald, Goenawan Mohamad, V. S. Naipaul, Sally Neighbour, Kevin O'Rourke, Richard Lloyd Parry, Daniel Pipes, Sayyid Qutb, Douglas E. Ramage, M. C. Ricklefs, Olivier Roy, Malise Ruthven, Adam Schwarz, Leo Suryadinata, Jean Gelman Taylor, Michael Vatikiotis, Esther Velthoen, Adrian Vickers, Bernard H. M. Vlekke and Simon Winchester. I am similarly grateful to *Indonesia Journal*, the International Crisis Group, Joyo News Service and the Van Zorge Report. Asia Society and the Bernard Schwartz fellows program gave me the gift of time to write. I'd also like to thank Ayesha Karim in London for her faith in this project, Alison Arnold and Michael Heyward in Melbourne for their invaluable suggestions, and Alyssa Ayres in too many places and in too many ways to list.